SONGS FOR BASS VOICE
An Annotated Guide to Works for Bass Voice

by
ALAN J. ORD

The Scarecrow Press, Inc.
Metuchen, N.J., & London
1994

British Library Cataloguing-in-Publication data available

Library of Congress Cataloging-in-Publication Data

Ord, Alan J., 1941-
  Songs for bass voice: an annotated guide to works for bass voice
/ by Alan J. Ord
    p. cm.
  Includes bibliographical references and Indexes.
  ISBN 0-8108-2897-9 (acid-free paper)
    1. Songs (Low voice)--Bibliography--Graded lists. 2. Sacred songs
  (Low voice)--Bibliography--Graded lists. I. Title.
  ML132.S6073 1994
  016.7838'9'0263--dc20   94-14392

To My Wife Kathleen and My Children

TABLE OF CONTENTS

PREFACE

The idea for this book came from my own frustration as a young bass at not finding suitable songs to sing both in range and tessitura. Much of the music attempted or assigned was too high in range or tessitura for an immature basso searching for high notes and very often the attempt was vocally unhealthy. Most of the songs most readily available were not low enough and were more appropriate for baritone or more advanced bass, not beginning bass. This led to my own search for, primarily, music composed specifically for bass voice and music specifically composed for low voice which would be suitable for bass. Secondarily I looked for appropriate songs originally composed for higher voices which were transposed to workable keys for bass voice. The results are the over two thousand songs entered in this volume. Some duplication occurs because some songs are found in more than one collection.

This book is not limited to the discussion of vocal music for the beginning student, but presents vocal literature for all levels from beginner to the total professional. The songs and arias annotated in this book obviously do not constitute all pieces composed for bass, low voice suitable for bass, or transposed for bass. Nor is it implied that if a song is not annotated in this book it is not worthy.

The first chapter pertains to songs in anthologies for the beginning bass. Special attention is given to songs of limited range and acceptable tessitura. The next several chapters outline songs in anthologies of increasing difficulty for the intermediate and more advanced levels. Chapter Five deals with some collections of songs by a single composer that are of special interest to the bass voice.

Perhaps the most important and illuminating chapter is the sixth which annotates song cycles and sets. With over one hundred song cycles and sets, most of which were composed specifically for the bass voice or low voice, this chapter presents a wealth of song material for the frustrated bass. Equally interesting and elucidating is Chapter Seven on songs with instruments from the baroque to the avant-garde. After that, the next several chapters compare anthologies of arias from opera and oratorio.

Often, the first experience a vocalist has as a soloist is in a church setting. Chapter Ten contains a sampling of those religious, inspirational, and Christmas songs of the type most often presented at churches of various denominations. A presentation of three anthologies of songs from musicals in Chapter Eleven is followed by three anthologies of spirituals, Russian folk songs, and sea shanties in Chapter Twelve. Chapter Thirteen contains additional noteworthy songs and arias for bass that are not included elsewhere in this book. Of great additional help are the various indexes found in the appropriate appendix at the end of the book.

Dr. Alan J. Ord

University of Alberta
Edmonton, Alberta
Canada

INTRODUCTION

In annotating the individual songs it was thought essential that all entries be as simple, straightforward, easy to understand, and meaningful as possible. For this reason it was felt that as few abbreviations as possible should be used, and all entries should follow the same basic layout or format.

Each annotation consists of the following information:

1. Composer - Last name is indicated first followed by the first name or initial.
2. Composer's birth and death dates.
3. Composer's nationality - In some cases the composer was born in one country and naturalized in another, in which case both nationalities are given.
4. Title - The title is indicated in italics with an alternate title in a different language in parenthesis, if applicable. If the song is from a larger work it is also indicated.
5. Language of the piece - If the song is in more than one language both are indicated.
6. Tempo indication.
7. Meter indication.
8. Range of vocal line - To avoid confusion the indicated pitch is the singing pitch, not necessarily the written pitch.
9. Tessitura - A subjective indication of the lie of the song for the average bass voice is noted.
10. Difficulty level - A subjective indication of the relative difficulty of the song based on musical, vocal, language, and interpretation factors is given.
11. Publisher.
12. Possible comments - Indications of: style; mood; recommendations; possible problems; occasional references to famous basses associated with the song.

The entries are listed in the following format:

No.	Composer	*Title* (Alternate title)(Language)	Publisher
	(Dates) Nationality	(from "opera or oratorio" if applicable)	
		Tempo & Meter (Range) Tessitura Difficulty	
		Possible comments: problems; style; mood; uses; recommendations; miscellaneous.	

A sample entry is as follows:

63.	Franz, Robert	*Widmung* (Dedication)(Ger./Eng.)	Schirmer
	(1815-1892) Ger.	Andante 2/4 (C3-D4) MH Med. diff.	
		Graceful, reflective love song; good introductory song to German Lieder.	

There are slight variations from this format in some chapters depending on need. If the item is from an anthology or collection the publisher is given only once at the beginning. In the chapter on song cycles and sets the comments section of the annotation is given at the beginning of the cycle. In Chapter Seven the entries require more information and the format is adjusted accordingly in an easily understood layout. Some additional variation in format is a result of the way each individual anthology or collection is organized.

In a few entries some information may be missing due to a lack of availability of primary sources in which case the author relied on secondary sources for the information given. In a very few cases quite limited information was available but it was thought that it was of such interest that inclusion was essential.

Most of the vocal literature annotated in this volume was in print at the time of this writing. Music that is out of print can often be found in many public and institutional libraries and performance of out-of-print music is possible. In addition, many out-of-the-way music stores may have a surprise and some specialty vocal music publishers, such as Classical Vocal Reprints or Recital Publications (see list of publishers) have much to offer.

ABBREVIATION AND USAGE KEY

Language indications:

    Eng. = English
    Fin. = Finnish
    Fr. = French
    Ger. = German
    Hun. = Hungarian
    Lat. = Latin
    Russ. = Russian
    Span. = Spanish

Octave placement indications (singing pitch):

    C2-C3 = great octave, bass clef
    C3-C4 = small octave, bass clef
    C4-C5 = first octave, treble clef

Note: C4 is middle C.
    + indicates additional publishers.

Tessitura indications:

    VH = very high
    H = high
    MH = medium high
    M = medium
    ML = medium low
    L = low
    VL = very low

Difficulty levels:

    Easy
    Moderately Easy
    Medium Difficulty
    Moderately Difficult
    Difficult
    Very Difficult

CHAPTER I

ART-SONG ANTHOLOGIES AND COLLECTIONS FOR BEGINNING BASS VOICE

There are a number of song anthologies for "low voice" available. Usually these "low voice" anthologies are more appropriate for baritone and with one exception are not included in this book. The song anthologies annotated in this chapter are suitable for the beginning bass voice.

EXPRESSIVE SINGING SONG ANTHOLOGY
For Low Voice
Second & Third Editions
Edited by Van A. Christy & John Glen Paton
Published by Wm. C. Brown, 1983 & 1990

Volume one of the two-volume second edition is annotated below in its entirety. The range and tessitura of most of the songs are well-suited to the young or undeveloped bass voice. In addition, volume two of the second edition and the one-volume third edition contain a number of excellent songs for bass voice. Some of these songs are found in Chapter Thirteen. A few of the songs in these three volumes are more suited to female voices and nearly all are transposed down from their original key.

ART SONGS

1. Beethoven, L. van (1770-1827) Ger.
   I Love Thee (Ich liebe dich)(Eng./Ger.)
   Andante 4/8   (Bb2-Db4)   M-MH   Mod. easy
   Gentle song with flowing lines.

2. Bohm, Carl (1844-1920) Ger.
   Still as the Night (Still wie die Nacht)(Eng./Ger)
   Tranquillo 6/4   (G2-Db4)   ML-MH Mod. easy
   Sustained; some command of dynamic variation.

3. Fontenailles, H. de
   A Resolve (Obstination)(Eng./Fr.)
   Andantino 4/4   (A2-C4)   ML-M   Mod. easy
   Happy beginning, sad ending; lyric legato line.

4. Franz, Robert (1815-1892) Ger.
   Dedication (Widmung)(Eng./Ger.)
   Andante 2/4   (Bb2-C4)   M   Mod. easy
   Gentle, flowing line; well-known song.

5.
   Good Night (Gute Nacht)(Eng./Ger.)
   Andante 6/8   (C3-C4)   M   Mod. easy
   Sad reflection; lyric sostenuto.

1

6.   *Out of My Soul's Great Sadness*
                                (Aus meinen grossen Schmerzen)(Eng./Ger.)
                                Andante 2/4   (G#2-B3)   ML-M   Mod. easy
                                Lyrical; subdued.

7. Grieg, Edvard   *I Love Thee* (Ich liebe dich)(Eng./Ger.)
    (1843-1907) Nor.   Andante 3/4   (C3-Db4)   M   Mod. easy
                                Well-known; often used for weddings; passionate climax.

8.   *Two Brown Eyes* (Zwei Braune Augen)(Eng./Ger.)
                                Allegretto 3/4   (B2-C3)   M-MH   Mod. easy
                                Lyric legato; tender love song.

9. Handel, George F.   *Verdant Meadows* (Verdi prati)(Eng./It.)
    (1685-1759) Ger./Eng.   Andante 3/4   (C3-Eb4)   MH   Mod. easy
                                Sustained legato; quiet contemplation; arranged as a duet.

10.   *Where'er You Walk* (Eng.)
                                Largo 4/4   (C3-D4)   M-MH   Med. diff.
                                Lyric legato; some agility required; well known.

11. Haydn, Joseph   *She Never Told Her Love* (Eng.)
    (1732-1809) Aus.   Largo 2/2   (B2-D4)   M-MH   Med. diff.
                                Gentle tragedy; lyric legato line.

12. Lully, Jean Baptiste   *Sombre Woods* (Bois épais)(Eng./Fr.)
    (1632-1687) It./Fr.   Andante 4/4   (Bb2-Db4)   M-MH   Med. diff.
                                Sustained with intense sadness; aria originally for tenor
                                voice; excellent piece.

13. MacDowell, E.   *The Sea* (Eng.)
    (1860-1908) Am.   Broad 6/8   (C3-C4)   M-MH   Med. diff.
                                Tragic; somewhat dramatic.

14. Martini, Giovanni   *The Joys of Love* (Plaisir d'amour)(Eng./Fr.)
    (1706-1784) It.   Allegretto 6/8   (G2-C4)   ML-M   Mod. easy
                                Sustained lyric legato; faithless love.

15. Mellish, Colonel R.   *Drink to Me Only with Thine Eyes* (Eng.)
    (c. 1777-1817)   Moderato 6/8   (C3-C4)   M-MH   Easy
                                Simple legato line; good beginning piece.

16. Mendelssohn, Felix   *On Wings of Song*
    (1809-1847) Ger.   (Auf Flügeln des Gesanges)(Eng./Ger.)
                                Andante 6/8   (Eb3-F4)   VH   Mod. easy
                                Solo or duet; melody for higher voice.

17. Nevin, Ethelbert   *Little Boy Blue* (Eng.)
    (1862-1901) Am.   Moderato 6/8   (C3-Bb3)   M   Easy
                                Simple; ballad-like; lyric, legato line.

18. Purcell, Edward   *Passing By* (Eng.)
    (d. 1932) Eng.   Andantino 2/4   (C3-C4)   M   Easy
                             Expressive; lyric legato; some command of soft dynamics.

19. Schubert, Franz   *Faith in Spring* (Frühlingsglaube)(Eng./Ger.)
    (1797-1828) Aus.   Andante 2/4   (Bb2-C4)   M   Mod. easy
                             Flowing, legato line; some command of agility required.

20.   *Morning Greeting* (Morgengrüss)
                             Moderato 3/4   (D3-C4)   M-MH   Mod. easy
                             Flirtatious; some agility required; limited range.

21. Schumann, Robert   *The Lotus Flower* (Die Lotusblume)(Eng./Ger.)
    (1810-1856) Ger.   Larghetto 6/4   (G2-D4)   M   Mod. easy
                             Warm, tender tone; sustained.

22.   *Thou'rt Lovely as a Flower* (Du bist wie eine Blume)
                             (Eng./Ger.)
                             Lento 2/4   (D3-C4)   M-MH   Med. diff.
                             Smooth legato line.

23. Scott, Alicia Ann   *Think on Me* (Eng.)
    (1810-1900) Scot.   Moderato 4/4   (C3-Db4)   M   Mod. easy
                             Folk-like; flowing line.

24. Sullivan, Sir Arthur   *The Lost Chord* (Eng.)
    (1842-1900) Eng.   Andante 4/4   (Bb2-Eb4)   M   Med. diff.
                             Excellent song for bass voice; sustained legato; lower key
                             than normally available.

25. Tchaikovsky, Peter   *None But the Lonely Heart*
    (1840-1893) Russ.   (Nur wer die Sehnsucht kennt)(Eng./Ger.)
                             Andante 4/4   (A2-D4)   M   Med. diff.
                             Melancholy; sustained.

OLD ITALIAN

26. Caccini, Giulio   *Amarilli, My Fair One* (Amarilli, mia bella)(Eng./It.)
    (1548-1618) It.   Moderato 4/4   (C3-D4)   MH   Med. diff.
                             Sostenuto; some agility required.

27. Caldara, Antonio   *Tho' Not Deserving* (Sebben, crudele)(Eng./It.)
    (1670-1736) It.   Allegretto 3/4   (C3-D4)   MH   Mod. easy
                             Flowing, legato line.

28. Paisiello, Giovanni   *Why Feels My Heart So Dormant*
    (1740-1816) It.   (Nel core più non mi sento)(Eng./It.)
                             Andantino 6/8   (C3-Eb4)   MH   Mod. easy
                             Flowing line.

29. Scarlatti, Alessandro   *Oh, No Longer Seek to Pain Me*
    (1660-1725) It.   (O cessate di piagarmi)(Eng./It.)
                             Andante 6/8   (C#3-C4)   M-MH   Mod. easy
                             Lyric, flowing line.

SACRED SONGS AND SPIRITUALS

30. Adams, Stephen   *The Holy City* (Eng.)
    (Maybrick, Michael)   Andante 4/4   (A2-C4)   M   Med. diff.
    (1844-1913) Eng.   Forthright; flowing, legato line.

31. Christy, Van (arr.)   *Beautiful Savior* (Eng.)
                             Andante 4/4   (C3-Db4)   M-MH   Mod. easy
                             Silesian folk song; sustained legato.

32.   *Joshua Fit the Battle of Jericho* (Eng.)
                             With spirit 2/2   (B2-D4)   M-MH   Mod. easy
                             Energetic; rhythmic.

33.   *Lonesome Valley* (Eng.)
                             Slowly 4/4   (Bb2-Db4)   M-MH   Mod. easy
                             Resignation; sustained.

34. Franck, César   *Bread of Angels* (Panis Angelicus)(Eng./Lat.)
    (1822-1890) Belg.   Moderato 4/4   (F3-F4)   VH   Mod. easy
                             Solo or duet; melody for higher voice.

35. Gaul, Alfred R.   *Eye Hath Not Seen* (Eng.)
    (1837-1913) Eng.   Largo Religioso 2/2 (A2-C4)   M-MH   Mod. easy
                             Sustained.

36. Homer, Sidney   *Requiem* (Eng.)
    (1864-1953) Am.   Adagio 4/4   (D3-C4)   MH   Mod. easy
                             Sustained.

37. Mendelssohn, Felix   *Oh, Rest in the Lord* (from "Elijah")(Eng.)
    (1809-1847) Ger.   Andantino 4/4   (A2-C4)   M   Mod. easy
                             Originally intended for female voice.

38. Mozart, W. A.   *Great Creator* (Ave Verum)(Eng./Lat.)
    (1756-1791) Austrian   Andantino 4/4   (B2-C4)   M   Mod. easy
                             Solo or duet; prayerful; sustained.

39. Tchaikovsky, Pyotr   *A Legend* (Eng.)
    (1840-1893) Russ.   Moderato 2/4   (Bb2-C4)   M   Mod. easy
                             Narrative; flowing line.

BALLADS

40. Chopin, Frédéric   *Lithuanian Song* (Litauisches Lied)(Eng./Ger.)

(1810-1849) Polish	Allegro moderato 4/4 (C3-D4) MH Med. diff. Folk ballad; lyric legato.
41. Christy, Van (arr.)	*The Old Woman and the Peddler* (Eng.) Allegretto 2/2 (C3-C4) MH Mod. easy English folk ballad; humorous; light.
42. Haydn, Franz J. (1732-1809) Austrian	*A Very Commonplace Story* (Eng.) (Ein sehr gewöhnliche Geschichte)(Eng./Ger.) Allegretto 2/4 (Ab2-Db4) M Mod. easy Humorous narrative.
43. Mozart, W. A. (1756-1791) Austrian	*A Tragic Story* (Eng.) Allegretto 2/4 (C3-Db4) MH Mod. easy Humorous narrative.
44. Storace, Stephen (1763-1796) Eng.	*The Pretty Creature* (Eng.) Allegro 2/4 (Bb2-C4) M-MH Mod. easy Arranged by H. Lane Wilson; humorous ballad; lower than normal key.

FOLK SONGS

45. Beethoven, L. van (1770-1827) Ger.	*The Miller of Dee* (Eng.) Gaily 6/8 (C3-C4) M-MH Mod. easy Arranged by Christy; vigorous, jolly folk song.
46. Brahms, J. (arr.) (1833-1897) Ger.	*Far Down in the Valley(Da unten im Tale)(Eng./Ger.)* Allegretto 3/4 (D3-C4) MH Mod. easy German folk song; flowing legato.
47.	*Oh, Calm of Night* (In stiller Nacht)(Eng./Ger.) Slowly 3/4 (C3-F4) H Mod. easy Duet; melody is sung by higher voice.
48. Christy, Van (arr.)	*All Through the Night* (Eng.) Andante 4/4 (Bb2-C4) M Easy Old Welch air.
49.	*Away Over Yandro* (He's Gone Away)(Eng.) Andante 4/4 (Bb2-D4) M-MH Mod. easy Southern mountain tune.
50.	*Begone Dull Care* (Eng.) Gaily 6/8 (C3-D4) MH Mod. easy Can be sung as solo or duet.
51.	*Go 'Way from My Window* (Eng.) Slowly 4/4 (A2-D4) M-MH Easy Can be sung as solo or duet.

52.   *Mister Banjo* (Eng.)
             Lively 2/4   (C3-D4)   MH   Mod. easy
             Energetic.

53.   *Poor Wayfaring Stranger* (Eng.)
             Slowly 3/4   (Bb2-D4)   M   Mod. easy
             Sustained.

54.   *Shenandoah* (Eng.)
             Slowly 3/4, 4/4   (G2-C4)   ML-M   Mod. easy
             Sea Chanty; sustained.

55.   *Tutu Maramba* (Eng.)
             Andante 4/4   (C3-C4)   M-MH   Mod. easy
             More for female voices.

THE FIRST BOOK OF BARITONE/BASS SOLOS
Compiled by Joan Frey Boytim
Published by G. Schirmer, Inc., 1991

An excellent new collection of songs in two volumes for beginning bass and baritone voices.
Most of the songs are suitable in range and tessitura for the bass voice and a good number are
in their original keys. The songs annotated below are from the first volume.

56. Arne, Thomas   *Why So Pale and Wan* (Eng.)
     (1710-1778) Eng.   Lively 4/4   (G2-D4)   ML-MH Mod. easy
                          Rhythmical and gay; strophic; some leaps; a good early
                          English song.

57. Beethoven, L. van   *There Was a Mighty Monarch* (Eng.)
     (1770-1827) Ger.   Steady 2/4   (C3-D4)   M-MH   Med. diff.
                          Humorous narrative; basically strophic; some patter; a
                          well-known song for bass voice.

58. Clarke, Robert   *The Blind Ploughman* (Eng.)
     (1879-1934) Eng.   Moderate 4/4   (C3-D4)   M-MH   Med. diff.
                          Sustained; somewhat forceful and dramatic; good sostenuto
                          study song.

59. Dibdin, Charles   *Blow High, Blow Low* (Eng.)
     (1745-1814) Eng.   Bright 4/4   (G2-C4)   ML-M   Med. diff.
                          Vigorous sea song; requires flexibility; excellent early
                          English song by a neglected composer.

60. Dougherty, C.   *Across the Western Ocean* (Eng.)
     (1902-1986) Am.   Broad 4/4   (D3-D4)   M-MH   Mod. easy
                          Sustained; sea shanty; from "Five Sea Chanties";
                          (see no. 702)

61.   *Shenandoah* (Eng.)
Sustained 3/4   (A2-D4)   M-MH   Mod. easy
Majestic sea shanty; excellent setting of this well-known
song. (see no. 704)

62. Fauré, Gabriel   *Le Secret* (The Secret)(Fr./Eng.)
(1830-1914) Fr.   Slow 2/4   (Db3-Eb4) H   Mod. diff.
Lyric love song; perhaps more suited to baritone voices.

63. Franz, Robert   *Widmung* (Dedication)(Ger./Eng.)
(1815-1892) Ger.   Andante 2/4   (C3-D4)   MH   Med. diff.
Graceful, reflective love song; good introductory song to
German Lieder.

64. Goodhart, A. M.   *The Bells of Clermont Town* (Eng.)
Brilliant 4/4   (A2-D4)   MH   Mod. diff.
Patter song; facile articulation required; good study song for
diction.

65. Gounod, Charles   *The King of Love My Shepherd Is* (Eng.)
(1818-1893) Fr.   Moderato 4/4   (B2-D4) M-MH Mod. easy
Inspirational; flowing legato line; strong ending.

66. Handel, G. F.   *Leave Me, Loathsome Light* (Eng.)
(1685-1759) Ger./Eng. Andante 6/4   (A2-D4) M   Mod. easy
Very sustained; ABA form; poignant; subdued.

67. Kilenyi, E. (arr.)   *Ecantadora Maria* (Maria, Dear)(Span./Eng.)
(1884-1968) Hung./Am. Moderato 2/4   (E3-C4)   MH   Med. diff.
Expressive; passionate; rhythmic; excellent introduction to
Spanish song.

68.   *La Paloma Blanca* (The White Dove)(Span./Eng.)
Spirited 6/8   (C3-D4) M-MH Med. diff.
Requires facile articulation; short song.

69. Leoni, Franco   *Tally-Ho!* (Eng.)
(1864-1949) It.   Quick 6/8   (C#3-D4) M-MH Mod. easy
Rhythmic; energetic; some leaps; strong ending.

70. MacDowell, E.   *The Sea* (Eng.)
(1861-1908) Eng.   Flowing 6/8   (D3-D4) MH-H Med. diff.
Somber; introspective; subdued; legato; wide contrast in
dynamics.

71. Mendelssohn, Felix *Jagdlied* (Hunting Song)(Ger./Eng.)
(1809-1847) Ger.   Andante 6/8   (B2-E4) MH-H Med. diff.
Strophic hunting song; alternate high and low sections; some
command of soft singing required.

72. Mueller, Carl F.   *Create in Me a Clean Heart* (Eng.)
    (b. 1892) Am.   Expressive 3/4   (B2-C4)   M   Mod. easy
                         Somewhat sustained; effective pianissimo ending.

73. Myers, Gordon (arr.) *Let Us Break Bread Together* (Eng.)
    (b. 1919) Am.   Steady 2/4   (A2-D4)   M-MH   Mod. easy
                          Simple straightforward interpretation; acappella sections.

74. Niles, John Jacob   *The Rovin' Gambler* (Eng.)
    (1892-1980) Am.   Allegro 2/4   (Bb2-Eb4)   H   Med. diff.
                         Bold; energetic; narrative; flexibility required; facile
                         articulation.

75. Payne, John (arr.)   *Lord, I Want to Be a Christian* (Eng.)
    (b. 1941) Am.   Slow 2/2   (Bb2-Db4)   M-MH   Med. diff.
                         Subdued African American spiritual; some command of soft
                         dynamics required.

76. Purcell, Henry   *Next Winter Comes Slowly* (Eng.)
    (1658-1695) Eng.   Slow 3/4   (G2-D4)   M-MH   Med. diff.
                         Sad; sustained.

77. Quilter, Roger   *Blow, Blow, Thou Winter Wind* (Eng.)
    (1877-1953) Eng.   Allegro 3/4   (C3-E4)   H   Med. diff.
                         Vigorous; energetic; demanding range; perhaps best suited
to   baritones in this key.

78.   *O Mistress Mine* (Eng.)
                         Allegro mod. 3/4   (A2-D4)   M-MH   Med. diff.
                         Delightful, lyric lovesong; gratefully for the bass voice, this
                         is in a key one half-step lower than normal.

79. Robertson, R. R.   *The Jolly Roger* (Eng.)
                         Allegro 3/4   (C3-D4)   MH   Med. diff.
                         Bold; declamatory; rhythmically vital; somewhat demanding
                         vocally.

80. Sarti, Guiseppe   *Lungi dal caro bene* (Far from My Love)(It./Eng.)
    (1729-1802) It.   Andante 2/4   (G2-D4)   M-MH   Med. diff.
                         Longing love song; requires some flexibility.

81. Schumann, Robert   *Hör' ich das Liedchen klingen* (E're When I Hear
    (1810-1856) Ger.   Them Singing)(Ger./Eng.)
                         Lento 2/4   (B2-Eb3)   ML-M   Mod. easy
                         Passionate; sustained; legato; short.

82.   *Intermezzo* (Thine Image Pure)(Ger./Eng.)
                         Slow 2/4   (B2-D4)   MH   Med. diff.
                         Dreamy, nostalgic, tranquil love song.

83. Shield, William   *The Friar of Orders Gray* (Eng.)
    (1748-1829) Eng.   Spirited 6/8   (G2-D4)   VH   Med. diff.
                             Energetic narrative; requires some agility; some large skips.

84. Speaks, Oley   *On the Road to Mandalay* (Eng.)
    (1874-1948) Am.   Alla Marcia 4/4   (Bb2-F4)   VH   Med. diff.
                             Strong, resolute; several mounting climaxes.

85. Tyson, Mildred Lund   *Sea Moods* (Eng.)
    (b. 1944) Am.   Andante 4/4   (B2-Eb4)   M-MH   Mod. diff.
                             Changing moods; stormy and passionate; interpretively not
                             easy.

86. Walthew, Richard   *The Splendour Falls* (Eng.)
    (1872-1951) Eng.   Allegretto 6/8   (Eb2-Eb4)   M-MH   Mod. diff.
                             Flowing line; some command of soft dynamics; Tennyson
                             poem.

87. Wilson, H. L. (arr.)   *False Phillis* (Eng.)
                             Allegretto 3/4   (A2-D4)   M-MH   Med. diff.
                             Lighthearted song of infidelity; some flexibility required;
                             early English.

SONGS FOR BASS IN A COMFORTABLE RANGE
Edited by Leonard Van Camp
Published by Carl Fischer, 1990

This new collection fills a very definite need of helping to provide appropriate vocal literature
for the low bass or beginning bass with a limited range. All of the songs have been transposed
and none of the songs go above C4. Included is an accompaniment cassette. Also arranged and
edited by Van Camp is *Songs for Low Voice in a Comfortable Range* published by C. Fischer.
Several of these songs are annotated in Chapter Thirteen. (see nos. 1834-5)

88. Bach, J. S.   *Now Comrades Be Jolly* (Eng.)
    (1685-1750) Ger.   Allegro 3/8   (F2-C4)   M   Med. diff.
                            Humorous; requires some flexibility; from "Judas
                            Maccabaeus."

89. Dvořák, Antonin   *I Will Sing New Songs of Gladness* (Eng.)
    (1841-1904) Bohem.   Andante 4/4   (C3-C4)   M   Mod. easy
                            Resolute and steady; from the set of "Biblical Songs." (see
                            no. 705)

90. Foster, Stephen   *Beautiful Dreamer* (Eng.)
    (1826-1864) Am.   Moderato 9/8   (A2-C4)   M   Easy
                            Simple and straightforward.

91. Franck, César   *Bread of the Angels* (Panis Angelicus)(Lat./Eng.)
    (1822-1890) Belg.   Slow 4/4   (C#3-B4)   M   Mod. easy

Resolute and steady.

92. Handel, G. F.   *Arm, Arm Ye Brave* (Eng.)
    (1685-1759) Ger./Eng.   Allegro 4/4   (G2-C4)   ML   Med. diff.
                            Energetic; requires flexibility; from "Judas Maccabaeus."

93. Haydn, Joseph   *Now Shines the Fullest Glory* (Eng.)
    (1732-1809) Austrian   Maestoso 3/4   (Eb2-C4)   L-M   Med. diff.
                            Majestic and demanding; from "The Creation."

94. Herbert, Victor   *The Streets of New York* (Eng.)
    (1859-1924) Irish/Am.   Waltz 3/4   (B2-C#4)   M   Mod. easy
                            Popular Broadway tune; from "The Red Mill."

95. Monro, George   *My Lovely Celia* (Eng.)
    (d. 1731) Eng.   Moderate 3/4   (G2-C4)   M   Mod. easy
                            Flowing love song; early English.

96. Purcell, Henry   *I Attempt from Love's Sickness to Fly* (Eng.)
    (1659-1695) Eng.   Allegretto 3/4   (A2-C4)   M   Med. diff.
                            Requires some flexibility.

97. Schubert, Franz   *Hark, Hark! The Lark!* (Eng.)
    (1797-1828) Austrian   Allegretto 6/8   (Bb2-C4)   M   Med. diff.
                            Buoyant and lyric; Shakespeare poetry.

98. Van Camp, L. (arr.)   *All Through the Night* (Eng.)
                            Andante 4/4   (A2-B4)   ML   Easy
                            Flowing and peaceful; a Welsh tune.

99.   *Let Me Fly* (Eng.)
                            Spirited 4/4   (Ab2-C4)   ML   Mod. easy
                            Lively and animated; a spiritual.

100.   *The Turtle Dove* (Eng.)
                            Moderato 4/4   (Bb2-C4)   M   Mod. easy
                            Melancholy and hopeful; an English folk song.

SELECTED SOLOS FOR CONTEST
For Low Voice
Edited by Gene and Audrey Grier
Published by Heritage Music, 1987

A small, quality collection of songs of limited range and fine lyrics for beginning students.
101. Artman, Ruth   *Beneath the Tree* (Eng.)
                            Moderato 4/4   (A2-D4)   M-MH   Med. diff.

102. Butler, Eugene   *Out of the Woods* (Eng.)
                            Moderato 4/4   (C3-D4)   M-MH   Med. diff.

| 103. | Grier, Gene (arr.) | *Shenandoah* (Eng.) | | | |
| | | Slowly 6/8 | (G2-D4) | M-MH | Mod. easy |

| 104. | Lantz, David | *I Saw Two Clouds at Morning* (Eng.) | | | |
| | | Andante 4/4 | (B2-D4) | M-MH | Mod. easy |

| 105. | Wagner, Douglas | *I Never Saw a Moor* (Eng.) | | | |
| | | Moderato 4/4 | (Bb2-C4) | M | Mod. easy |

THE YOUNG SINGER
For Baritone/Bass
Compiled by Richard D. Row
Published by Carl Fischer, Inc., 1965

An excellent collection of songs by various composers for beginning students. Many of the songs have a limited upper range and appropriate tessitura for the young bass voice. Most of the songs are in transposed keys.

106.	Bishop, Sir Henry	*Love Has Eyes* (Eng.)			
	(1786-1855) Eng.	Allegretto 4/4	(C3-D4)	MH	Mod. easy
		Simple and straightforward; flowing line.			

107.	Dix, J. Airlie	*The Trumpeter* (Eng.)(1904)			
		Maestoso 4/4	(B2-D4)	M-MH	Med. diff.
		Grand and broad; long song with big ending.			

108.	Folk Song	*Jesus, Jesus Rest Your Head* (Eng.)			
		Calm 2/4	(A2-D4)	M	Mod. easy
		Tranquil and legato; Christmas song.			

109.	Foote, Arthur	*I'm Wearing Awa' to the Land o' the Leal* (Eng.)			
	(1853-1937) Am.	Moderato 9/8	(Bb2-D4)	ML	Mod. easy
		Warm and sweet.			

110.	Franz, Robert	*Dedication* (Widmung)(Eng./Ger.)			
	(1815-1892) Ger.	Andante 2/4	(C3-D4)	MH	Mod. easy
		Legato and flowing; original key.			

111.		*For Music* (Für Music)(Eng./Ger.)			
		Andante 3/4	(C3-D4)	M	Mod. easy
		Sustained and with feeling.			

112.	German, Edward	*Rolling Down to Rio* (Eng.)			
	(1862-1936) Welch	Allegro 2/4	(G2-D4)	M-MH	Med. diff.
		Energetic with solid tone; Kipling poem.			

113.	Grieg, Edward	*A Swan* (Ein Schwan)(Eng./Ger.)			
	(1843-1907) Norweg.	Andante 3/4	(A2-C4)	M	Med. diff.
		Dynamically varied and interpretively demanding; command			

of soft dynamics required.

114. Handel, George F.   *When First We Met* (Eng.)
      (1685-1759) Ger./Eng.   Andante 4/4   (C3-D4)   MH   Mod. easy
                               Liltingly; from the opera "Ptolemy."

115.   *Where'er You Walk* (Eng.)
                               Largo 4/4   (C3-D4)   M-MH   Mod. easy
                               Sustained with tender feeling; a favorite tune.

116. Haydn, Joseph   *Serenade* (Eng.)
      (1732-1809) Austrian   Andante 2/4   (C3-C4)   M   Mod. easy
                               Simple love song.

117. Homer, Sidney   *Requiem* (Eng.)
      (1864-1953) Am.   Adagio 4/4   (Eb3-Db4)   MH-H   Med. diff.
                               Sustained; perhaps more suited to baritone voice.

118. Löhr, Herman   *The Little Irish Girl* (Eng.)
      (1872-1943) Eng.   Moderato 4/4   (Bb2-D4)   M-MH   Mod. easy
                               Rhythmic lilt; humorous ballad.

119. Mendelssohn, Felix   *On Wings of Song*
      (1809-1847) Ger.   (Auf Flügeln des Gesanges)(Eng./Ger.)
                               Andante 6/8   (C3-D4)   MH   Mod. easy
                               Tranquil and flowing.

120. Old English Song   *Come Let's Be Merry* (Eng.)
                               Allegro 3/4   (Bb2-Eb4)   MH-H   Mod. easy
                               Gaily with solid tone; perhaps better suited to baritone in
                               this key. (see no. 1850.)

121. Purcell, Edward   *Passing By* (Eng.)
      (1689-1740) Eng.   Andante 2/4   (C3-C4)   M-MH   Mod. easy
                               Simple, easy delivery.

122. Quilter, Roger   *Now Sleeps the Crimson Petal* (Eng.)
      (1877-1953) Eng.   Andante 3/4; 5/4   (B2-D4)   M-MH   Mod. easy
                               Lyrically with tenderness; Tennyson poem.

123. Reichardt, Louise   *When the Roses Bloom* (Eng.)
      (1779-1826) Ger.   Moderato 4/8   (C3-D4)   M-MH   Med. diff.
                               Simply with a light touch; demands flexibility with
                               ornaments.

124. Respighi, Ottorino   *Nebbie* (Mists)(It./Eng.)
      (1879-1936) It.   Lento 4/2   (B2-E4)   MH-H   Med. diff.
                               Very sustained; perhaps best suited to baritone in this key.

125. Strauss, Richard   *Morgen* (Tomorrow)(Ger./Eng.)

(1864-1949) Ger.   Lento 4/4   (B2-C4)   **M**   Med. diff.
                            Tranquil with deep feeling; interpretively not easy; lower
                            key than normally available.

126.   Tchaikovsky, Peter   *Pilgrim's Song* (Eng.)
       (1840-1893) Russ.   Andante 4/4   (A2-D4)   **M-MH**   Med. diff.
                                Sustained and broadly felt; effective climax with this
                                excellent song.

127.   Vaughan Williams, R.   *Roadside Fire* (Eng.)
       (1872-1958) Eng.   Allegro 4/4   (Bb2 -Eb4)   **M-MH**   Med. diff.
                                Flowing and sustained; vocally demanding.

128.   *Silent Noon* (Eng.)
                                Largo 3/4   (Bb2-Db4)   **M-MH**   Mod. diff.
                                Sostenuto; command of soft dynamics.

CHAPTER II

ART-SONG ANTHOLOGIES AND COLLECTIONS FOR INTERMEDIATE BASS VOICE

The song anthologies annotated in this chapter are somewhat more difficult vocally, musically, and interpretively and are suitable for the intermediate level bass voice.

ARIE ITALIANE FROM 13TH TO 18TH CENTURIES
For Bass-Baritone
Edited by Raffaele Mingardo
Published by Zerboni, 1976

An important collection of early Italian songs and arias for intermediate or possibly advanced bass or bass-baritone most of which are in their original keys.

129. Anonimo XVI   *E dirgli: Orlando fa che ti raccordi*
                             Grave 2/2   (G#2-C4)   ML   Mod. easy
                             Sustained.

130. Bassani, Giovanni   *Ite o furie*
      (1647-1716) It.   Allegro 4/4   (G2-E4)   M-MH   Mod. diff.
                             An excellent melismatic showpiece for bass voice.

131. Caccini, Giulio   *Amarilli*
      (1550-1618) It.   Andante 2/2   (A2-B3)   ML-M   Med. diff.
                             A favorite early Italian song; sustained; not the original key.

132.   *Aria di romanesca*
                             Moderato 2/2   (C3-Bb3)   M   Med. diff.
                             Agility required; short song.

133.   *Chi mi confort'ahime!*
                             Adagio 2/2   (F2-G3)   ML   Med. diff.
                             Flexibility required; sustained.

134.   *Deh! Se tue belle ciglia*
                             Andante 2/2   (Bb1-C4)   VL-M   Mod. diff.
                             Employment of pulse register; wide range; highly
                             melismatic.

135.   *Vocalizzo*
                             Moderato 4/4   (G2-Ab3)   ML   Mod. diff.
                             Extremely melismatic; excellent command of agility
                             required; only five words in the song; short song.

136. Carissimi, Giacomo   *Amante sciolto d'Amore* (Vittoria, Vittoria!)

    (1605-1674) It.   Allegro 3/4   (Bb2-Eb4) MH   Med. diff.
                    Lower keys of this well-known song are available.

137. Falconieri, Andrea   *Armilla ingrata*
     (1585-1656) It.   Allegro/Mod. 3/2, 4/4 (D2-D4) L-M   Mod. diff.
                    Excellent melismatic piece for low bass.

138.   *Begl'occhi lucenti*
                    Allegretto 3/2   (C3-F4) MH   Med. diff.
                    Flowing legato line.

139.   *Filli vezzosa, Filli amorosa*
                    Allegro 4/4   (C2-E4) VL-M Mod. diff.
                    Excellent show piece for low bass; very wide range;
                    melismatic.

140. Fallamero, G.   *O faccia che rallegri il paradiso*
     (16th century) It.   Andante 4/4   (C#3-B3) M   Mod. easy
                    Strophic with small amounts of agility.

141.   *Siate avvertiti o voi cortesi amanti*
                    Allegro 2/2   (C3-C4) M   Mod. easy
                    Facile articulation.

142. Marcello, B.   *Nave che solca*
     (1686-1739) It.   Allegro/Lento 2/2, 6/8 (E2-E4) L-MH Mod. diff.
                    Agility; facile articulation; large leaps.

143.   *Udite, amanti udite*
                    Adagio/Allegro 8/4, 3/8 (G2-F4) ML-MH Mod. diff.
                    An extended scene with agility, facile articulation and large
                    leaps.

144. Monteverdi, C.   *Perchè se m'odiavi*
     (1567-1643) It.   Andante 6/2, 3/2   (C#3-D4) M-MH Med. diff.
                    Sustained.

145.   *Più lieto il guardo*
                    Allegro 6/2, 4/4   (A2-D4) M-MH Mod. easy
                    Facile articulation in recitato section.

146. Stefani, Giovanni   *Partenza*
     (17th century) It.   Moderato 4/4   (C3-Bb4) M   Mod. easy
                    Strophic with few problems.

147.   Strozzi, Barbara   *Amor dormiglione*
     (ca. 1625- ?) It.   Allegretto 6/2, 4/4 (G#2-C#4) ML-MH Med. diff.
                    Soft, flowing line; some agility required.

148.   *Costume de grandi*

| | | Allegretto/Mod. 6/8, 4/4 (D3-D4) Agility required. | M-MH | Med. diff. |

149.

La Crudele, che non sente, non vede
Allegro/Lento 4/4   (E2-C4)   L-ML   Med. diff.
Agility required.

150. Todi, Jacopone da   *Troppo perde 'l tempo*
      (ca. 1228-1306) It.   Andante 4/4   (C3-D4)   M-MH   Mod. easy
                               Flowing line.

151. Vicentino, Don M.   *Che farala, che dirala*
      (15-16th century) It.   Allegro 3/2, 2/2   (A2-A3)   ML   Mod. easy
                               Some syncopation; rhythmical.

BASS SONGS
Edited by Martin Mason
Previously Published by Oliver Ditson
Currently Published by Theodor Presser, 1990

A useful edition of songs, many in their original keys, for beginning or intermediate bass voice.

152. Braine, Robert   *Brown Men* (Eng.)
      (1896-?) Am.   Allegro moderato 2/4 (Bb2-Eb4)   MH   Med. diff.
                               Requires rapid articulation; rhythmic.

153. Bullard, Frederic F.   *The Indifferent Mariner* (Eng.)
      (1864-1901) Am.   Andante 4/4   (G2-Eb4)   M-MH   Med. diff.
                               Energetic; rhythmic.

154.   *When Good Fellows Get Together* (Eng.)
                               Andante 4/4   (Bb2-D4)   M   Mod. easy
                               Drinking song.

155. Cowles, Eugene   *A Gypsy King Am I* (Eng.)
      (1868-?) Am.   Boldly 4/4   (G2-D4)   M-MH   Mod. easy
                               Descriptive; energetic.

156. Fischer, Ludwig   *Down Deep Within the Cellar* (Eng.)
      (1745-1825) Ger.   (Im kühlen Keller sitz' ich hier)
                               Moderato 4/4   (F2-D4)   L-MH   Mod. easy
                               Drinking song; large leaps; wide range.

157. Flégier, Ange   *The Horn* (Le Cor)(Eng./Fr.)
      (1846-1927) Fr.   Various tempo & meter (D2-D4)   ML-M   Med. diff.
                               Vigorous; several sustained low notes; his most well-known
                               song.

158. Gaul, Harvey   *A Song of Fellowship* (Eng.)

	(1881-1945)	Strong 4/4 Energetic.	(A2-D4)	ML-M	Med. diff.
159.	Hasse, Gustav (1890-?) Ger.	*The Vesper-Hymn* (Die Vesper-Hymne)(Eng./Ger.) Andantino 6/4 Sustained.	(C3-D#4)	MH	Med. diff.
160.	Jude, William H. (1851-1922) Eng.	*The Skipper* (Eng.) Con molto 6/8 Vigorous song of the sea; some flexibility required.	(G2-E4)	ML-MH	Med. diff.
161.	Mozart, W. A. (1756-1791) Austrian	*O Isis and Osiris* (Possenti numi)(Eng./It.) Slow 3/4 Very sustained; warm tone; excellent beginning aria of its type for low bass.	(F2-C4)	L-M	Med. diff.
162.		*Within This Sacred Dwelling* (Eng./Ger) (In diesen heil'gen Hallen) Slow 4/4 Sustained; flowing line; warm tone; excellent beginning aria of its type for low bass.	F#2-C#4)	L-M	Med. diff.
163.	Nevin, George B. (1859-1933) Am.	*Song of the Armourer* (Eng.) Con spirito 4/4 Vigorous.	(C3-D4)	M-MH	Mod. easy
164.	O'Hara, George B.	*Leetle Bateese* (Eng.) Brightly 6/8 Humorous.	(B2-D4)	ML-MH	Mod. easy
165.	Pergolesi, G. B. (1710-1736) It.	*Nina* (Tre giorni)(Eng./It.) Andante 4/4 Flowing legato.	(C3-D4)	MH	Mod. easy
166.	Schubert, Franz (1797-1828) Austrian	*By the Sea* (Am Meer)(Eng./Ger.) Molto lento 4/4 Sustained.	(Bb2-Db4)	MH	Med. diff.
167.		*The Wanderer* (Der Wanderer)(Eng./Ger.) Molto adagio 2/2 Sustained; rather demanding vocally; energetic; excellent song for bass voice.	(D2-D4)	MH	Mod. diff.
168.	Schumann, Robert (1810-1856) Ger.	*The Two Grenadiers* (Die beiden Grenadiere)(Eng./Ger.) Moderato 4/4 Vigorous; vocally demanding final section; well-known.	(Bb2-D4)	MH	Mod. diff.
169.	Scott, Lady John (1810-1900) Scot.	*Annie Laurie* (Eng.) Moderato 4/4	(D3-D4)	MH	Mod. easy

Flowing legato.

170. Shield, William   *The Friar of Orders Gray* (Eng.)
     (1748-1829) Eng.   Con spirito 6/8   (G2-D4)   ML-MH   Med. diff.
                              Energetic; requires flexibility.

171. Tchaikovsky, Peter   *Don Juan's Serenade* (Eng.)
     (1840-1893) Russ.   Allegro 3/4   (A2-D4(E4)) MH   Mod. diff.
                              Vocally demanding in places; some agility required;
                              well-known.

172. Wagner, Richard   *O Thou Sublime, Sweet Evening Star*
     (1813-1883) Ger.   (O! du mein holder Abendstern)(Eng./Ger.)
                              Slowly 4/4, 6/8   (G2-C#4)   ML-MH   Med. diff.
                              Baritone aria transposed to lower key for bass; very
                              sustained; well-known.

BASS SONGS
Imperial Edition
Edited by Sydney Northcote
Published by Boosey & Hawkes, 1953

This well-known and important edition contains songs that are generally more demanding and
suited to the intermediate or possibly advanced bass singer. The songs, most in their original
keys, are from the standard repertoire with a wide variety in style.

173. Arne, T. A.   *Bacchus, God of Mirth and Wine* (Eng.)
     (1710-1778) Eng.   Moderato 4/4   (Ab2-Eb4)   MH   Med. diff.
                              Humorous and energetic; drinking song.

174. Beethoven, L. van   *The Song of the Flea* (Eng./Ger.)
     (1770-1827) Ger.   Allegretto 2/4   (C3-D4)   MH   Med. diff.
                              Humorous ballad; strophic design; some patter.

175. Blow, John.   *The Self-Banished* (Eng.)
     (1648-1708) Eng.   Andante 3/4   (A2-D4)   MH   Med. diff.
                              Introspective; early English.

176. Brahms, Johannes   *Earth and Sky* (Feldeinsamkeit)(Eng./Ger.)
     (1833-1897) Ger.   Lento 4/4   (B2-Eb4)   MH-H   Med. diff.
                              Sustained and soft; demands command of soft dynamics.

177.   *I Said I Will Not Forget Thee*
                              (Nicht mehr zu dir zu gehen)(Eng./Ger.)
                              Lento 3/2   (C3-Eb4)   M-MH   Med. diff.
                              Sustained and somber; interpretively difficult.

178. Buononcini, G. B.   *Love Leads to Battle* (Pupille nere)(Eng./It.)
     (1672-1755) It.   Allegro 3/4   (C3-D4)   MH   Med. diff.

Energetic; requires some flexibility.

179. Carissimi, Giacomo   *I Triumph! I Triumph!* (Vittoria! Vittoria!)(Eng./It.)
     (1604-1674) It.   Allegro 3/4   (A2-D4)   M-MH   Med. diff.
                              Vigorous; melismatic; requires considerable agility.

180. English Air   *Down Among the Dead Men* (Eng.)
                              Allegro 4/4   (A2-D4)   M-MH   Mod. easy
                              Vigorous drinking song.

181. German Trinklied   *Drinking* (Eng.)
                              Allegretto 4/4   (F2-D4)   L-MH   Mod. easy
                              Spirited; wide leaps; attributed to Ludwig Fischer, bass.

182. Gounod, Charles   *The Valley* (Le Vallon)(Eng./Fr.)
     (1818-1893) Fr.   Andante 4/4   (A2-C#4)   M-MH   Mod. easy
                              Sustained and reflective.

183. Handel, George F.   *Droop Not Young Lover* (Eng./It.)
     (1685-1759) Ger./Eng   Allegretto 3/8   (G2-E4)   ML-MH   Med. diff.
                              Bold melodic line; vocal agility required.

184.   *Love That's True Will Live Forever* (Eng./It.)
                              Allegro 4/4   (B2-D4)   MH   Mod. diff.
                              Majestic and energetic; a popular aria from the opera
                              "Berenice."

185. Harty, Hamilton   *My Lagen Love* (Eng.)
     (1879-1941) Irish   Quasi without tempo (Bb2-Eb4)   MH   Mod. diff.
                              Expressively free.

186. Head, Michael   *Money, O!* (Eng.)
     (1900-1976) Eng.   Moderate 4/4   (G2-D4)   MH   Med. diff.
                              Philosophical and thoughtful.

187. Hume, Tobias   *Tobacco* (Eng.)
     (d. 1645) Eng.   Lively 2/2   (Bb2-Db4)   M-MH   Mod. easy
                              Humorous song of love.

188. Lully, J. B.   *All Your Shades* (Bois épais)(Eng./Fr.)
     (1632-1687) Fr.   Andante 4/4   (B2-D4)   M-MH   Med. diff.
                              Legato, sustained; a favorite French aria originally composed
                              for tenor.

189. Mendelssohn, Felix   *I Am a Roamer* (Eng./Ger.)
     (1809-1847) Ger.   Quick 2/4   (E2-E4)   L-H   Mod. diff.
                              Demanding patter song with wide range; facile articulation
                              required.

190. Mozart, W. A.   *Thoughts at Eventide* (Abendempfindung)(Eng./Ger.)

| | (1756-1791) Austrian | Andante 4/4   (C3-Db4)   MH   Mod. diff.
Flowing, legato; interpretively difficult. |

191. Purcell, Henry
     (1658-1695) Eng.

Arise, Ye Subterranean Winds (Eng.)
Allegro 4/4   (E2-D4)   L-MH   Mod. diff.
Vigorous; agility required; vocally demanding.

192.

Hear! Ye Gods of Britain (Eng.)
Lento 2/4   (G2-Eb4)   MH   Mod. diff.
Dramatic and demanding.

193.

The Owl Is Abroad (Eng.)
Moderato 4/4   (G2-D4)   ML-MH   Mod. easy
Humorous, nonsense song.

194. Rachmaninoff, S.
     (1873-1943) Russ.

By the Grave (Sur la tombe encore fraiche)(Eng./Fr.)
Largo 4/4   (C3-E4)   M-H   Mod. diff.
Dramatic, expressive; interpretively difficult.

195. Schubert, Franz
     (1797-1828) Ger.

Lay of the Imprisoned Huntsman
(Lied des gefangenen Jägers)(Eng./Fr.)
Allegretto 3/4   (C3-C4)   M-MH   Med. diff.
Descriptive song of hunting and love.

196.

The Lime Tree (Der Lindenbaum)(Eng./Ger.)
Moderato 3/4   (A2-D4)   M-MH   Med. diff.
Expressive, legato; command of mezzo voice.

197.

My Last Abode (Aufenthalt)(Eng./Ger.)
Vigorous 2/4   (G2-Eb4)   L-H   Mod. diff.
Demanding and dramatic; requires solid low notes.

198. Schumann, Robert
     (1810-1856) Ger.

The Last Toast (Auf das Trinkglass)(Eng./Ger.)
Lento 4/4   (Ab2-Eb4)   M-MH   Med. diff.
Legato with deep feeling.

199.

The Two Grenadiers (Die beiden Grenadiere)(Eng./Ger.)
Moderato 4/4   (A2-D4)   M-MH   Med. diff.
Dramatic ballad; demanding climax.

200. Strauss, Richard
     (1864-1949) Ger.

The Solitary One (Der Einsame)(Eng./Ger.)
Adagio 4/4   (Eb2-C4)   L-M   Mod. diff.
Restrained and sensitive; one of two songs in a set for bass
voice.

201. Tchaikovsky, Peter
     (1840-1893) Russ.

To the Forest (Eng.)
Andante 4/4   (A2-D4)   M-MH   Med. diff.
Sustained and deeply felt; effective climax.

202. Wood, Charles

Ethiopia Saluting the Colours (Eng.)

(1866-1926) Irish   Alla marcia 4/4   (Ab2-Db4)   M-MH   Med. diff.
                           Descriptive and effective.

BASS SONGS AND ARIAS
Published by C. F. Peters

This volume of bass songs is in German only, but contains several songs not easily found
elsewhere.

203. Bach, J. S.   *Todessehnsucht* (Ger.)
     (1865-1750) Ger.   Langsam 3/4   (Bb2-F4)   M-H   Med. diff.
                           Sustained.

204. Beethoven, L. van   *Bitten* (Ger.)
     (1770-1827) Ger.   Grave 2/2   (C3-C4)   MH   Med. diff.
                           Very sustained; not original key.

205.   *Die ehre Gottes* (Ger.)
                           Majestically 2/2   (Ab2-Db4)   MH   Med. diff.
                           Sustained; not original key.

206.   *Hat Man nicht auch Gold daneben* (from "Fidelio")(Ger.)
                           Allegro moderato 2/4 (Bb2-D4)   MH   Med. diff.
                           Rapid articulation required.

207. Brückler, Hugo   *Sonne taucht in Meeresfluten* (Ger.)
     (1845-1871) Ger.   Langsam 4/2   (C3-Db4)   M   Mod. diff.
                           Sustained.

208. Fischer, Ludwig   *Der Trinker* (Ger.)
     (1745-1825) Ger.   Moderato 4/4   (F2-F4)   M   Mod. easy
                           Wide range; drinking song; folk song.

209. Grieg, Edward   *Ich liebe dich* (Ger.)
     (1843-1907) Norweg.   Andante 3/4   (C3-Eb4)   MH   Med. diff.
                           Old favorite; sustained; not original key.

210. Handel, G. F.   *Ombra mai fu* (Ger. trans.)
     (1685-1759) Ger./Eng. Largo 3/4   (Ab2-Db4)   M-MH   Med. diff.
                           Sustained; not original key.

211. Loewe, Carl   *Heinrich der Vogler* (Ger.)
     (1796-1869) Ger.   Slow/Fast 4/8,6/8   (G#2-D4)   L-MH   Med. diff.
                           Ballad; some agility required; not original key.

212.   *Prinz Eugen* (Ger.)
                           Comodo 5/4   (F2-D4(F4)) M-MH   Med. diff.
                           Ballad; rhythmical; not original key.

213. Lortzing, Gustav   *Auch ich war ein Jüngling* (Ger.)
      (1801-1851) Ger.   Andante 3/8   (A2-D4)   M   Med. diff.
                                Strophic; rhythmic; original key.

214. Lyra, Justus   *Reiterlied* (Ger.)
      (1822-1882) Ger.   Mässig 6/8   (C#3-D4)   MH   Mod. easy
                                Strophic folk song.

215. Mendelssohn, Felix   *Herr Gott Abrahams* (from "Elijah")(Ger.)
      (1809-1847) Ger.   Adagio 4/4   (Bb2-Eb4)   MH   Mod. diff.
                                Sustained, original key.

216. Mozart, W. A.   *In diesen heil'gen Hallen*
      (1756-1791) Austrian   (from "Die Zauberflöte")(Ger.)
                                Larghetto 2/4   (F#2(E2)-C#4)   L-M   Med. diff.
                                Sustained; good introductory aria of its type for beginning
                                students; original key.

217.   *O Isis und Osiris* (from "Die Zauberflöte")(Ger.)
                                Andante 3/4   (F2-C4)   L-M   Med. diff.
                                Sustained; good introductory aria of its type for beginning
                                students; original key.

218.   *Warnung* (Ger.)
                                Scherzhaft 2/4   (C3-D4)   MH   Med. diff.
                                Some rapid articulation; original key.

219. Schubert, Franz   *Der Lindenbaum* (Ger.)
      (1797-1828) Austrian   Mässig 3/4   (G2-C4)   ML-M   Med. diff.
                                Flowing legato; not original key.

220.   *Der Wanderer* (Ger.)
                                Slow/Fast 2/2, 6/8   (E2(C2)-C4)   L-MH   Mod. diff.
                                Sustained section; animated section; one whole-step lower
                                than original key.

221. Schumann, Robert   *Die beiden Grenadiere* (Ger.)
      (1810-1856) Ger.   Mässig 4/4   (A2-D4)   MH   Med. diff.
                                Demanding climax; sustained; original key.

222.   *Frühlingsfahrt* (Ger.)
                                Frisch 4/4   (A2-D4)   M-MH   Med. diff.
                                Energetic; not original key.

223. Sommer, W.   *Vagans Scholasticus* (Ger.)
                                Andante 4/4   (A2-D4)   M-MH   Mod. easy
                                Strophic folk song.

224. Wolf, Hugo   *Biterolf* (Ger.)
      (1860-1903) Austrian   Ziemlich gehalten 3/2 (Bb2-Db4)   M-MH   Med. diff.

Sustained; somewhat chromatic; original key.

225.   *Heimweh* (Ger.)
                             Mässig 4/4   (A2-E4)   M-H   Mod. diff.
                             Sustained; somewhat chromatic; not original key.

226.   Zahn, C. Johannes   *Reiterlied* (Ger.)
       (1817-1895) Ger.   Marchmässig 4/4   (G2-D4)   **M-MH**   Mod. easy
                             Strophic folk song.

227.   Zelter, Carl   *Der König in Thule* (Ger.)
       (1758-1842) Austrian   Sanft und frei 6/4   (A2-A3)   ML   Mod. easy
                             Strophic ballad; original key.

THE RUSSIAN SONG BOOKS
SONGS FOR BASS VOICE
Edited by Rosa Newmarch
Published by Breitkopf

An important collection of songs by Russian composers suitable for intermediate or advanced
bass voice. The songs in this edition are in their original keys and are in English only.

228.   Arensky, Antony S.   *The Spirit of Poesy* (Eng.)
       (1861-1906) Russ.   Andante 4/4   (Bb2-G4)   VH   Mod. diff.
                             For baritone.

229.   *The Wolves* (Eng.)
                             Andante 9/8   (A2-Eb4)   M-MH   Mod. diff.
                             Dedicated to Feodor Chaliapin; ballad; interpretively
                             demanding.

230.   Balakirev, Mily   *The Desert* (Eng.)
       (1836-1910) Russ.   Various tempo 4/4   (C#3-E4)   M-H   Mod. diff.
                             Mystical; interpretively demanding.

231.   Bleichmann, Julius   *The Convoy* (Eng.)
       (1868-1909) Russ.   Tempo di Marcia 4/4   (C#3-E4)   M-H   Mod. diff.
                             A favorite of Feodor Chaliapin and dedicated to him; ballad;
                             interpretively challenging.

232.   Kalinnikov, Vassily   *A Prayer* (Eng.)
       (1966-1900) Russ.   Various tempo & meter (C3-E4)   M-H   Mod. diff.
                             Sustained; interpretively demanding.

233.   Koenemann, T.   *The Blacksmith* (Eng.)
       (Keneman, Feodor)   Various tempo & meter (B2-E#4)   M-H   Mod. diff.
       (1873-1937) Russ.   Dedicated to Feodor Chaliapin; vocally and interpretively
                             demanding.

234.   *The Three Roads* (Eng.)

Various tempo & meter (B2-E4)   M-H   Mod. diff.
Descriptive; interpretively challenging.

235.   *When the King Went Forth to War* (Eng.)
                              Various tempo & meter (A2-E4)   M-H   Mod. diff.
                              Composed for Feodor Chaliapin; vocally and interpretively
                              demanding; ballad.

236. Korestchenko, A.   *Autumn Melody* (Eng.)
      (1870-1921) Russ.   Allegro non troppo 6/8   (D3-F4)   M-H   Med. diff.
                              Flowing legato.

237. Slonov, Mikhail   *O Thou Sun, Thou Blessed, Glowing Sun* (Eng.)
      (1869-1930) Russ.   Andante 2/4   (D3-C4(E4)) M   Med. diff.
                              Sustained.

238. Sokolov, Vladimir   *Through the Fields in Winter* (Eng.)
      (1830-1890) Russ.   Various tempo & meter (B2-E4)   M-H   Med. diff.
                              Ballad; interpretively demanding.

239. Tchaikovsky, Pyotr   *Benediction* (Pilgrim's Song)(Eng.)
      (1840-1893) Russ.   Andante 4/4   (A2-D4)   M-MH   Med. diff.
                              Well-known; sustained; flowing legato; effective climax.

240. Tcherepnin, Nikolai   *Menaeceus* (Eng.)
      (1873-1845) Russ.   Various tempo & meter (G2-Eb4)   ML-MH   Mod. diff.
                              Interpretively challenging; requires command of soft
                              dynamics.

CHAPTER III

ART-SONG ANTHOLOGIES AND COLLECTIONS FOR ADVANCED BASS VOICE

The song anthologies annotated in this chapter are musically, vocally, and interpretively difficult and are suitable for the more advanced bass voice.

THE CONTEMPORARY ART SONG
For Bass-Baritone
Edited by Hermann Reutter
Published by Schott

An important collection of extremely challenging songs by a prominent group of 20th-century composers. From late romantic style to polytonal, atonal, and serial models, these songs bring arduous musical, vocal, and interpretive requirements. These songs are in their original keys.

241.	Bartók, Béla (1881-1945) Hung.	*Im Tale* (Hun./Ger./Eng.) Sostenuto 4/4	(Db3-Eb4)	M-MH	Diff.
242.	Fortner, Wolfgang (1907-1987) Ger.	*Abbitte* (Ger.) Langsam 4/4, 3/4	(B2-Eb4)	MH	Diff.
243.		*Hyperions Schicksalslied* (Ger.) Varied tempo & meter	(A2-F4)	M-H	Diff.
244.		*Lied vom Weidenbaum* (Ger./Eng.) Langsam 3/4	(A2-Db4)	ML-M	Diff.
245.	Hindemith, Paul (1895-1963) Ger.	*Fragment* (Ger.) Langsam 4/4	(B2-D4)	M-MH	Diff.
246.	Mahler, Gustav (1860-1911) Ger.	*Wo die schönen Trompeten blasen* (Ger./Eng.) Varied tempo and meter	(G2-F4)	M-H	Diff.
247.	Milhaud, Darius (1892-1974) Fr.	*Lamentation* (Fr.) Allant 4/4, 3/4	(A2-E4)	M-MH	Diff.
248.	Pfitzner, Hans (1869-1949) Ger.	*Hussens Kerker* (Ger.) Langsam 3/2, 4/2	(B2-E4)	M-MH	Diff.
249.	Reutter, Hermann (1900-1985) Ger.	*Johann Kepler* (Ger.) Varied tempo & meter	(Bb2-Db4)	M-MH	Diff.
250.		*Trommel* (Ger./Eng.) Alla marcia 3/4, 4/4	(C3-E4)	MH-H	Diff.

251.   *Lied für ein dunkles Mädchen* (Ger./Eng.)
                       Langsam 2/4, 3/4   (B2-D4)   M-MH   Diff.

252.   Schoeck, Othmar *Peregrina* (Ger.)
       (1886-1957) Ger. Langsam 3/4   (Bb2-Gb4)   H   Diff.

TEN SONGS FOR LOW MAN'S VOICE
Published by Mobart Music Publications, 1978

The following is an interesting and challenging collection of songs for bass or bass-baritone by contemporary composers.

       Hall, Jeffrey   *Two Settings from Ahab* (Eng.)
These two songs are extremely complex and demanding.
253.   No. I
                       Andante; complex meters (F#2-E4)   ML-H   Very diff.

254.   No. II
                       Complex tempo & meter (E2-E4)   L-H   Very diff.

255.   Hobson, R. Bruce   *A Busy Man Speaks* (Eng.)
                       Slow; varied meter   (A2-F#4)   ML-VH   Very diff.

       Leibowitz, René   *Trois poèmes* (Fr./Eng.)
       (1913-1972) Polish/Fr.
These three very short songs are musically and interpretively complex and require a fine technique.
256.   No. I
                       Lento 2/2   (G2-Eb4)   MH   Diff.

257.   No. II
                       Moderato 6/8, 9/8   (Ab2-Eb4)   MH   Diff.

258.   No. III
                       Andante 3/4   (F#2-Fb4)   ML-MH   Diff.

       Vier Lieder (Ger./Eng.)
These four very short songs require excellent musicianship, technique, and interpretive skills.
259.   No. I
                       Andante 2/4, 3/4   (F2-Eb4)   ML-MH   Diff.

260.   No. II
                       Adagio 3/4   (F#2-D4)   ML-MH   Diff.

261.   No. III
                             Allegro 6/8   (E2-D#4)   L-H   Very diff.

262.   No. IV
                             Largo 2/2, 3/4   (A2-E4)   ML-H   Diff.

CHAPTER IV

ADDITIONAL ART-SONG ANTHOLOGIES AND COLLECTIONS FOR BASS VOICE

The following collections and anthologies are out of print and in many cases contain songs that are dated or that can be found in volumes that are presently available. A number of jewels do appear in these collections, however, in the form of neglected noteworthy pieces or songs that are in a lower key than are found elsewhere. For these reasons and in an effort toward completeness the following volumes are included, although less fully annotated.

ALBUM OF BASS SONGS
In Four Volumes
G. Schirmer, 1890

VOLUME I

263. Beethoven, L. van (1770-1827) Ger.
In This Sepulchral Darkness
(In questa tomba)(Eng./It.)
Lento 2/4   (C3-E4)   M-MH   Med. diff.

264. Esser, Heinrich (1818-1872) Ger.
The Dead Soldier (Der Todte Soldat)(Eng./Ger.)
Moderato 4/4   (G2-E4)   M-MH   Med. diff.

265. Gounod, Charles (1818-1893) Fr.
Nazareth (Eng.)
Moderato 6/4   (G2-D4)   ML-M   Med. diff.

266. Henrion, Paul (1819-1901) Fr.
The Muleteer of Tarrangona
(Le Muletier de Tarrangone)(Eng./Fr.)
Tempo di Bolero 3/4   (Ab2-D4)   MH   Mod. diff.

267. Kreutzer, Conradin (1780-1849) Ger.
Forest Song (Waldeslied)(Eng./Ger.)
Moderato 4/4   (E2-D4)   L-M   Med. diff.

268. Loewe, Carl (1796-1869) Ger.
Phosphorescence (Meeresleuchten)(Eng./Ger.)
Andante 9/8   (E2-B3)   L-M   Med. diff.

269. Löhr, Frederic (1872-1943) Eng.
Out on the Deep (Eng.)
Allegro moderato 6/8   (G2-C4)   ML-M   Med. diff.

270. Lortzing, G. A. (1801-1851) Ger.
In Childhood I Dallied (Sonst spielt ich)(Eng./Ger.)
Andante 3/4   (E3-F4)   VH   Med. diff.

271. Mozart, W. A. (1756-1791) Austrian
To Scenes of Peace Retiring
(In diesen heil'gen Hallen)(Eng./Ger.)

		Slowly 4/4	(F#2(E2)-C#4)	L-M	Med. diff.

272.   *O Isis and Osiris* (O Isis und Osiris)(Eng./Ger.)
Slowly 3/4   (F2-C4)   L-M   Med. diff.

273.   Nessler, Victor   *It Was Not So to Be*
      (1841-1890) Ger.   (Es hat nicht sollen sein)(Eng./Ger.)
Andante 4/4   (A2-C#4)   M   Med. diff.

274.   Rodney, Paul   *The Brave Sentinel* (Eng.)
Con spirito 4/4   (Bb2-D4)   M-MH   Med. diff.

275.   *Calvary* (Eng.)
Maestoso 12/8   (A2(F#2)-C#4)   ML-M   Med. diff.

276.   *The Old Guard* (Eng.)
Con spirito 4/4   (A2-D4)   ML-MH   Med. diff.

277.   *The Soldier's Dream* (Eng.)
Moderato 4/4   (G2-D4)   M-MH   Med. diff.

278.   Roeckel, Joseph   *Happy Three* (Eng.)
      (1838-1923) Ger.   Allegretto 4/4   (Bb2-D4)   M   Med. diff.

279.   Schubert, Franz   *Erlking* (Erlkönig)(Eng./Ger.)
      (1797-1828) Austrian   Schnell 4/4   (A2-E4)   M-H   Mod. diff.

280.   Schumann, Robert   *The Poet's Love* (Ich grolle nicht)(Eng./Ger.)
      (1810-1856) Ger.   Nicht zu schnell 4/4 (Bb2-D4(G4))   M-MH   Med. diff.

281.   *The Two Grenadiers*
(Die beiden Grenadiere)(Eng./Ger.)
Mässig 4/4   (C3-D4)   MH   Med. diff.

282.   Vogrich, Max   *The Clover Blossoms Kiss Thy Feet* (Eng.)
      (1852-1916) Transyl.   Moderato 4/4   (Bb2-Db4)   M-MH   Med. diff.

283.   *Thy True Heart* (Eng.)
Andante 3/4   (B2-D4)   M   Med. diff.

VOLUME II

284.   Brüll, Ignaz   *How Times Have Changed*
      (1846-1907)   Austrian   (Wie anders war es)(Eng./Ger.)
Allegro moderato 4/4   (G2-C4)   ML-M   Med. diff.

285.   Carissimi, Giacomo   *Victorious My Heart Is* (Vittoria mio core!)(Eng./It.)
      (1605-1674) It.   Allegro 3/4   (A2-D4)   M-MH   Med. diff.

286.   Graben-Hoffmann, G.   *I at Thy Feet*

	(1820-1900) Ger.	(Zu deinen Füssen möcht ich liegen)(Eng./Ger.)		
		Allegro moderato 6/8 (C#3-E4) M-H Med. diff.		
287.	Gumbert, Ferdinand	*The Pirate* (Der Sceräuber)(Eng./Ger.)		
	(1818-1896) Ger.	Allegro moderato 6/8 (G#2-D4) M-MH Med. diff.		
288.	Hatton, John L.	*Simon the Cellarer* (Eng.)		
	(1808-1886) Eng.	Allegretto 6/8 (G2-D4) M-MH Med. diff.		
289.	King, Oliver	*Israfel* (Eng.)		
	(1855-1923) Eng.	Andante 4/4 (B2-E4) MH Med. diff.		
290.	Kreutzer, Conradin	*What Noble Joys a Hunter's Life*		
	(1780-1849) Ger.	(Ein Schütz bin ich)(Eng./Ger.)		
		Allegro moderato 6/8 (Bb2-Eb4) MH Med. diff.		
291.	Lassen, Eduard	*The Captive Admiral* (Der gefangene Admiral)(Eng./Ger.)		
	(1830-1904) Danish	Molto lento 4/4 (G2-F4) ML-H Mod. diff.		
292.		*Greeting* (Grüssen)(Eng./Ger.)		
		Langsam 3/4 (G2-D4) M Med. diff.		
293.	Mattei, Tito	*My Native Land* (Patria)(Eng./It.)		
	(1841-1914) It.	Andante 4/4 (G2-D4) ML-MH Med. diff.		
294.	Mendelssohn, Felix	*Show Me, Almighty* (Eng.)		
	(1809-1847) Ger.	Adagio/Allegro 4/4 (B2-D4) MH Med. diff.		
295.	Meyerbeer, G.	*Song of the Trappist*		
	(1791-1864) Ger./Fr.	(Cantique du Trappiste)(Eng./Fr.)		
		Andante 4/4 (F2-D4) ML-MH Mod. diff.		
296.	Pinsuti, Ciro	*Bedouin Love Song* (Eng.)		
	(1829-1888) It.	Allegretto 3/4 (F#2-D34) M-MH Med. diff.		
297.	Randegger, A.	*The Gold-Beater* (Eng.)		
	(1832-1911) It./Eng.	Boldly 6/8 (B2-E4) M-H Med. diff.		
298.	Reissiger, F.	*The Silesian Toper and the Devil*		
	(1809-1883) Ger.	(Der schlesische Zecher und der Teufel)(Eng./Ger.)		
		Moderato 4/4 (F#2-D4) M-MH Med. diff.		
299.	Schäffer, August	*The Jolly Friar* (Das Pfäfflein)(Eng./Ger.)		
	(1814-1879) Ger.	Moderato 4/4 (C3-D4) M-H Med. diff.		
300.	Vogrich, Max	*I Love But Thee* (Eng.)		
	(1852-1916) Transyl.	Molto vivo 4/4 (A2-D4(E4)) MH Med. diff.		
301.		*Poor Wounded Heart* (Eng.)		
		Andante 2/4 (Gb2(Eb2)-Db4) L-M Med. diff.		

302. Watson, W. M.   *Anchored* (Eng.)
(1840-1889) Eng.   Con spirito 6/8   (C3-D4)   M-MH   Med. diff.

303.   *Thy Sentinel Am I* (Eng.)
Bold 4/4   (F2-D4)   M-MH   Med. diff.

304. Widor, Charles   *Invocation* (Eng.)
(1844-1937) Fr.   Lento 6/8   (Bb2-D4)   M   Med. diff.

VOLUME III

305. Becker, Valentin E.   *The Forest Cross* (Das Kreuz im walde)(Eng./Ger.)
(1814-1890) Ger.   Various tempo & meter   (G2(E2)-D4)   M   Med. diff.

306. Binder, Carl   *If Power Divine*
(1816-1860) Austrian   (Wenn ich einmal der Herrgott wär)(Eng./Ger.)
Allegro 3/4   (B2-E4)   M-MH   Med. diff.

307. D'Alquen, F. (arr.)   *In Cellar Cool* (Im tiefen Keller sitz' ich hier)(Eng./Ger.)
Con spirito 4/4   (F2-D4)   L-MH   Mod. easy
The melody is attributed to Ludwig Fischer.

308. Dorn, Alexander   *Snowdrops* (Schneeglöckchen)(Eng./Ger.)
(1833-1901) Ger.   Allegretto 2/4   (E2-D4)   L-M   Med. diff.

309. Gailhard, Pierre   *The Giant* (Le Géant)(Eng./Fr.)
(1848-1918) Fr.   Largamente 3/4   (B2-E4)   M-H   Med. diff.

310. Giorza, Paolo   *Alone* (Eng.)
(1832-1914) It./Am.   Andante 4/4   (A2(D2)-E4)   M-MH   Med. diff.

311. Hartmann, Ludwig   *I Dream'd of a Pallid Princess Maid*
(1836-1910) Ger.   (Mir träumte von einem Königskind)(Eng./Ger.)
Tranquillo 4/4   (G2-Eb4)   M-MH   Med. diff.

312. Hölzel, Gustave   *Belltones* (Glockengeläute)(Eng./Ger.)
(1813-1883) Hung.   Allegro moderato 6/8   (G#2-D4)   M-MH   Med. diff.

313. Kleffel, Arno   *Primula veris* (Eng./Ger.)
(1840-1913) Ger.   Moderato 9/8   (D3-Eb4)   H   Med. diff.

314. Lassen, Edward   *What Dost Before* (Was machst du mir)(Eng./Ger.)
(1830-1904) Danish   Allegretto 3/4   (D3-Eb4)   H   Med. diff.

315. Mariani, Angelo   *Invocation* (Invocazione a Dio)(Eng./It.)
(1822-1873) It.   Andante grave 4/4   (A2-Eb4)   MH-H   Med. diff.

316. Marschner, H.   *Upon That Day* (An jenem Tag)(Eng./Ger.)
(1795-1861) Ger.   Various tempo & meter   (B2-D4)   M-MH   Med. diff.

317. Massenet, Jules   *Vision Fair* (Vision fugitive)(Eng./Fr.)
      (1842-1912) Fr.   Allegro 4/4   (A2-Eb4)   MH   Med. diff.

318. Mattei, Tito   *Oh Hear the Wild Wind Blow* (Eng.)
      (1841-1914) It.   Allegretto mosso 3/4   (G#2-E4)   ML-H   Med. diff.

319. Matys, Carl   *The Warder* (Der Thürmer)(Eng./Ger.)
                               Andante 4/4   (F#2-E4)   MH   Med. diff.

320. Pfeil, Heinrich   *Calm Is the Lake* (Still ruht der See)(Eng./Ger.)
      (1835-1899) Ger.   Lento 3/4   (C3-Db4)   M-MH   Mod. easy

321. Reissiger, Carl   *Noah* (Eng.)
      (1798-1859) Ger.   Moderato 3/4   (F#2-D4)   MH   Med. diff.

322. Schnecker, Peter   *The Old Stone Wall* (Eng.)
      (1850-1903) Am.   Andante 3/4   (G2-E4)   M-H   Med. diff.

323. Schubert, Franz   *The Wanderer* (Der Wanderer)(Eng./Ger.)
      (1797-1828) Austrian   Lento 2/2   (D2-D4)   MH   Mod. diff.

324. Shield, William   *The Friar of Orders Gray* (Eng.)
      (1748-1829) Eng.   Con spirito 6/8   (G2-D4)   ML-MH   Med. diff.

325. Vogrich, Max   *From Greenland's Icy Mountain* (Eng.)
      (1852-1916) Transyl.   Andante 4/4   (G2-D4)   ML-MH   Med. diff.

326. Wallnöfer, Adolf   *Vale carissima* (Eng./Ger.)
      (1854-1946) Austrian   Lento 4/4   (F3-Db4)   MH   Med. diff.

327. Weidt, Heinrich   *How Fair Art Thou* (Wie schön bist du)(Eng./Ger.)
      (1828-1901) Ger.   Moderato/Agitato 3/4 (Bb2-Eb4)   MH   Med. diff.

328. Wurda, J.   *Soldier's Love* (Soldatenliebe)(Eng./Ger.)
                               Various tempo & meter (G2-Eb4)   MH   Med. diff.

VOLUME IV

329. Gounod, Charles   *Vulcan's Song*
      (1818-1893) Fr.   (Au bruit des lourds mateaux)(Eng./Fr.)
                               Allegro moderato 2/4   (Ab2-Eb4)   M-MH   Mod. diff.

330. Jude, William H.   *The Mighty Deep* (Eng.)
      (1851-1922) Eng.   Andante serioso 4/4   (F2-E4)   L-MH   Med. diff.

331. Lachner, Franz   *The Repentance* (Reue)(Eng./Ger.)
      (1803-1890) Ger.   Andante 2/4   (Eb2-Eb4)   L-MH   Med. diff.

332. Lindpainter, P. von   *The Standard Watch* (Die Fahnenwacht)(Eng./Ger.)
     (1791-1856) Ger.   Allegro 4/4   (C3-E4)   H   Med. diff.

333. Loewe, C.   *The Watch* (Die Uhr)(Eng./Ger.)
     (1796-1869) Ger.   Andantino 6/8   (Ab2-Eb4)   M-MH   Med. diff.

334. Lortzing, Albert   *Stadinger's Song*
     (1801-1851) Ger.   (from "Der Waffenschmied")(Eng.)
                             Andante 3/8   (A2-D4)   M-MH   Med. diff.

335. Mendelssohn, F.   *I Am a Roamer Bold* (from "Son and Stranger")(Eng.)
     (1809-1847) Ger.   Allegro vivace 2/4   (F2-E4)   L-H   Mod. diff.

336. Mililotti, Leopoldo   *Heart-Broken Sailor Boy*
                             (Povero Marinar)(Eng./Ger./Fr.)
                             Lento 3/4   (C3-E4)   MH   Med. diff.

337. Moszkowski, M.   *Maiden Fair* (Mädchenaug'! Mädchenaug'!)(Eng./Ger.)
     (1854-1925) Pol./Ger.   Lively 3/4, 9/8   (E3-E4)   H   Med. diff.

338. Nicolai, Otto   *A Weanling Small* (Als Büblein klein)(Eng./Ger.)
     (1810-1849) Ger.   Various tempo & meter (E2-E4)   L-MH   Med. diff.

339. Pressel, Gustav   *The Woodlands All Were Turning*
     (1827-1890) Ger.   (Ich sah den Wald sich färben)(Eng./Ger.)
                             Andante/Allegro 4/4 (F#2-D4)   ML-MH   Med. diff.

340. Proch, Heinrich   *Recognition* (Das Erkennen)(Eng./Ger.)
     (1809-1878) Austrian   Tempo di Marcia 4/4 (Db3-Eb4)   MH   Med. diff.

341. Ries, Franz   *Rhinewine Song*
     (1755-1846) Ger.   (Am Rhein und beim Wein)(Eng./Ger.)
                             Moderato 4/4   (B2-E4)   M-H   Med. diff.

342. Sieber, Ferdinand   *Undaunted* (Senza tinore!)(Eng./It.)
     (1822-1895) Austrian   Lento 4/4   (F2-C4)   L-M   Med. diff.

343. Slansky, L.   *Huntsman's Song* (Waidmannslied)(Eng./Ger.)
                             Various tempo & meter (Bb2-F4)   H   Med. diff.

344. Spohr, L.   *Love's a Tender Flow'ret*
     (1784-1859) Ger.   (Liebe ist die zarte Blüthe)(Eng./Ger.)
                             Larghetto 3/4   (G2-F4)   M-H   Mod. diff.

345. Tchaikovsky, Pyotr   *Don Juan's Serenade*
     (1840-1893) Russ.   (Tout sommeille dans Grenade)(Eng./Fr.)
                             Allegro 3/4   (A2-D4(E4)) MH   Mod. diff.

346. Weidt, Heinrich   *Watchman's Song* (Thurmwächter's Lied)(Eng./Ger.)
     (1828-1901) Ger.   Moderato 12/8   (E2-E4)   L-H   Med. diff.

THE ARTISTIC BASSO
Published by M. Witmark & Sons

347. Bohm, Carl   *Calm as the Night* (Still wie die Nacht)(Eng./Ger.)
      (1844-1844) Ger.   Poco tranquillo 6/4   (A2-Eb4)   M-H   Med. diff.

348. Clay, Frederic   *Gipsy John* (Eng.)
      (1840-1889) Eng.   Allegro 3/4   (A2-D4)   M-MH   Mod. easy

349. Elliott, James W.   *Song of Hybrias the Cretan* (Eng.)
      (1833-?) Eng.   Allegretto 6/8   (F2-Db4)   L-M   Med. diff.

350. Fischer, Ludwig   *My Lodging Is the Cellar Here*
      (1745-1825) Ger.   (Im kühlen keller sitz' ich hier)(Eng./Ger.)
                                Con spirito 4/4   (F2-D4)   L-MH   Med. diff.

351. Flegier, Ange   *The Horn* (Le Cor)(Eng./Fr.)
      (1846-1927) Fr.   Allegro 6/8   (D2-D4)   L-MH   Med. diff.

352. Hatton, John L.   *Simon the Cellarer* (Eng.)
      (1808-1886) Eng.   Allegretto 6/8   (G2-D4)   M-MH   Med. diff.

353. Hullah, John   *Three Fishers* (Eng.)
      (1812-1884) Eng.   Andantino 6/8   (A2(E2)-D4(F4))   M-MH   Mod. easy

354. Jude, William H.   *The Mighty Deep* (Eng.)
      (1851-1922) Eng.   Andante 4/4   (F2-E4)   L-MH   Med. diff.

355. Keller, Carl   *The Exile* (Eng.)
      (1784-1855) Ger.   Adagio 4/4   (D2-D4)   L-M   Med. diff.

356. Löhr, Frederic   *Out on the Deep* (Eng.)
      (1872-1943) Eng.   Allegro moderato 6/8   (G2-D4)   ML-M   Mod. easy

357. Mozart, W. A.   *Within This Sacred Dwelling*
      (1756-1791) Austrian   (In diesen heil'gen Hallen)(Eng./Ger.)
                                Larghetto 4/4   (F#2-C#4)   L-M   Med. diff.

358. Nessler, Victor   *It Was Not So to Be* (Eng./Ger.)
      (1841-1890) Ger.   Andante con moto 4/4   (A2-C#4)   M   Med. diff.

359. Pinsuti, Ciro   *I Fear No Foe* (Eng.)
      (1829-1888) It.   Allegro moderato 4/4   (E2-E4)   ML-H   Med. diff.

360. Poniatowski, (Prince)   *The Yeoman's Wedding Song* (Eng.)
      (1816-1873) Polish   Allegretto 6/8   (C3-D4)   M-MH   Mod. easy

361. Schubert, Franz   *The Wanderer* (Der Wanderer)(Eng./Ger.)

	(1797-1828) Austrian	Molto adagio 2/2	(D2-D4)	MH	Med. diff.
362.	Schumann, Robert (1810-1856) Ger.	*Die beiden Grenadiere* (Eng./Ger.) Mässig 4/4	(Bb2-D4)	MH	Med. diff.
363.	Shield, William (1748-1829) Eng.	*The Friars of the Orders Gray* (Eng.) Con spirito 6/8	(G2-D4)	M-MH	Med. diff.
364.	Stuart, Leslie (Barrett, Thomas) (1866-1928) Eng.	*The Bandolero* (Eng.) Spirited 3/4	(Ab2-Db4)	ML-M	Mod. easy
365.	Tours, Frank (1877-1963) Eng./Am.	*A Year Ago* (Eng.) Andante 4/4	(D3-D4)	M-H	Mod. easy

BASS ALBUM
24 ARIEN UND LIEDER FÜR EINE TIEFE MÄNNERSTIMME
Published by Wilhelmiana

This volume contains a few interesting songs not readily available elsewhere. The songs are in German only.

366.	Beethoven, L. van (1770-1827) Ger.	*In questa tomba oscura* (In dieses Grabes Dunkel)(Ger.) Lento 2/4	(C3-E4)	M-MH	Med. diff.
367.	Binder, Carl (1816-1860) Austrian	*Wenn ich einmal der Herrgott wär'* (Trinklied)(Ger.) Allegro moderato 3/4	(B2-D4)	M-MH	Mod. easy
368.	Blume, Karl (1883-1947) Ger.	*Es träumt ein Fass* (Ger.) Langsam 3/4	(C#3-D4)	MH	Mod. easy
369.	Fischer, Ludwig (1745-1825) Ger.	*Im tiefen Keller* (Ger.) Moderato 4/4	(F2-D4)	L-MH	Mod. easy
370.	Flotow, F. (1812-1883) Ger.	*Lasst mich euch fragen* (Porterlied aus "Martha")(Ger.) Andante 6/8	(G2-F4)	ML-H	Mod. diff.
371.	Fürst, Fritz	*Der Wagen rollt* (Ger.) Animated 6/8	(G2-D4)	ML-MH	Med. diff.
372.	Graben-Hoffmann, G. (1820-1900) Ger.	*Fünfmalhunderttausend Teufel* (Ger.) Various tempo & meter	(G2-E4)	ML-MH	Med. diff.
373.	Heiser, Wilhelm (1815-1897) Ger.	*Das Grab auf der Heide* (Ger.) Allegro 4/4	(A#2-E4)	M-H	Med. diff.

374. Loewe, Carl   *Die Uhr* (Ger.)
      (1796-1869) Ger.   Andantino 6/8   (G2-D4)   L-MH   Med. diff.

375. Lortzing, G. A.   *Auch ich war ein Jüngling* (aus "Waffenschmied")(Ger.)
      (1801-1851) Ger.   Andante 3/8   (A2-D4)   M   Med. diff.

376. Millöcker, Carl   *Ach ich hab' sie ja nur*
      (1842-1899) Austrian   (aus der Operette "Bettelstudent")(Ger.)
                                 Various tempo & meter (A2-E4)   MH   Med. diff.

377. Mozart, W. A.   *In diesen heil'gen Hallen* (aus "Zauberflöte")(Ger.)
      (1756-1791) Austrian   Larghetto 2/4   (F#2(E2)-C#4)   L-M   Med. diff.

378.   *O Isis und Osiris* (aus "Zauberflöte")(Ger.)
                                 Adagio 3/4   (F2-C4)   L-M   Med. diff.

379.   *Wer ein Liebchen hat gefunden*
                                 (aus "Die Entführung aus dem Serail")(Ger.)
                                 Andante 6/8   (G2-D4)   ML-MH   Med. diff.

380. Mussorgsky, M.   *Flohlied* (Ger.)
      (1839-1881) Russ.   Moderato giusto 4/4   (A#2-G4)   M-H   Mod. diff.

381. Nicolai, Otto   *Als Büblein klein* (aus "Die lustigen Weiber")(Ger.)
      (1810-1849) Ger.   Various tempo & meter (E2-E4)   L-H   Mod. diff.

382. Peuschel, Moritz   *Die drei Weinkenner* (Ger.)
      (1838-1892) Ger.   Various tempo & meter (G2-C4)   M-MH   Med. diff.

383. Schubert, Franz   *Der Lindenbaum* (Ger.)
      (1796-1828) Austrian   Mässig 3/4   (C3-C4)   M   Med. diff.

384. Schumann, R.   *Wanderlied* (Ger.)
      (1810-1856) Ger.   Sehr lebhaft 4/4   (G2-D4)   L-M   Med. diff.
                                 Lower than normally available keys.

385. Simon, Rudolf   *In der Waldschenke* (Ger.)
                                 Mässig schnell 6/8   (F2-C4)   L-M   Mod. easy

386. Wagner, Richard   *Gebet des Königs* (aus "Lohengrin")(Ger.)
      (1813-1883) Ger.   Adagio 3/4   (F2-Eb4)   ML-H   Med. diff.

387.   *O, Du mein holder Abendstern* (aus "Tannhäuser")(Ger.)
                                 Moderato 4/4, 6/8   (A2-D4)   M-MH   Med. diff.

388. Weber, C. M. von   *Hier im ird'schen Jammertal*
      (1786-1826) Ger.   (aus "Freischütz")(Ger.)
                                 Allegro 2/4   (D3-F#4)   H   Med. diff.

BASS SONGS
Published by Boosey

This well-conceived volume contains many important songs for the true bass voice. Although an older edition this collection would be an asset to any bass singer's library.

389. Aylward, Florence   *Mavourneen* (Eng.)
     (1862-?) Eng.   Andante 3/4   (Bb2-D4)   MH   Med. diff.

390. Balfe, Michael   *From Rushy Beds of Silver Nile*
     (1808-1870) Irish   (from the opera "Keolanthe")(Eng.)
                           Allegro moderato 3/4 (Bb2-D4)   MH   Med. diff.

391. Boyce, William   *Hearts of Oak* (Eng.)
     (1711-1779) Eng.   Moderato 4/4   (G2-D4)   M-MH   Mod. easy

392. Buononcini, G.   *Love Leads to Battle* (Pupille nere)(Eng./It.)
     (1670-1747) It.   Allegro maestoso   (C3-D4)   MH   Med. diff.

393. Carissimi, Giacomo   *I Triumph, I Triumph* (Vittoria, vittoria)(Eng./It.)
     (1605-1674) It.   Allegro 3/4   (A2-D4)   MH   Med. diff.

394. English Air   *Down Among the Dead Men* (Eng.)
                           Allegro 4/4   (A2-D4)   M   Mod. easy

395. German Air   *My Lodging Is the Cellar Here* (Eng.)
                           Andante 4/4   (F2-D4)   L-MH   Mod. easy

396. Gounod, Charles   *Maids May Boast* (Si les Filles d'Arles)(Eng./Fr.)
     (1818-1893) Fr.   Andantino 2/4   (A2-D4)   M-MH   Med. diff.

397.   *Nazareth* (Eng.)
                           Moderato 6/4   (G2-C#4)   ML-MH   Med. diff.

398.   *Vulcan's Song* (from the opera "Philemon et
                           Baucis")(Eng./Fr.)
                           Allegro moderato 2/4 (G2-D4)   ML-MH   Med. diff.

399. Halévy, Jacques   *Though Faithless Men* (Si la rigueur)
     (1799-1862) Fr.   (from "La Juive")(Eng./Fr.)
                           Andante 2/4   (E2-C4)   L-M   Med. diff.

400. Handel, George F.   *Born Among the Rugged Wildwood*
     (1685-1726) Ger./Eng. (Nasce al Bosco)(from the opera "Ezio")(Eng./It.)
                           Allegro moderato 4/4 (Eb2-Eb4)   L-MH   Mod. diff.

401.   *Clouds May Rise* (Sorge infausta)
                           (from "Orlando")(Eng./It.)
                           Allegro 4/4   (G2-Eb4)   ML-MH   Mod. diff.

402.   *Love That's True Will Live Forever*

		(Si, tra i ceppi)(Eng./It.)			
		Allegro 4/4	(B2-D4)	MH	Med. diff.
403.		*O Ruddier Than the Cherry* (from "Acis and Galatea")(Eng.)			
		Moderato 4/4	(G2-F4)	M-H	Mod. diff.
404.		*Pour Forth No More Unheeded Prayers* (from "Jephtha")(Eng.)			
		Vivace 3/4	(A2-Eb4)	MH	Mod. diff.
405.		*Ye Verdant Hills* (from "Susanna")(Eng.)			
		Larghetto 3/4	(Bb2-D4)	M-MH	Med. diff.
406.	Hatton, John L. (1808-1886) Eng.	*Simon the Cellarer* (Eng.)			
		Allegretto 6/8	(G2-D4)	M-MH	Med. diff.
407.	Irish Air	*The Harp That Once Thro' Tara's Halls* (Eng.)			
		Andante 4/4	(Bb2-D4)	M-MH	Easy
408.		*The Minstrel Boy* (Eng.)			
		Spirited 4/4	(A2-D4)	MH	Easy
409.	Leveridge, Richard (1670-1758) Eng.	*The Roast Beef of Old England* (Eng.)			
		Allegro 6/8	(A2-D4)	M	Easy
410.	Loder, Edward (1813-1865) Eng.	*The Brave Old Oak* (Eng.)			
		Boldly 4/4	(G2-D4)	M-MH	Mod. easy
411.	MacFarren, G. (1813-1887) Eng.	*The Monk Within His Cell* (from the opera "Robin Hood")(Eng.)			
		Tempo giusto 4/4	(F2-E4)	ML-MH	Mod. diff.
412.	Mendelssohn, F. (1809-1847) Ger.	*I Am a Roamer* (Eng.)			
		Allegro vivace 2/4	(F2-E4)	L-H	Mod. diff.
413.	Mozart, W. A. (1756-1791) Austrian	*Within These Sacred Bowers* (In diesen heil'gen Hallen)(Eng./Ger.)			
		Larghetto 2/4	(F#2-C#4)	L-M	Med. diff.
414.	Purday, Charles (1791-1885) Eng.	*The Old English Gentleman* (Eng.)			
		Allegretto 4/4	(A2-D4)	M	Mod. easy
415.	Schubert, Franz (1797-1828) Austrian	*The Erlking* (Der Erlkönig)(Eng./Ger.)			
		Vivace 4/4	(G2-D4)	ML-MH	Mod. diff.
		One whole-step lower than the original key.			
416.		*The Wanderer* (Der Wanderer)(Eng./Ger.)			
		Molto adagio 2/2	(D2-D4)	MH	Med. diff.

417. Schumann, Robert   *I Will Not Grieve* (Ich grolle nicht)(Eng./Ger.)
     (1810-1856) Ger.   Moderato 4/4   (Bb2-D4(G4))   M-MH   Med. diff.

418. Scottish Air   *Auld Lang Syne* (Eng.)
                               Moderato 2/4   (A2-D4)   M   Easy

419.   *Bonnie Dundee* (Eng.)
                               Allegretto 6/8   (A2-D4)   M-MH   Easy

420.   *The Hundred Pipers* (Eng.)
                               Allegro 6/8   (A2-D4)   ML-MH   Easy

421.   *Scots, Wha Hae Wi' Wallace Bled!* (Eng.)
                               Andante 2/4   (D3-D4)   M-MH   Easy

422. Sullivan, Arthur   *I Would I Were a King* (Eng.)
     (1842-1900) Eng.   Allegro con brio 3/4   (C#3-E4)   M-H   Med. diff.

423. Tchaikovsky, P.   *A Pleading* (Eng.)
     (1840-1893) Russ.   Andante 4/4   (A2-D4)   MH   Med. diff.

424.   *Ah, Weep No More* (Eng.)
                               Moderato assai 4/4   (C3-Eb4)   MH   Med. diff.

425.   *Oh, But to Hear Thy Voice* (Eng.)
                               Allegro agitato 4/4 (B2-Db4)   MH   Med. diff.

426. Thomas, Ambroise   *The Drum-Major's Song* (Air du Tambour Major)
     (1811-1896) Fr.   (from the opera "Le Caïd")(Eng./Fr.)
                               Moderato/Allegro 4/4, 2/4 (G2-E4) M-H   Mod. diff.

427. Wagner, Richard   *O Pure and Tender Star of Eve* (Eng./Ger.)
     (1813-1883) Ger.   (O du, mein holder Abendstern)(from "Tannhäuser")
                               Moderato 4/4, 6/8   (A2-D4)   M-MH   Med. diff.
                               One whole-step lower than original key.

428. Wallace, W. V.   *The Bell-Ringer* (Eng.)
     (1812-1865) Irish   Andante 4/4   (G2-Eb4)   MH   Med. diff.

EZIO PINZA ALBUM OF CONCERT SONGS AND ARIAS
Published by G. Schirmer

429. Edwards, Clara   *Into the Night* (Eng.)
     (1887-1974) Am.   Tranquillo 4/4   (C3-Db4)   MH   Mod. easy

430. Flègier, A.   *Le Cor* (The Horn)(Fr./Eng.)
     (1846-1927) Fr.   Allegro/Andante 6/8, 4/4 (D2-D4)   L-MH   Med. diff.

431. Gounod, Charles   *Le veau d'or* (from "Faust")(Fr.)
     (1818-1893) Fr.   Allegro maestoso 6/8   (C3-Eb4)   H   Mod. diff.

432. Halévy, Jacques   *Though Faithless Men* (Si la rigueur)
     (1799-1862) Fr.   (from "La Juive")(Eng./Fr.)
                             Andante 2/4   (E2-C4)   L-M   Med. diff.

433. Levitzki, Mischa   *Do You Remember?* (Eng.)
     (1898-1941) Am.   Allegretto 4/4   (Bb2-Eb4(G4)) MH   Med. diff.

434. Mozart, W. A.   *Finch' han dal vino* (from "Don Giovanni")(It.)
     (1756-1791) Austrian   Presto 2/4   (D3-Eb4)   H   Mod. diff.

435.   *Non più andrai* (from "Le Nozze di Figaro")(It.)
                             Allegro 4/4   (C3-E4)   MH   Mod. diff.

436. Mussorgsky, M.   *Song of the Flea* (Eng.)
     (1839-1881) Russ.   Moderato 4/4   (A#2-G4)   M-H   Mod. diff.

437. Pergolesi, G. B.   *Nina* (Tre Giorni)(It.)
     (1710-1736) It.   Andante 4/4   (C3-D4)   MH   Mod. easy

438. Rossini, Gioachino   *La calunnia* (from "Il Barbiere di Siviglia")(It.)
     (1792-1868) It.   Allegro 4/4   (C#3-F#4)   MH-VH   Mod. diff.

439. Tosti, F. Paolo   *La serenata* (Serenade)(It.)
     (1846-1916) It.   Andantino 4/4   (B2-C4)   M-MH   Mod. easy

440. Tschaikowsky, P.   *To the Forest* (Pilgrim's Song)(Eng.)
     (1840-1893) Russ.   Andante 4/4   (A2-D4)   M-MH   Med. diff.

441. Verdi, Giuseppe   *Dormirò sol*
     (1813-1901) It.   (Recitative and Aria from "Don Carlos")(It.)
                             Andante 4/4   (G2-E4)   M-H   Mod. diff.

442.   *Infelice! e tuo credevi* (Recitative and Aria from
                             "Ernani")(It.)
                             Andante 4/4   (G2-Eb4)   MH   Mod. diff.

FAMOUS SONGS
For Bass
Edited by H. E. Krehbiel
Published by John Church

This is a useful edition with several noteworthy songs not readily available.
443. Beethoven, L. van   *In questa tomba oscura* (Eng./It.)
     (1770-1827) Ger.   Lento 2/4   (C3-E4)   M-MH   Med. diff.

444.		*Nature's Adoration* (Eng.) Andante 4/4	(Ab2-Eb4)	MH	Med. diff
445.	Brahms, Johannes (1833-1897) Ger.	*Wie bist du meine Königin* (Eng./Ger.) Adagio 3/8	(C3-Eb4)	MH	Med. diff.
446.	Chopin, Frédéric (1810-1849) Polish	*Bacchanal* (Eng.) Vivace 3/4	(B2-D4)	M-MH	Med. diff.
447.	Clay, Frederic (1838-1889) Eng.	*Gipsy John* (Eng.) Allegro 3/4	(A2-D4)	M-MH	Med. diff.
448.	Cornelius, Peter (1824-1874) Ger.	*Ein Ton* (Eng./Ger.) Un poco agitato 3/4	(G3-G3)	M	Mod. easy
449.	Dvorák, Anton (1841-1904) Bohem.	*Als die alte Mutter* (Eng./Ger.) Andante 6/8, 2/4	(D#3-E4)	H	Mod. easy
450.	English Air	*Drink to Me Only with Thine Eyes* (Eng.) Andantino 6/8	(C3-C4)	M	Easy
451.	Faure, Jean (1830-1914) Fr.	*Les Rameaux* (Eng./Fr.) Andante 2/2	(C3-Eb4)	MH-H	Med. diff.
452.	Fesca, Alexander (1820-1849) Ger.	*Der Wanderer* (Eng./Ger.) Allegro vivo 12/8	(C#3-E4)	MH	Med. diff.
453.	Fischer, Ludwig (1745-1825) Ger.	*Im tiefen Keller sitz' ich hier* (Eng./Ger.) Con spirito 4/4	(F2-D4)	L-MH	Med. diff.
454.	Folk Song	*All Through the Night* (Eng.) Moderato 4/4	(Bb2-C4)	M	Easy
455.	Franz, Robert (1815-1892) Ger.	*Aus meinen grossen Schmerzen* (Eng./Ger.) Andante 2/4	(C#3-Eb4)	MH	Mod. easy
456.		*Für Musik* (Eng./Ger.) Andante 3/4	(Eb3-F4)	H	Mod. easy
457.		*Ständchen* (Eng./Ger.) Andante 2/4	(C3-Eb4)	MH	Mod. easy
458.	German Air	*In einem Kühlen Grunde* (Eng./Ger.) Allegretto 6/8	(C3-D4)	MH	Mod. easy
459.	Giordani, Tommaso (1733-1806) It.	*Caro mio ben* (Eng./It.) Larghetto 2/2	(B2-D4)	MH	Mod. easy
460.	Gounod, Charles (1818-1893) Fr.	*Nazareth* (Eng.) Moderato 6/4	(G2-C#4)	M-MH	Med. diff.

461.   *Le Vallon* (Eng./Fr.)
                             Andante 4/4   (D3-F4)   H   Mod. diff.

462.   Grieg, Edward   *Ich liebe Dich* (Eng./Ger.)
       (1843-1907) Norweg.   Andante 3/4   (D3-Eb4)   MH   Mod. easy

463.   *Mit einer Primula veris* (Ger.)
                             Allegretto 6/8   (B2-E4)   MH   Med. diff.

464.   Hiller, Ferdinand   *Gebet* (Eng./Ger.)
       (1811-1885) Ger.   Moderato 2/4   (G2-D4)   M-MH   Med. diff.

465.   Himmel, Friedrick   *Battle Prayer* (Eng.)
       (1765-1814) Ger.   Slow 4/4   (D2-D4)   M   Med. diff.

466.   Hullah, John   *Three Fishers Went Sailing* (Eng.)
       (1812-1884) Eng.   Andantino 6/8   (A2-F4)   MH   Med. diff.

467.   Jensen, Adolf   *Alt Heidelberg, du feine* (Eng./Ger.)
       (1837-1879) Ger.   Un poco agitato 3/4   (A2-E4)   MH   Med. diff.

468.   *Ständchen* (Eng./Ger.)
                             Very lively 3/4   (D3-F4)   H   Med. diff.

469.   Jude, William H.   *The Mighty Deep* (Eng.)
       (1851-1922) Eng.   Andante 4/4   (F2-E4)   ML-H   Med. diff.

470.   Kjerulf, Halfdan   *Sehnsucht* (Eng./Ger.)
       (1815-1868) Norweg.   Andante 3/8   (Bb2-D4)   M   Mod. easy

471.   Lassen, Edward   *Es war ein Traum* (Eng./Ger.)
       (1830--1904) Danish   Lento 9/8   (B2-E4)   M-H   Med. diff.

472.   Liszt, Franz   *Du bist wie eine Blume* (Eng./Ger.)
       (1811-1886) Hung.   Adagio 3/4   (C#3-E4)   MH   Med. diff.

473.   Loewe, Carl   *Archibald Douglass* (Eng./Ger.)
       (1796-1869) Ger.   Grave 4/4   (F2-D4)   ML-MH   Mod. diff.

474.   *Edward* (Eng./Ger.)
                             Agitato 6/8   (F2-E4)   L-H   Mod. diff.

475.   Marschner, H.   *Der Himmel in Thale* (Eng./Ger.)
       (1795-1861) Ger.   Moderato 4/4   (Bb2-F4)   M-H   Med. diff.

476.   Mattei, Tito   *Oh, Hear the Wild Wind Blow* (Eng.)
       (1841-1914) It.   Allegretto 3/4   (G#2-E4)   ML-MH   Med. diff.

477.   Mendelssohn, F.   *Reiselied* (Eng./Ger.)
       (1809-1847) Ger.   Presto 12/8   (C3-Db4)   MH   Med. diff.

478. Meyerbeer, G.   *Der Moench* (Eng./Ger.)
      (1791-1864) Ger.   Allegro 6/8   (F2-E4)   L-H   Mod. diff.

479. Mililotti, Leopoldo   *Povero marinar* (Eng./It.)
                             Lento 3/4   (C3-E4)   MH   Med. diff.

480. Nessler, Victor   *Es hat nicht sollen sein* (Eng./Ger.)
      (1841-1890) Ger.   Andante con moto 4/4 (A2-C#4)   M   Med. diff.

481. Pergolesi, G.   *Nina* (Eng./It.)
      (1710-1736) It.   Andante 4/4   (C3-D4)   MH   Mod. easy

482. Pressel, Gustav   *Ich sah den Wald sich färben* (Eng./Ger.)
      (1827-1890) Ger.   Andante 4/4   (F#2-D4)   ML-M   Med. diff.

483. Purcell, Henry   *I Attempt from Love's Sickness to Fly* (Eng.)
      (1659-1695) Eng.   Andante 3/4   (B2-D4)   MH   Med. diff.

484. Radecke, Rudolph   *Aus der Jugendzeit* (Eng./Ger.)
      (1829-1893) Ger.   Semplice 3/4   (C3-D4)   M   Mod. easy

485. Rubinstein, Anton   *Der Asra* (Eng./Ger.)
      (1829-1894) Russ.   Moderato 3/4   (B2-F4)   MH   Med. diff.

486.   *Gelb rollt mir zu Füssen* (Eng./Ger.)
                             Andante 2/4   (C3-F4)   H   Med. diff.

487. Saint-Saëns, C.   *Le pas d'armes du roi Jean* (Eng./Fr.)
      (1835-1921) Fr.   Allegro 2/4   (D2-Eb4)   L-MH   Med. diff.

488. Schubert, Franz   *Erlkönig* (Eng./Ger.)
      (1797-1828) Austrian   Schnell 4/4   (A2-E4)   ML-H   Mod. diff.

489.   *Der Wanderer* (Eng./Ger.)
                             Moderato 4/4   (E2(C2)-C4) L-MH   Mod. diff.
                             One whole-step lower than normally available.

490.   *Was ist Sylvia* (Eng./Ger.)
                             Moderato 4/4   (C3-D4)   MH   Med. diff.

491. Schumann, Robert   *Die beiden Grenadiere* (Eng./Ger.)
      (1810-1856) Ger.   Mässig 4/4   (Bb2-D4)   MH   Med. diff.

492.   *Ich grolle nicht* (Eng./Ger.)
                             Nicht zu schnell 4/4 (Bb2-D4(G4)) M-MH   Med. diff.

493. Shield, William   *The Friars of Orders Gray* (Eng.)
      (1748-1829) Eng.   Con spirito 6/8   (G2-D4)   ML-MH   Med. diff.

494. Wagner, Richard   *Les deux Grenadiers* (Eng./Fr.)

(1813-1883) Ger.	Moderato 4/4	(A2-F#4)	H	Diff.

495. Weidt, Heinrich — *Wie schön bist du* (Eng./Ger.)
(1828-1901) Ger. — Moderato 3/4 — (Bb2-Eb4) — MH — Med. diff.

FAVORITE BASS SONGS
Edited by Max Spicker
Published by G. Schirmer

496. Allitsen, Frances — *Since We Parted* (Eng.)
(1848-1912) Eng. — Lento 4/4 — (D3-Eb4) — MH — Mod. easy

497. Behrend, A. H. — *Daddy* (Eng.)
Moderato 6/8 — (C3-D4) — MH — Easy

498. Cowen, Frederic — *For a Dream's Sake* (Eng.)
(1852-1935) Eng. — Adagio 4/4 — (C3-D4) — MH — Med. diff.

499. Davis, L. S. — *A Jolly Fat Friar* (Drinking-Song)(Eng.)
Tempo comodo 6/8 — (G2-Eb4) — MH — Mod. easy

500. Elliott, James W. — *Song of Hybrias the Cretan* (Eng.)
(1833-?) Eng. — Allegretto 6/8 — (F2-Db4) — ML-M — Mod. easy

501. Hawley, Charles — *Ah! 'Tis a Dream* (Eng.)
(1858-1915) Am. — Moderato 3/4 — (G2-C4) — ML-M — Easy

502. — *Bedouin Love-Song* (Eng.)
Allegro vivace 4/4 — (D2-D4) — L-M — Mod. easy

503. Haynes, W. Battison — *Off to Philadelphia* (Eng.)
(1859-1900) Eng. — Animato 4/4 — (G2-D4) — M — Mod. easy

504. Hiller, Ferdinand — *Be Thou with Me* (Eng.)
(1811-1885) Ger. — Moderato 2/4 — (G2-D4) — M — Mod. easy

505. Hullah, John — *The Three Fishers* (Eng.)
(1812-1884) Eng. — Andantino 6/8 — (G2-Eb4) — M — Mod. easy

506. Jude, William H. — *The Skipper* (Eng.)
(1851-1922) Eng. — Energetic 6/8 — (G2-E4) — M — Mod. easy

507. Knight, Joseph P. — *Rocked in the Cradle of the Deep* (Eng.)
(1812-1887) Eng. — Andante tranquillo 4/4 (F2-C4) — M — Mod. easy

508. Löhr, Frederic N. — *Paradise Square* (Eng.)
(1857-1925) Eng. — Moderato 6/8 — (G2-C4) — M-MH — Mod. easy

509. Marzials, Theo   *The Miller and the Maid* (Eng.)
     (1850-1920) Eng.   Moderato 4/4   (C3-Eb4)   H   Easy

510. Pinsuti, Ciro   *'Tis I!* (Eng.)
     (1829-1888) It.   Andante 4/4   (A2-D4)   M-MH   Mod. easy

511. Rodney, Paul   *Time and Tide* (Eng.)
                             Moderato 4/4   (Bb2-D4)   MH   Easy

512. Roeder, Otto   *On Venice Waters* (Gondolier Waltz)(Eng.)
                             Andantino 4/4   (Bb2-F4)   MH   Mod. easy

513. Somerset, Henry   *A Song of Sleep* (Eng.)
     (1849-1932) Eng.   Slowly 4/4   (D3-D4)   MH   Mod. easy

514. Storch, M. Anton   *Nächtlicher Gruss* (Greeting at Night)(Ger./Eng.)
     (1813-1888) Austrian   Andante grazioso 4/4 (D3-D4)   MH   Mod. easy

515. Tosti, F. Paolo   *La serenata* (Serenade)(It.)
     (1846-1916) It.   Andantino 4/4   (B2-C4)   M-MH   Mod. easy

516. Trotère, Henry   *In Old Madrid* (Eng.)
     (1855-1912) Eng.   Tempo di bolero 3/4 (C3-Db4)   MH   Mod. easy

517. Wellings, Milton   *Only a Rose* (Eng.)
     (1850-1929) Am.   Moderato 3/4   (C3-C4)   MH   Easy

RADIO CITY ALBUM OF BASS SOLOS
Published by Edward B. Marks Music

Aside from the Koenemann piece, this volume consists mainly of somewhat dated sea songs.

518. Gabriel, Charles H.   *The Wanderer* (Eng.)
     (1856-1932) Am.   Moderato 6/8   (F2-D4)   ML-MH Mod. easy

519. Koenemann, T.   *When the King Went Forth to War* (Eng./Russ.)
     (1873-1937) Russ.   Various tempo & meter (A2-E4)   M-H   Mod. diff.

520. Petrie, H. W.   *As High as the Stars and as Deep as the Sea* (Eng.)
     (1857-1925) Am.   Cantabile 12/8   (F2-D4)   L-M   Mod. easy

521.   *Down in the Deep Let Me Sleep When I Die*
                             Cantabile 12/8   (G2-D4)   ML-MH Mod. easy

522.   *Good Fellows* (Eng.)
                             Animato 6/8   (A2-D4)   M-MH   Mod. easy

523.   *Ho! For a Sail in a Piping Breeze* (Eng.)
                             Moderato 6/8   (A2-D4)   M-MH   Mod. easy

524.		*The Miller* (Eng.)			
		Moderato 6/8	(E2-D4)	L-M	Mod. easy
525.		*Out Where the Breakers Roar* (Eng.)			
		Cantabile 12/8	(Eb2-C4)	L-M	Mod. easy
526.		*Roll On Thou Deep and Dark Blue Ocean*			
		Cantabile 12/8	(G2-C4)	ML	Mod. easy
527.		*The Sea Is the Home for Me* (Eng.)			
		Cantabile 12/8	(F2-C4)	L-M	Mod. easy
528.		*When the Winds O'er the Sea Blow a Gale*			
		Allegro giocoso 6/8	(G2-D4)	ML-MH	Mod. easy
529.	Solman, Alfred	*If I Had a Thousand Lives to Live* (Eng.)			
	(1868-1937) Am.	Animato 12/8	(Ab2-C4)	M	Mod. easy
530.		*The Sexton and the Bell* (Eng.)			
		Andante 12/8	(Eb2-C4)	L-M	Mod. easy
531.		*When the Bell in the Lighthouse Rings* (Eng.)			
		Moderato 12/8	(F2-Bb4)	ML	Mod. easy
532.		*When the Ocean Rolls No More* (Eng.)			
		Andante 12/8	(A2-D4)	ML	Mod. easy

CHAPTER V

ART-SONG COLLECTIONS OF A SINGLE COMPOSER FOR BASS VOICE

Collections of songs by a single composer are quite numerous and collections in low voice of Brahms, Schubert, Schumann, Wolf, Debussy, Duparc, Fauré, and others are important. However, many of the songs in these low voice collections are not low enough for bass. Some individual songs by the above mentioned composers that are appropriate for bass are treated in Chapter Thirteen. Only those collections that are specifically for bass or require special attention are included in this chapter.

Handel, G. F.   *A Collection of Songs,* Vol. VII (Bass)(Eng.)   B & H
(1685-1759) Ger./Eng.

The songs and arias of Handel are numerous. However, only a few dozen well-known pieces are generally available. The following appealing collection contains worthy pieces that are less well-known. These selections as with all Handel songs and arias are generally characterized as being vocally demanding with most animated pieces requiring considerable agility. In addition most all of his vocal works exhibit a wide range, large leaps, and a relatively high tessitura. The performing pitch of Handel's day was between one half-step and one whole-step lower than the performing pitch of today and it would be quite acceptable to transpose any of his works down accordingly. Additional important songs and arias by Handel are outlined in Chapter Thirteen.

533.	*Alcides' Name in Latest Story* (from "Hercules") Allegro 4/4	(G2-D4)	ML-MH	Mod. diff.
534.	*The God of War* (from "Hercules") Allegro 6/8	(Bb2-Eb4)	M-H	Mod. diff.
535.	*His Sceptre Is the Rod of Righteousness* (from "Occasional Oratorio") Pomposo 4/4	(F#2-E4)	MH	Med. diff.
536.	*Leave Me, Loathsome Light* (from "Semele") Andante 6/4	(A2-D4)	M-MH	Med. diff.
537.	*Like the Shadow* (from "Time and Truth") Andante 3/8	(A2- D4)	M-MH	Med. diff.
538.	*More Sweet Is That Name* (from "Semele") Allegro 6/8	(A2-D4)	M-MH	Mod. diff.

539.   *O Praise the Lord*
                        (from "Chandos Anthems," No. 12)
                        Moderato 4/4   (B2-E4)   H   Mod. diff.

540.   *The Oak That for a Thousand Years*
                        (from "Susanna")
                        Allegro moderato 4/4 (F2-E4)   ML-MH   Med. diff.

541.   *Peace, Peace Crowned with Roses*
                        (from "Susanna")
                        Larghetto 3/4   (A2-E4)   MH   Med. diff.

542.   *A Serpent in My Bosom Warmed*
                        (from "Saul")
                        Allegro 4/4   (Bb2-Eb4)   MH   Mod. diff.

543.   *Since the Race of Time Has Run*
                        (from "Joseph")
                        Allegro 4/4   (G2-E4)   MH   Mod. diff.

544.   *Thrice Blest That Wise Discerning King*
                        (from "Solomon")
                        Allegro 4/4   (G2-D4)   MH   Mod. diff.

545.   *To Power Immortal*
                        (from "Belshazzar")
                        Largo 12/8   (G2-D4)   MH   Med. diff.

546.   *Vouchsafe, O Lord!*
                        (from Dettingen "Te Deum")
                        Largo 4/4   (D#3-D#4)   H   Med. diff.

547.   *When Nature Groans*
                        (from "2nd Passion")
                        Allegro 4/4   (G2-Eb4)   MH   Mod. diff.

548.   *When Storms the Proud*
                        (from "Athalia")
                        Allegro 4/4   (G2-F4)   M-H   Mod. diff.

549.   *Why Do the Gentiles Tumult?*
                        (from "Occasional Oratorio")
                        Allegro 4/4   (A2-E4)   MH   Mod. diff.

550.   *Wide Spread His Name*
                        (from "Theodora")
                        Allegro 3/4   (A2-D4)   MH   Med. diff.

| Loewe, Carl | ***Balladen und Lieder***, Band I (Ger.) | | | Peters |

(1796-1869) Ger.

The ballads and songs of Loewe are a must for investigation by any bass. Though the following songs are not originally composed for bass they are extremely well-suited and this transposed volume for low voice published by Peters contains some of the best. The songs are generally of a wide range with few tessitura problems and often the highest notes are just touched on. Although a few of these songs could be attempted by beginning basses, such as "Der Pilgrim vor Sankt Just," the majority of the ballads are more appropriate for intermediate or advanced bass voices. (See Chapter Thirteen for additional songs specifically composed for bass voice.)

551.	*Archibald Douglas*			
	Various tempo & meter (F2-D4)	Ml-MH	Mod. diff.	
552.	*Edward*			
	Agitato 6/8, 2/4	(G2-E4)	ML-MH	Mod. diff.
553.	*Erlkönig*			
	Geschwind 9/8, 6/8	(F#2-E4)	ML-MH	Diff.
554.	*Die Glocken zu Speier*			
	Lento 2/2	(C3-Db4)	MH	Med. diff.
555.	*Heinrich der Vogler*			
	Various tempo & meter (G#2-D4)	ML-MH	Mod. diff.	
556.	*Herr Oluf*			
	Allegro 4/4, 2/4	(G2(D2)-E4)	ML-MH	Mod. diff.
557.	*Kleiner Haushalt*			
	Vivace, various meter	(G2-E4)	ML-MH	Diff.
558.	*Die nächtliche Heerschau*			
	Alla Marcia 4/4	(F2-Eb4)	M-MH	Med. diff.
559.	*Der Nöck*			
	Various tempo & meter (F2-Eb4)	M-MH	Mod. diff.	
560.	*Odins Meeresritt*			
	Andante/Allegro 4/4, 6/8 (A2-E4)	ML-MH	Mod. diff.	
561.	*Der Pilgrim vor Sankt Just*			
	Allegro 12/8	(A2-B3)	M	Mod. easy
562.	*Prinz Eugen*			
	Moderato 5/4	(F2-D4(F4))	M	Med. diff.
563.	*Tom der Reimer*			
	Allegretto 4/4	(Ab2-Eb4)	M-MH	Med. diff.
564.	*Die Uhr*			
	Andante 6/8	(Ab2-Eb4)	ML-MH	Med. diff.

565.   *Der Woywode*
                                  Various tempo & meter (B2-E4)   MH-H   Mod. diff.

Purcell, Henry   ***Six Songs for Bass*** (Eng.)   International
(1659-1695) Eng.
Composed specifically for bass voice, these pieces generally have wide ranges and require
considerable vocal flexibility.

566.   *Anacreon's Defeat*
                                  Allegro/Andante 4/4, 3/2 (F2-E4) ML-H   Mod. diff.

567.   *Arise, Ye Subterranean Winds*
                                  Allegro 2/2   (E2-D4)   L-M   Mod. diff.

568.   *Hence with Your Trifling Deity*
                                  Brisk/Slow 3/4   (F2-Eb4)   L-H   Mod. diff.

569.   *Next, Winter Comes Slowly*
                                  Moderato 3/2   (A2-E4)   M-H   Med. diff.

570.   ***Wondrous Machine***
                                  Moderato 4/4   (B2-E4)   M-H   Mod. diff.

571.   *Ye Twice Ten Hundred Deities*
                                  Various tempo & meter (G2-Eb4)   M-H   Mod. diff.

Schubert, Franz   ***Schubert Album,*** Band I   Peters+
(1797-1828) Aus.   (Ger.)(Tiefer Alt oder Bass)
Originally composed for higher voices, many important songs contained in this edition are in
lower keys than are generally accessible. The extensive downward transpositions may be
excessive, however, causing the accompaniments to sound muddy. *Die schöne Müllerin*, which
is felt by many to be more appropriate for higher voices is not annotated. Schubert composed
numerous songs specifically for bass voice and low voice which are found in Chapter XIII.

                                  Die Winterreise
These songs are annotated in the normal order of presentation.

572.   *Gute Nacht*
                                  Mässig 2/4   (A2-C#4)   M   Med. diff.

573.   *Die Wetterfahne*
                                  Ziemlich geschwind 6/8 (A2-C4)   M   Med. diff.

574.   *Gefrorne Tränen*
                                  Nicht zu langsam 2/2   (F#2-C#4)   M   Med. diff.

575.   *Erstarrung*
                                  Ziemlich schnell 4/4   (C3-Eb4)   MH   Med. diff.

576.   *Der Lindenbaum*
                   Mässig 3/4   (Ab2-C4)   M   Med. diff.

577.   *Wasserflut*
                   Langsam 3/4   (F#2-D4)   M   Med. diff.

578.   *Auf dem Flusse*
                   Langsam 2/4   (Ab2-D4)   ML-M   Med. diff.

579.   *Rückblick*
                   Nicht zu geschwind 3/4 (A2-D4)   M   Med. diff.

580.   *Irrlicht*
                   Langsam 3/8   (F2-D4)   M   Med. diff.

581.   *Rast*
                   Mässig 2/4   (G2-D4)   M   Med. diff.

582.   *Frühlingstraum*
                   Etwas bewegt 6/8   (C3-Db4)   MH   Med. diff.

583.   *Einsamkeit*
                   Langsam 2/4   (C3-D4)   MH   Med. diff.

584.   *Die Post*
                   Etwas geschwind 6/8 (G2-C4)   M   Med. diff.

585.   *Der greise Kopf*
                   Etwas geschwind 3/4 (A2-D4)   M   Med. diff.

586.   *Die Krähe*
                   Etwas geschwind 2/4 (G2-D4)   M   Med. diff.

587.   *Letzts Hoffnung*
                   Nicht zu geschwind 3/4 (F2-D4)   M   Med. diff.

588.   *Im Dorfe*
                   Etwas langsam 12/8   (C3-C4)   M   Med. diff.

589.   *Der stürmische Morgen*
                   Ziemlich geschwind 4/4 (A#2-C4)   M-MH   Med. diff.

590.   *Täuschung*
                   Etwas geschwind 6/8 (D3-D4)   MH   Med. diff.

591.   *Der Wegweiser*
                   Mässig 2/4   (C#3-D4)   M-MH   Med. diff.

592.   *Das Wirtshaus*
                   Sehr langsam 4/4   (C3-D4)   MH   Med. diff.

593.   *Mut*
                        Ziemlich geschwind 2/4   (A2-D4)   M   Med. diff.

594.   *Die Nebensonnen*
                        Nicht zu langsam 3/4   (F3-Db4)   MH   Med. diff.

595.   *Der Leiermann*
                        Etwas langsam 3/4   (C3-Db4)   MH   Med. diff.

                        Schwanengesang
These songs are annotated in normal order of presentation.
596.   *Liebesbotschaft*
                        Ziemlich langsam 2/4   (A2-C4)   M   Mod. diff.

597.   *Kriegers Ahnung*
                        Nicht zu langsam 3/4   (F#2-D4)   M-MH   Mod. diff.

598.   *Frühlingssehnsucht*
                        Geschwind 2/4   (A2-C4)   M   Mod. diff.

599.   *Ständchen*
                        Mässig 3/4   (A2-D4)   M-MH   Mod. diff.

600.   *Aufenthalt*
                        Nicht zu geschwind 2/4   (F#2-D4)   L-MH   Mod. diff.

601.   *In der Ferne*
                        Ziemlich langsam 3/4   (G2-Eb4)   M-MH   Mod. diff.

602.   *Abschied*
                        Mässig geschwind 4/4   (G2-D4)   ML-M   Mod. diff.

603.   *Der Atlas*
                        Etwas geschwind 3/4   (A2-Eb4)   M-MH   Mod. diff.

604.   *Ihr Bild*
                        Langsam 2/2   (D3-D4)   MH   Mod. diff.

605.   *Das Fischermädchen*
                        Etwas geschwind 6/8   (G2-Db4)   M-MH   Mod. diff.

606.   *Die Stadt*
                        Mässig geschwind 3/4   (G2-D4)   M   Mod. diff.

607.   *Am Meer*
                        Sehr langsam 2/2   (Bb2-Db4)   MH   Mod. diff.

608.   *Der Doppelgänger*
                        Sehr langsam 3/4   (F#2-D4)   ML-MH   Mod. diff.

609.   *Die Taubenpost*
                   Ziemlich langsam 2/2   (C#3-D4)   MH   Mod. diff.

                   Ausgewählte Lieder
These songs are annotated in alphabetical order.
610.   *Auf dem Wasser zu singen*
                   (Not suitable)

611.   *Ave Maria*
                   (Women's voices)

612.   *Du bist die Ruh*
                   Langsam 3/8   (C3-Eb)   MH-H   Med. diff.

613.   *Erlkönig*
                   Schnell   (G2-D4)   ML-MH   Mod. diff.

614.   *Die Forelle*
                   Etwas lebhaft 2/4   (C3-C4)   M-MH   Med. diff.

615.   *Frühlingsglaube*
                   Ziemlich langsam 2/4 (A2-B3)   M   Med. diff.

616.   *Geheimes*
                   Etwas geschwind 2/4 (A2-D4)   M   Med. diff.

617.   *Gretchen am Spinnrade*
                   (Women's voices)

618.   *Heidenröslein*
                   (Women's voices)

619.   *Jägers Abendlied*
                   Sehr langsam 2/4   (D3-Db4)   MH   Med. diff.

620.   *Die junge Nonne*
                   (Women's voices)

621.   *Lied der Mignon*
                   (Women's voices)

622.   *Lob der Tränen*
                   Ziemlich langsam 3/4 (C#3-C#4)   MH   Med. diff.

623.   *Des Mädchens Klage*
                   (Women's voices)

624.   *Rastlose Liebe*
                   Schnell 2/4   (G2-C#4)   MH   Med. diff.

625.   *Romanze aus Rosamunde*
                       Andante 6/8   (A2-C4)   M   Med. diff.

626.   *Schäfers Klagelied*
                       Mässig 6/8   (A2-Db4)   M-MH   Med. diff.

627.   *Sei mir gegrüsst*
                       Langsam 3/4   (E3-D4)   MH   Med. diff.

628.   *Ständchen*
                       Allegretto 6/8   (C3-D4)   MH   Med. diff.

629.   *Der Tod und das Mädchen*
                       Mässig 2/2   (A2(D2)-Eb4)   M-MH   Med. diff.
                       (Although many feel this work should be only for women's
                       voices, a number of notable basses have performed or
                       recorded this excellent piece; this is the original key)

630.   *Der Wanderer*
                       Slow, Fast, 2/2, 6/8   (F2(C2)-C4)   L-MH   Mod. diff.

631.   *Wanderers Nachtlied*
                       Langsam 4/4   (D3-D4)   MH   Med. diff.

CHAPTER VI

SONG CYCLES AND SETS

This chapter contains a wealth of song literature much of which can be sung as individual pieces if desired. Many of the cycles and sets were composed specifically for bass voice and most of the remaining were composed for low voice. The cycles and sets are organized alphabetically by composer. The songs within a cycle or set are in the order indicated by the composer.

632. Ahrens, Sieglinde   *Drei Gesänge* (Ger.) 1969   Müller
      (b. 1936) Ger.   (three songs for bass and organ)(see no. 1058)

      Amram, David   *Three Shakespeare Songs* (Eng.)   Peters
      (b. 1930) Am.
This musically exacting and interpretively challenging group of Shakespeare songs for bass voice, trombone, flute, and piano is contemporary in musical design and is difficult to execute.
633.   *Malvolio's Aria* ("Tis But Fortune")
                          Moderato 4/4,5/4   (F#2-E4)   M-H   Diff.

634.   *Blow, Blow Thou Winter Wind*
                          Moderato 4/4   (A2-Db4)   M   Mod. diff.

635.   *Fool's Song*
                          Allegretto 6/8   (B2-E4)   MH   Mod. diff.

      Amram, David   *Three Songs for America* (Eng)   Peters
These three unique songs for advanced bass voice, woodwind quintet, and string quartet are musically complex and interpretively difficult.
636.   I (John F. Kennedy)
                          Lento 4/4   (F#2-Eb4)   M-MH   Diff.

637.   II (Martin Luther King, Jr.)
                          Lento 6/8   (F2-E4)   M-MH   Diff.

638.   III (Robert F. Kennedy)
                          Animato 4/4   (F#2-D4)   M-MH   Diff.

      Bate, Stanley   *Five Songs by James Joyce* (Eng.)   Ricordi
      (1911-1959) Eng.
A set of five songs for low voice and piano suitable for bass-baritone or possibly bass.
639.   *Bahnhofstrasse*
                          Lento   (C3-D4)   MH   Mod. diff.

640.   *Simples*
                       Moderato   (D#3-D4)   MH   Mod. diff.

641.   *Tilly*
                       Very fast   (Bb2-E4)   MH   Mod. diff.

642.   *Tutto è sciolto*
                       Lento   (A2-E4)   M-MH   Mod. diff.

643.   *Watching the Needle Boats at San Sabba*
                       Allegretto   (D3-D4)   MH   Mod. diff.

644. Beethoven, Ludwig van *An die ferne Geliebte* (Ger./Eng.)   Belwin
      (1770-1827) Ger.
This well-known cycle of six connected songs usually sung by higher male voices is available
in an edition for low voice.
                       Various tempo & meter (C3-E4)   M-H   Med. diff.

      Beethoven, Ludwig van *Two Humorous Arias* (Ger./Eng.)   International
These two arias, printed separately by International Music Co. provide a combination of patter,
agility, wide leaps, and high tessitura that is challenging to even the most accomplished bass.
645.   *Die Prüfung des Küssens*
                       Andante 2/4   (G2-E4)   M-H   Mod. diff.

646.   *Mit Mädeln sich vertragen*
                       Allegro 6/8   (A2-E4)   MH-H   Mod. diff.

      Berger, Jean   *Five Shelley Poems* (Eng.)   Sheppard
      (b. 1909) Ger./Am.
With sensitive lyrics by Percy Bysshe Shelley these musically challenging songs are well-suited
to the intermediate or advanced bass voice.
647.   *Where Art Thou?*
                       Slow 6/4   (A2-D#4)   M-MH   Med. diff.

648.   *The Fountains Mingle with the River*
                       Allegro 3/4   (G2-E4)   ML-MH   Diff.

649.   *The Flower That Smiles Today*
                       Flowing 3/2; 6/4   (Bb2-Eb4)   M-MH   Med. diff.

650.   *Of Times Past*
                       Andante 4/4   (A2-E4)   M-MH   Med. diff.

651.   *On a Cat*
                       Allegro 6/4   (A2-D4)   ML-MH   Med. diff.

Brahms, Johannes   ***Vier ernste Gesänge***   Simrock+
(1833-1897) Ger.   (Four Serious Songs)(Ger./Eng.)

This important song cycle for low voice is fortunately available in a low bass edition in the
range indicated below published by N. Simrock. A must for intermediate or advanced bass.

652.   *Denn es gehet*
                          Andante 4/4   (G2-Eb4)   ML-MH   Mod. diff.
                          Sober and introverted; musically and interpretively
                          demanding.

653.   *Ich wandte mich*
                          Andante 3/4   (F#2- D#4) M-MH   Mod. diff.
                          Oppressive and dark; supreme legato; command of soft
                          dynamics.

654.   *O Tod, wie bitter bist du*
                          Grave 3/2   (A2-E4)   M-MH   Diff.
                          Solemn and dignified with command of high mezzo voce.

655.   *Wenn ich mit Menschen*
                          Andante 4/4   (Gb2-F4)   M-H   Diff.
                          Noble and stirring; deeply felt; wide range; command of
                          high notes.

Branscombe, Gena   ***A Lute of Jade*** (Eng.)   Recital Pub.
(1881-1977) Can.

Translated from Chinese texts of the 8th and 9th centuries A.D., the songs in this group are
for any voice but are suitable for bass in this low voice edition.

656.   *A Lovely Maiden, Roaming*
                          Allegretto 6/8   (Bb2-Eb4)   M-MH   Mod. diff.

657.   *My Fatherland*
                          Andante 4/4   (C3-D4)   M-MH   Mod. diff.

658.   *There Was a King of Liang*
                          Allegretto 4/4   (B2-D4)   M-MH   Mod. diff.

659.   *Fair Is the Pine Grove*
                          Allegretto 6/8   (B2-Eb4)   M-MH   Mod. diff.

660. Chausson, Ernest   ***Chansons de Shakespeare*** (Fr.)   Rouart
      (1855-1899) Fr.

A group of four songs, three of which are for low male voice suitable for bass-baritone or
possibly bass. The three songs are: 1. *Chanson de clown*, 2. *Chanson d'amour*, 4. *Chanson
d'Ophélie*. 3. *Chant funèbre* is for women's chorus and is published separately.

Cornelius, Peter   ***Christmas Songs*** (Ger./Eng.)   Well-Temp.
(1824-1874) Ger.

Formerly only readily available in higher keys, this newly distributed edition by Masters Music Publications is available for bass voice in the ranges indicated below.

| 661. | *The Christmas Tree* (Christbaum) | | | |
| | Allegretto 6/8 | (C3-D4) | M-MH | Med. diff. |

| 662. | *The Shepherds* (Die Hirten) | | | |
| | Andante 9/8 | (C3-D4) | M-MH | Med. diff. |

| 663. | *The Shepherds* (Die Hirten) | | | |
| | Tranquillo 9/8 | (B2-Db4) | M-MH | Med. diff. |

| 664. | *The Kings* (Die Könige) | | | |
| | Andante 4/4 | (B2-C4) | M | Mod. easy |

| 665. | *The Kings* (Die Könige) | | | |
| | Lento 4/4 | (A2-D4) | M | Med. diff. |

| 666. | *Simeon* | | | |
| | Legato 2/4 | (A2-D4) | M | Med. diff. |

| 667. | *Christ, the Friend of Children* (Christus der Kinderfreund) | | | |
| | Lento 2/4 | (Bb2-Bb3) | M | Mod. easy |

| 668. | *The Christ-Child* (Christkind) | | | |
| | Animato 9/8 | (Bb2-Db4) | M | Mod. diff. |

Cornell, Douglas   *Retrospective* (Eng.)   UMI
Am.

This song cycle was composed for Eldon Udell Black (bass) and first performed in 1968. As of this printing this cycle is only available from the author or from Black's treatise, *A Performance Edition of Repertoire for the Profondo Bass*, available from University Microfilms International. This unique and musically demanding cycle is for the more advanced low bass voice.

| 669. | I. | | | |
| | Moderato 4/4 | (F#2-C4) | L-M | Mod. diff. |

| 670. | II. | | | |
| | Scherzando 3/4 2/4 | (F#2-E4) | ML-MH | Diff. |

| 671. | III. | | | |
| | Tranquillo 4/4 | (Eb2-C#4) | L-M | Diff. |

Cumming, Richard   *We Happy Few* (Eng.)   B & H
(b. 1928) Am.

This cycle was commissioned by bass-baritone Donald Gramm under a grant from the Ford Foundation. The songs in this appealing cycle with excellent prose (Shakespeare, Housman, Whitman, the Bible) are musically challenging, and are appropriate to the intermediate or more advanced bass-baritone.

672.   *The Feast of Chrispian*

		Maestoso 6/4	(G2-E4)	ML-MH	Diff.
673.		*To Whom Can I Speak Today?*			
		Adagio 2/2	(A2-C4)	M	Mod. diff.
674.		*Fife Tune*			
		Andante 6/8	(A2-Eb4)	M-MH	Mod. diff.
675.		*Here Dead Lie We*			
		Adagio 4/4	(Cb2-B3)	M	Med. diff.
676.		*A Ballad of the Good Lord Nelson*			
		Allegro	(A2(D2)-D4)	M-MH	Med. diff.
677.		*Going to the Warres*			
		Allegro 3/4	(A2-D4)	ML-MH	Med. diff.
678.		*A Sight in Camp*			
		Lento 2/2	(Ab2-E4)	ML-MH	Med. diff.
679.		*The End of the World*			
		Moderato 3/4	(A2-Eb4)	MH	Diff.
680.		*Grave Hour*			
		Adagio 4/4	(B2-E4)	M-H	Med. diff
681.		*The Song of Moses*			
		Fast 5/8 6/8	(G2-E4)	ML-MH	Diff.

	Debussy, Claude (1862-1918) Fr.	*Fêtes Galantes II* (Fr.)			International

This cycle is contained in "43 Songs" for low voice.

		Les ingénus			
682.		Modéré 3/8	(C3-F4)	H	Mod. diff.
683.		*La faune*			
		Andantino 3/4	(C3-C4)	MH	Mod. diff.
684.		*Colloque sentimental*			
		Triste et lent 3/4	(Ab2-Fb4)	M-H	Mod. diff.

	Diamond, David (b. 1915) Am.	*Four Ladies* (Eng.)			Southern

With prose by Ezra Pound these four humorous songs are set here in this edition in their original keys. They are musically intricate and require subtlety in interpretation.

		Agathas			
685.		Moderato 3/4	(E3-C#4)	M	Diff.

| 686. | *Young Lady* | | | |
| | Lento 3/4 | (A2-D4) | M-MH | Diff. |

| 687. | *Lesbia Illa* | | | |
| | Allegro 7/8 | (D3-D4) | M-MH | Diff. |

| 688. | *Passing* | | | |
| | Lento 5/4 | (D3-D#4) | M-MH | Diff. |

Diamond, David   ***The Midnight Meditation*** (Eng.)   Southern

A very demanding cycle of four songs for bass-baritone (dedicated to bass-baritone William Warfield) on the dark lyrics of Elder Olson. Composed in 1951 the songs are vocally taxing, musically complex, dissonant, and interpretively demanding.

| 689. | I. | | | |
| | Lento 2/4 | (F2-D4) | L-MH | Diff. |

| 690. | II. | | | |
| | Moderato 3/2 | (F#2-F4) | ML-H | Very diff. |

| 691. | III. | | | |
| | Allegretto 2/4 | (F#2-E4) | L-H | Very diff. |

| 692. | IV. | | | |
| | Grave 4/4 | (F2-E4) | ML-H | Very diff. |

DiGiovanni, Rocco   ***Arcobaleno*** (It.)   Recital Pub.
(b.1924) Am.

These seven short songs for bass set to the poetry of and written for Nicola Rossi-Lemeni (famous Italian basso) are in a conservative range but are rather complex musically and are interpretively subtle. Translations of the Italian text into English are found at the back of the volume.

| 693. | *Rosso* | | | |
| | Espressivo 5/4 | (Bb2-C#4) | M | Diff. |

| 694. | *Arancione* | | | |
| | Andante 3/4 | (Bb2-D4) | M | Diff. |

| 695. | *Giallo* | | | |
| | Andante 6/4, 4/4 | (C3-C#4) | M | Diff. |

| 696. | *Verde* | | | |
| | Moderato 2/4 | (Db3-Db4) | M | Diff. |

| 697. | *Azzurro* | | | |
| | Andante 4/4 | (C#3-C#4) | M | Diff. |

| 698. | *Indaco* | | | |
| | Andante 2/2 | (Gb3-Eb4) | MH | Diff. |

699.	*Violetto*			
	Espressivo 5/4	(Gb3-D4)	MH	Diff.

Dougherty, C. (arr.)   ***Five Sea Chanties*** (Eng.)   Schirmer
(1902-1986) Am.

Five popular sea chanties arranged for low voice and piano are appropriate for beginning or intermediate bass or bass-baritone.

700.	*Rio Grande*			
	Flowing 6/4	(Eb3-Eb4)	M-MH	Mod. easy
701.	*Blow Ye Winds*			
	Fast and light 4/4	(C3-D4)	M-MH	Mod. easy
702.	*Across the Western Ocean*			
	Broad 4/4	(D3-D4)	M-MH	Mod. easy
703.	*Mobile Bay*			
	Jolly 4/4	(D3-Eb4)	M-MH	Mod. easy
704.	*Shenandoah*			
	Majestic sweep 3/4	(A2-D4)	M-MH	Mod. easy

Dvorák, Antonin   ***Biblical Songs*** (Eng.)   Schirmer
(1841-1904) Czech.

Appropriate for most any voice, these tastefully composed religious songs in the keys presented are well-suited to the beginning or intermediate bass voice and present few musical or vocal problems.

705.	*Clouds and Darkness*			
	Andantino 3/8	(B2-D4)	M-MH	Med. diff.
706.	*Lord Thou Art My Refuge*			
	Andante 4/4	(B2-C4)	M	Mod. easy
707.	*Hear My Prayer*			
	Andante 3/4	(Bb2-E4)	MH	Med. diff.
708.	*God Is My Shepherd*			
	Andante 4/4	(B2-C#4)	M	Mod. easy
709.	*I Will Sing New Songs*			
	Risoluto 4/4	(Eb3-Eb4)	MH	Med. diff.
710.	*Hear My Prayer, O Lord*			
	Andante 4/4	(B2-D4)	M-MH	Mod. easy
711.	*By the Waters of Babylon*			
	Andante 3/8	(Bb2-Eb4)	M-MH	Med. diff.

| 712. | *Turn Thee to Me* | | | |
| | Andante 4/4 | (Db3-Db4) | MH | Med. diff. |

| 713. | *I Will Lift Mine Eyes* | | | |
| | Andante 3/8 | (D3-Eb4) | MH | Med. diff |

| 714. | *Sing Ye a Joyful Song* | | | |
| | Allegro 2/4 | (C3-D4) | M-MH | Med. diff. |

Finzi, Gerald   ***Let Us Garlands Bring*** (Eng.)   B & H
(1901-1956) Eng.

A lovely cycle of songs for low voice and suitable for intermediate bass or bass-baritone. These songs present few problems but the last song may need to be transposed.

| 715. | *Come Away, Come Away, Death* | | | |
| | Lugubre 2/4 | (A#2-D4) | M-MH | Med. diff. |

| 716. | *Who Is Silvia* | | | |
| | Allegro 2/4 | (A2-D4) | M-MH | Med. diff. |

| 717. | *Fear No More the Heat o' the Sun* | | | |
| | Grave 6/4 | (Bb2-Eb4) | MH | Med. diff. |

| 718. | *O Mistress Mine* | | | |
| | Allegretto 2/2 | (Bb2-Eb4) | MH | Med. diff. |

| 719. | *It Was a Lover and His Lass* | | | |
| | Allegretto 2/4 | (A2-E4) | M-H | Mod. diff. |

Flagello, Nicolas   ***The Land*** (Eng.)   General
(b. 1928) Am.

This cycle of songs on nature is musically demanding and is for a more advanced bass with a secure top.

| 720. | *The Eagle* | | | |
| | Andante 4/4 | (A2-C#4) | M | Mod. diff. |

| 721. | *The Owl* | | | |
| | Varied tempo & meter | (Bb2-D4) | M-MH | Diff. |

| 722. | *The Throstle* | | | |
| | Allegro; varied meter | (Db3-E4) | M-H | Diff. |

| 723. | *The Oak* | | | |
| | Andante 4/4 | (D3-Eb4) | M-MH | Diff. |

| 724. | *The Snowdrop* | | | |
| | Allegro 3/8 | (D3-E4) | MH | Diff. |

| 725. | *Flower in the Cranny* | | | |

	Lento 4/4	(Db3-C4)	M-MH	Diff.

Gibbs, C. Armstrong   ***Songs of the Mad Sea-Captain*** (Eng.)   B & H
(1889-1960) Eng.

A well-crafted and effective cycle of sea songs for intermediate or advanced bass voice.

726.	*Hidden Treasure*			
	Con moto 2/4	(G2-D4)	M-MH	Med. diff.

727.	*Abel Wright*			
	Alla marcia 4/4	(Ab2-D#4)	M-MH	Med. diff.

728.	*Toll the Bell*			
	Lento 6/8	(A2-D4)	ML-MH	Med. diff.

729.	*The Golden Ray*			
	Ma non troppo 2/2	(B2-D4)	MH	Med. diff.

Hall, Jeffrey   ***Two Settings from Ahab*** (Eng.)(see no. 253-4)

730. Head, Michael   ***Six Sea Songs*** (Eng.)   B & H
(1900-1976) Eng.

A group of songs of sea for low voice suitable for bass-baritone. The group consists of *A Sea Burthen, Limehouse Reach, Back to Hilo, A Dog's Life, Lavender Pond,* and *Sweethearts and Wives.*

	Various tempo & meter (A2-F4)	MH-H	Med. diff.

Honegger, Arthur   ***Quatre Chansons*** (Fr.)   Salabert
(1892-1955) Swiss

An effective and highly recommended set of songs for low voice suitable for intermediate or advanced bass-baritone or possibly bass voice by this influential composer of French music.

731.	I			
	Allegretto 2/2	(C#3-E4)	MH	Mod. diff.

732.	II			
	Largo 12/8	(A2-C4)	M	Mod. diff.

733.	III			
	Adagio 4/4	(G2-C#4)	M	Mod. diff.

734.	IV			
	Giocoso 2/4	(A#2-E4)	MH	Mod. diff.

Hovhaness, Alan   ***Four Songs*** (Op. 238)(Eng./Armenian)   Peters
(b. 1911) Am.

This interesting, modal work for low voice is nicely suited to intermediate bass-baritone or perhaps bass. The ability to handle higher tessitura and long phrases is required.

735.	*Inconsequential Journey*			
	Allegro 3/8	(C3-C4)	M-MH	Med. diff.

736.	*Time Passes*			
	Adagio 4/4, 5/8	(C3-Eb4)	MH	Med. diff.

737.	*Singing, Singing*			
	Allegro 2/4	(E3-D4)	MH	Med. diff.

738.	*Old Dome of Ararat*			
	Slow, no meter	(D3-F4)	MH-H	Med. diff.

Hovhaness, Alan   *Four Songs* (Op. 242)(Eng.)   Peters

This cycle is for low voice suitable for bass-baritone or bass. It requires some command of higher tessitura, agility and long phrases for this interesting, modal group.

739.	*Distant Lake of Sighs*			
	Adagio 2/2	(E3-E4)	MH-H	Med. diff.

740.	*Under a Byzantine Dome*			
	Andante 7/4, 4/4	(G2-E4)	ML-MH	Med. diff.

741.	*In Early Dawn Time*			
	Andante 4/4	(D3-D4)	MH	Med. diff.

742.	*From High Armenia Mountain*			
	Maestoso, no meter	(Gb2-Eb4)	ML-MH	Med. diff.

Hovhaness, Alan   *Three Odes of Solomon* (Eng.)   Peters

This modal setting of these songs gives this cycle a unique quality and is appropriate for intermediate level bass.

743.	*No Way Is Hard*			
	Lento 5/4	(C3-D4)	MH	Med. diff.

744.	*As the Wings of Doves*			
	Andante 6/4	(C3-E4)	MH	Med. diff.

745.	*As the Work of the Husbandman*			
	Andante 4/4	(D3-D4)	MH	Med. diff.

Hyman, Dick   *Songs from the Plays of Shakespeare*   General
(b. 1927) Am.

This jazzy cycle of songs for low voice is generally well suited in range and tessitura for bass voice and is more applicable to beginning and intermediate level students.

746.	*When That I Was and a Little Tiny Boy*			
	Moderate 4/4	(C3-C4)	M	Mod. easy

747.	*Under the Greenwood Tree*			
	Expressive 4/4	(C3-D4)	MH	Mod. easy
748.	*When Daffodils Begin to Peer*			
	Allegro 4/4	(D3-C4)	M	Mod. easy
749.	*It Was a Lover and His Lass*			
	Allegro 2/2	(C3-Eb4)	M-MH	Mod. easy
750.	*Come Away, Come Away, Death*			
	Moderate 2/2	(B2-D4)	M-MH	Mod. easy
751.	*Winter*			
	Lento 3/4	(Bb2-D4)	M-MH	Mod. easy
752.	*Spring*			
	Allegro 2/2	(D3-D4)	MH	Mod. easy
753.	*Sigh No More, Ladies, Sigh No More*			
	Alla marcia 2/4	(C3-D4)	M-MH	Mod. easy
754.	*Will You Buy Any Tape?*			
	Alla marcia 2/2	(Bb2-D4)	M-MH	Mod. easy
755.	*O Mistress Mine*			
	Andante 3/4	(A2-C4)	M	Mod. easy
756.	*Take, O Take Those Lips Away*			
	Expressive 2/2	(C3-Eb4)	MH-H	Mod. easy
757.	*Blow, Blow, Thou Winter Wind*			
	Allegro	(C#3-E4)	M-H	Mod. easy
758.	*Lawn As White As Driven Snow*			
	Allegretto 3/4	(Bb2-D4)	ML-MH	Mod. easy
759.	*Who Is Silvia?*			
	Allegro 6/8	(A2-D4)	ML-M	Mod. easy

| Ibert, Jacques (1890-1962) Fr. | ***Don Quichotte*** (Fr.) | | | Leduc |

An excellent cycle of songs for bass-baritone or possibly bass and orchestra (piano reduction also available) at an intermediate or advanced level with command of high mezza voce and good proficiency with French required. They are dedicated to Feodor Chaliapin.

760.	*Chanson du départ*			
	Various tempo 3/8	(A2-E4)	MH	Mod. diff.
761.	*Chanson à Dulcinée*			
	Allegro, various meter	(Bb2-Eb4)	M-H	Mod. diff.

762.   *Chanson du Duc*
                            Various tempo 4/4, 2/4 (Ab2-Db4)   ML-MH   Mod. diff.

763.   *Chanson de la mort*
                            Andante molto 2/4   (D3-E4)   MH-H   Mod. diff.

Keel, Frederick   ***Three Salt-Water Ballads*** (Eng.)   B & H
(1871-1950) Br.

An excellent cycle of sea songs for low voice and well suited to the bass voice at the
intermediate level. The third song requires facile articulation with high tessatura, but few
problems are apparent in this effective cycle.

764.   *Port of Many Ships*
                           Allegretto 4/4   (C3-Eb4)   M-MH   Med. diff.

765.   *Trade Winds*
                           Allegretto 3/4   (Bb2-Eb4)   M-MH   Med. diff.

766.   *Mother Cary*
                           Briskly 3/4   (C3-Eb4)   MH   Mod. diff.

Kirk, Theron   ***Prayers from the Ark*** (Vol. 3.)(Eng.)   MCA
(b. 1919) Am.

The third of a three part cycle for soprano, tenor, and bass-baritone. All four of these
interesting songs for bass-baritone are tonal with some musical demands and can be performed
as a separate group.

767.   *Noah's Prayer*
                           Allegro 4/4   (F2-Eb4)   MH   Mod. diff.

768.   *The Prayer of the Elephant*
                           Largo 4/4   (A2-Db4)   M-MH   Mod. diff.

769.   *The Prayer of the Donkey*
                           Largo 4/4   (D2-D#4)   L-MH   Med. diff.

770.   *The Prayer of the Giraffe*
                           Allegro 4/4   (E3-D#4)   MH   Med. diff.

Kodály, Zoltán   ***Two Songs*** (Op. 5)(Hun./Ger.)   B & H
(1882-1967) Hung.

Two demanding songs for bass-baritone and piano.

771.   *A Közelitö Tél* (Der nahende Winter)
                           Andante 4/4   (A#2-Gb4)   MH-VH   Diff.

772.   *Sirni, Sirni, Sirni* (Weinen, Weinen)
                           Lento 2/2   (G2-E4)   M-H   Diff.

Laderman, Ezra   ***Songs from Michelangelo*** (Eng.)   Oxford
(b. 1924) Am.

This cycle of songs was first performed by Sherrill Milnes (baritone), but the range and tessitura indicate bass. Only accomplished singers should attempt this effective cycle with its wide leaps, many accidentals, and vocal demands.

773.	*Who Is the One Who Draws Me to You?*				
	Andantino 3/4, 2/4	(A2-D4)	M-MH	Diff.	
774.	*Oh Sweeter a Sudden Death Would Be*				
	Presto, various meter	(A2-Db4)	M-MH	Very diff.	
775.	*Your Face Is Sweeter Than Mustard*				
	Gaily 4/4, 2/4	(G#2-E4)	M-H	Very diff.	
776.	*The More You See the Torment on My Face*				
	Moderato 2/4, 3/4,	(Ab2-Db4)	MH	Very diff.	
777.	*If In a Part a Woman Is Beautiful*				
	Lento 6/8	(Ab2-E4)	MH-H	Diff.	
778.	*For All This Anguish*				
	Lento, various meter	(F#2- D4)	L-MH	Diff	

779. Leguerney, Jacques   ***Le Carnaval*** (Fr.)   Salabert
(b. 1908) Fr.

Originally composed for baritone, these three songs: *Le grotesque, La belle brune*, and *Le carnaval* are suited to bass-baritone and possibly bass as well. It contains sections of difficult French and is musically not easy.

780. Leguerney, Jacques   ***La Solitude*** (Fr.)   Mondia

This cycle of four songs: *Les ormeaux, Corine, La source*, and *A la forêt* was also originally composed for baritone but is appropriate for bass-baritone and possibly bass. The work is musically and interpretively demanding with sections requiring high, soft dynamics. The overall range is (Bb2-F4) with M-H tessitura.

781. Leibowitz, René   ***Trois poèmes*** (Fr./Eng.)(see nos. 256-8)

Leichtling, Alan   ***Three Songs of Emily Dickinson***   Seesaw
(b. 1947)

This unique group of songs is for bass voice and cello.

782.	*There Is No Silence*			
	Lento 2/2	(C3-B3)	ML	Diff.
783.	*The Hallowing of Pain*			
	Largo, varied meter	(C3-A#3)	ML	Diff.

784.   *Success Is Counted Sweetest*
                             Andante 2/2   (B2-Eb4)   MH   Diff.

         Loewe, Carl   ***Liederkranz für Bass*** (op. 145)(Ger.)   Peters
         (1796-1869) Ger.
Composed for August Fricke, great German bass, these four largely strophic songs are excellent
for low bass voice at the beginning and intermediate level and present few problems.
785.   *Meeresleuchten*
                             Andante 9/8   (E2-B3)   L-M   Med. diff.

786.   *Im Sturme*
                             Vivace 4/4   (A2-C4)   ML-M   Med. diff.

787.   *Heimlichkeit*
                             Andante 6/8   (F2-B3)   L-ML   Med. diff.

788.   *Reiterlied*
                             Vivace 3/4   (E2-B3)   L-ML   Med. diff.

         Mahler, Gustav   ***Kindertotenlieder*** (Ger.)   International
         (1860-1911) Aus.
Emotionally and interpretively demanding, this cycle for low voice is appropriate for
bass-baritones with a wide range and good command of both high and low notes.
789.   *Nun will die Sonn' so hell aufgehn!*
                             Langsam 4/4   (D3-Eb4)   MH   Mod. diff.

790.   *Nun seh' ich wohl, warum so dunkle Flammen*
                             Ruhig 4/4   (A2-F4)   M-H   Mod. diff.

791.   *Wenn dein Muetterlein*
                             Schwer 4/4   (G2-F4)   ML-H   Diff.

792.   *Oft denk' ich, sie sind nur ausgegangen!*
                             Ruhig bewegt 2/2   (Bb2-Gb4)   M-VH   Diff.

793.   *In diesem Wetter!*
                             Mit ruhelos 4/4   (Bb2-F4)   MH-H   Diff.

         Martino, Donald   ***Three Songs for Bass Voice*** (Eng.)   E. C. Schirmer
         (b. 1931) Am.
An extremely demanding cycle of songs for bass-baritone employing avant-garde techniques.
The poetry is by James Joyce. The final song requires an F#4 and a sustained F4.
794.   *Alone*
                             Slow, various meter (B2-Eb4)   M-MH   Very diff.

795.   *Tutto è sciolto* (Eng.)
                             Slow, varied meter   (F#2-Eb4)   ML-MH   Very diff.

| 796. | | *A Memory of the Players in a Mirror* | | | |
| | | Slow 2/4 | (G2-F#4) | ML-VH | Very diff. |

| | Marx, Karl | *Vier Gesänge vom Tage* (Ger.) | | | Bärenreiter |
| | (1897-1985) Ger. | | | | |

These four unique and complex songs are for bass and string quartet or orchestra.

| 797. | | *Komme, o Tag* | | | |
| | | Slow 2/2 | (A2-F4) | M-H | Diff. |

| 798. | | *Morgenlied* | | | |
| | | Joyous 2/2 | (C3-F4) | MH-H | Diff. |

| 799. | | *Die Quelle* | | | |
| | | Quiet 3/4 | (F#2(B1)-E4) | L-MH | Diff. |

| 800. | | *Regen* | | | |
| | | Stormy 3/4 | (G2-Eb4) | M-H | Diff. |

| | Mason, Daniel G. | *Nautical Lays of a Landsman* (Eng.) | | | Schirmer |
| | (1873-1953) Am. | | | | |

A humorous group of songs of the sea for bass-baritone or bass with few demands.

| 801. | | *I Ain't Afeard o' the Admiral* | | | |
| | | Moderato 4/4 | (A2-E4) | M-MH | Med. diff. |

| 802. | | *A Grain of Salt* | | | |
| | | Moderato 3/4 | (A2-D4) | MH | Med. diff. |

| 803. | | *The Constant Cannibal Maiden* | | | |
| | | Moderato 3/2, 3/4 | (C3-E4) | MH | Med. diff. |

| | Mathieu, Rodolphe | *Saisons Canadiennes* (Fr.) | | | Composer |
| | (1890-1962) Fr. Can. | | | | |

A cycle of four songs by a French Canadian composer for bass-baritone and piano. The manuscript is available through the University of Laval in Quebec, Canada.

| 804. | | *Automne* | | | |
| | | Moderato 4/4 | (Bb2-E4) | MH | Diff. |

| 805. | | *Hiver* | | | |
| | | Moderato 4/4 | (Bb2-E4) | MH | Diff. |

| 806. | | *Été* | | | |
| | | Moderato 3/4 | (Bb2-Eb4) | M-MH | Diff. |

| 807. | | *Printemps* | | | |
| | | Allegro 3/4 | (C3-F4) | MH-H | Diff. |

Milhaud, Darius   ***Chansons bas*** (Fr.)   Eschig
(1892-1974) Fr.

For the intermediate or advanced bass-baritone or perhaps bass with good command of high
notes, this cycle for low voice requires command of the French language and an appropriate
sense of style.

808.   *Le Savetier*
                         Various tempo & meter (Bb2-F4)   MH-H   Mod. diff.

809.   *La Marchande d'herbes aromatiques*
                         Various tempo & meter (C3-F4)   MH-H   Mod. diff.

810.   *Le Cantonnier*
                         Various tempo & meter (G2-Bb3)   M   Mod. diff.

811.   *Le Marchand d'ail et d'oignons*
                         Various tempo & meter (C#3-D#4)   MH   Mod. diff.

812.   *La Femme de l'ouvrier*
                         Various tempo & meter (C3-B3)   M   Mod. diff.

813.   *Le Vitrier*
                         Various tempo & meter (C3-C4)   M-MH   Mod. diff.

814.   *Le Crieur d'imprimes*
                         Various tempo & meter (Bb2-Ab3)   M   Mod. diff.

815.   *La Marchande d'habits*
                         Various tempo & meter (C#3-E4)   MH   Mod. diff.

816. Milhaud, Darius   ***Trois poèmes de J. Supervielle*** (Fr.)   Heugel
These songs, *Ce peu, Compagnon du silence, Ce bruit de la mer,* for low voice are musically
somewhat complex with high tessitura but are vocally quite sympathetic.

Mussorgsky, Modest   ***Songs and Dances of Death*** (Russ./Eng.)   International
(1835-1881) Russ.

An excellent cycle of songs for low voice at the intermediate to advanced level. Interpretively
demanding and vocally challenging, these songs require a mature sound and an excellent sense
of appropriate style. The last song of the group is vocally arduous and must be paced
accordingly.

817.   *Lullaby*
                         Lento 4/4   (Ab2-F4)   M-MH   Mod. diff.

818.   *Serenade*
                         Moderato 2/4   (A2-Eb4)   M-MH   Mod. diff.

819.   *Trepak*
                         Lento 4/4   (C3-Eb4)   M-MH   Mod. diff.

| 820. | *Commander-in-Chief* | | | |
| | Vivace 4/4 | (B2-Eb4) | MH-H | Diff. |

Mussorgsky, Modest   ***Without Sun*** (Russ./Eng)   International
An introspective, cheerless, and deeply felt cycle for bass-baritone or possibly bass. The songs are interpretively challenging with limited range and require some command of soft dynamics.

821.	*Within Four Walls*			
	Moderato	(C#3-D4)	MH	Mod. diff.
822.	*In the Crowd*			
	Moderato	(A2-Eb4)	MH	Mod. diff.
823.	*An End at Last to a Senseless Day*			
	Moderato	(B2-E4)	M-H	Mod. diff.
824.	*Ennui*			
	Moderato	(B2-D#4)	M-H	Mod. diff.
825.	*Elegy*			
	Andantino/Allegro	(C#3-E4)	M-H	Mod. diff.
826.	*On the River*			
	Moderato	(C#3-D#4)	M-H	Mod. diff.

Myers, Gordon   ***Crows and Other people*** (Eng.)   Eastlane
(b. 1919) Am.
A very short cycle of light, humorous songs. He has composed many other humorous songs.

827.	*Crows*			
	Brisk 4/4	(F3-D4)	MH	Mod. easy
828.	*A Hippopotamus*			
	Slow 4/4	(A2-E4)	MH	Med. diff.
829.	*A Thousand Species*			
	Andante 3/4	(C3-Eb4)	MH	Mod. easy

Orland, Henry   ***Two Ballads by Goethe*** (Ger.)   Seesaw
(b. 1918) (Ger.)
Exhibiting a wide range with many large leaps, and rhythmic complexity, this impressive show-piece is almost formidable in its vocal demands, and equally so musically and interpretively.

830.	*Der Zauberlehrling* (The Sorcerer's Apprentice)			
	Varied tempo, meter	(E2-F4)	L-MH	Very diff.
831.	*Der Totentanz* (The Dance of the Dead)			
	Varied tempo, meter	(Eb2-E4)	L-MH	Very diff.

Orthel, Léon   *Twee Liederen*   Donemus
(1905-1985) Dutch
Dedicated to bass-baritone Chris Verhoog these two songs are set to the verses of Rilke. They
are musically complex and interpretively challenging.
832.   *Schlangenbeschwörung*
                            Allegro, varied meter (G#2-F4)   MH   Diff.

833.   *Die Versuchung*
                            Andante, varied meter (F2-E4)   MH   Diff.

Persichetti, V.   *Two Chinese Songs*   Elkan-Vogel
(b. 1915) Am.
Two short songs employing the dorian mode for bass voice.
834.   *All Alone*
                            Slowly 5/4, 4/4   (Ab2-Bb3) ML-M   Mod. easy

835.   *These Days*
                            Spirited 2/4   (C3-D4)   M-MH   Med. diff.

Pfitzner, Hans   *Drei Sonette* (Op. 41)(Ger.)   Peters
(1869-1949) Ger.
The songs in this set are for bass voice and are generally sustained, requiring some command
over softer dynamics.
836.   *Auf die Morgenröte*
                            Slow   (A#2-D4)   M-MH   Diff.

837.   *Der verspätete Wanderer*
                            Moderato   (Ab2-E4)   MH   Diff.

838.   *Das Alter*
                            Moderately slow   (C#3-Eb4) M-H   Diff.

Pfitzner, Hans   *Vier Lieder* (Ger.)   B & H
A group of challenging songs for bass-baritone. The first three songs are appropriate for bass.
The last song, however, has a baritone tessitura and range.
839.   *Hussens Kerker*
                            Sehr langsam 3/2   (B2-E4)   M-MH   Diff.

840.   *Säerspruch*
                            Grave 4/4   (C3-D4(F4)) MH   Diff.

841.   *Eingelegte Ruder*
                            Adagio 4/4   (D3-D4)   MH   Diff.

842.   *Lass scharren deiner Rosse Huf . . .*
                            Quickly 2/2   (C3-F4)   MH-H   Diff.

Poulenc, Francis   *Le Bestiaire* (Fr./Eng.)   Eschig
(1899-1963) Fr.

This amusing and less demanding cycle of very short songs for low voice was originally scored
for string quartet, flute, clarinet, and bassoon. The songs are well suited to the bass voice, only
the third song presents range problems.

| 843. | *Le Dromadaire* (The Dromedary) | | | |
| | Slowly 2/4 | (D3-C4) | M | Mod. easy |

| 844. | *La Chèvre du Thibet* (The Goat from Tibet) | | | |
| | Moderate 4/4 | (D3-Bb3) | M | Mod. easy |

| 845. | *La Sauterelle* (The Grasshopper) | | | |
| | Slowly 4/4 | (E3-E4) | H | Med. diff. |

| 846. | *Le Dauphin* (The Dolphin) | | | |
| | Animated 4/4 | (B2-B3) | M | Med. diff. |

| 847. | *L'Écrevisse* (The Crab) | | | |
| | Allegretto 4/4 | (B2-Cb3) | M-MH | Med. diff. |

| 848. | *La Carpe* (The Carp) | | | |
| | Slow 4/4 | (B2-Cb3) | M | Mod. easy |

849.   Poulenc, Francis   *Quatre poèmes de G. Apollinaire* (Fr.)   Rouart
       (1899-1863) Fr.

These four songs were originally composed for baritone or mezzo, but are suitable for
bass-baritone. The songs: *L'Anguille, Carte postale, Avant le cinéma, 1904,* contain sections
of difficult French.

Presser, William   *Seven Secular Songs* (Eng.)   Presser
(b. 1916) Am.

An interesting and useful group of seven songs on various themes, some humorous and some
serious for bass at an intermediate level.

| 850. | *Madrigal* | | | |
| | Allegretto 3/4 | (G2-Eb4) | M-MH | Med. diff. |

| 851. | *To Electra* | | | |
| | Fast 2/2 | (G2-Eb4) | M-MH | Mod. diff. |

| 852. | *To Daisies* | | | |
| | Slow 4/4 | (G2-C4) | ML-M | Med. diff. |

| 853. | *Eaper Weaper* | | | |
| | Allegro 4/4 | (F#2(D2)-E4(G4)) | ML-H | Mod. diff. |

| 854. | *Requiem* | | | |
| | Slow 4/4, 5/4 | (Bb2-Eb4) | M-MH | Mod. diff. |

855.   *To Celia*
                              Andante 6/4   (C3-C4)   M   Mod. easy

856.   *The Shoe Tying*
                              Moderate 3/4   (F2-D4)   ML-MH   Mod. diff.

Quilter, Roger   ***Three Shakespeare Songs*** (Eng.)   B & H
(1877-1953) Br.

Quilter wrote many songs but none specifically for bass. A number of his works are available in lower keys but few of these are truly suitable for bass. The second song of the following very popular set of songs is transposed into a key low enough for most basses.

857.   *Come Away, Death*
                              Poco andante 4/4   (C3-Eb4)   MH-H   Mod. easy

858.   *O Mistress Mine*
                              Allegro moderato 3/4   (Bb2-Eb4)   MH   Mod. easy
                              (available in lower key, see no. 78)

859.   *Blow, Blow, Thou Winter Wind*
                              Non troppo allegro 3/4   (C3-E4)   MH-H   Mod. easy

Ravel, Maurice   ***Chantes populaire***   International+
(1875-1937) Fr.

An excellent cycle of songs for low voice and fine for bass voice provided the second song is transposed into an appropriate key. The cycle demands a keen sense of style, a light touch, vocal agility, and facile articulation in four languages.

860.   *Chanson Espagnole* (Span.)
                              Andantino 6/8   (D3-Bb3)   M   Med. diff.

861.   *Chanson Française* (Fr.)
                              Allegretto 3/4   (G3-F4)   H   Med. diff.

862.   *Chanson Italienne* (It.)
                              Largamente 2/4   (C3-Eb4)   M-MH   Med. diff.

863.   *Chanson Hébraïque* (Hebrew)
                              Allegro moderato 4/4   (E3-E4)   M-MH   Mod. diff.

864. Reif, Paul   ***Five Finger Exercises*** (Eng.)   Leslie Prod.
      (1910-1978) Am.

Originally composed for low voice suitable for bass at the intermediate level this effective cycle is now available only in high voice through General Music Publishing.

Reutter, Hermann   ***Chamber Music*** (Eng.)   Schott's
(1900-1985) Ger.

This cycle of four songs for low male voice and piano with words by James Joyce is musically very challenging.

865.   *Strings in the Earth and Air*
                                 Flowing 6/16 4/16   (B2-D4)   M   Diff.

866.   *Lean Out of the Window, Goldenhair*
                                 Fast 5/4   (B2-E4)   MH   Diff.

867.   *My Dove, My Beautiful One*
                                 Allegro 3/4   (B2-Eb4)   MH-H   Diff.

868.   *Sleep Now*
                                 Andante 3/8   (B2-E4)   MH   Diff.

          Reutter, Hermann   ***Drei altägyptische Gedichte*** (Ger.)   Schott's
With old Egyptian text, this musically demanding cycle is for low male voice and piano.

869.   *Memento*
                                 Andante, varied meter   (C3-E4)   MH   Diff.

870.   *Echnatons Sonnengesang*
                                 Slow, varied meter   (G2-F4)   M-H   Diff.

871.   *Finale*
                                 Slow, varied meter   (A2-C4)   ML   Diff.

872.   Rhené-Baton   ***Chansons pour Marycinthe*** (Fr.)   Durand
         (Baton, René)
         (1879-1940) Fr.

This is a cycle of six songs for baritone, but is suitable for bass-baritone or possibly bass. The
songs are *Le premier jour où je vis, Le claquement bref des sabots, Douceur du soir dans le
village, Pendant que vous dormiez, Vous ne pouviez savoir, Vous aurez une maison blanche,* and
may be sung separately.

          Rickard, Jeffrey   ***Four Plus One*** (Eng.)   UMI
A humorous cycle on the verses of Ogden Nash for bass (composed for Eldon Udell Black) with
a low Db2 and a high F4. A useful group for the appropriate beginning or intermediate bass.
This is available in *A Performance Edition of Repertoire for the Profondo Bass,* by Eldon Udell
Black published on demand by University Microfilms International.

873.   *The Termite*
                                 Quick 4/4   (G2-C4)   ML   Med. diff.

874.   *The Canary*
                                 Allegro 8/8   (D3-C4)   MH   Mod. easy

875.   *The Octopus*
                                 In a slow groove 4/4   (F2-C4)   ML-M   Mod. easy

876.   *The Cow*

	Bravura 4/4	(Db2-C#4)	ML-M	Mod. easy
877.	*The Germ* Allegro 4/4	(F2-F4)	ML-MH	Med. diff.

878. Ropartz, Guy   ***Veilles de Départ*** (Fr.)   Rouart
      (1864-1955) Fr.
This cycle of five songs is for low voice and is suitable for bass-baritone or possibly bass. The
songs are *Les veilles de départ, Pourquoi pleurer?, Derniers jours d'un amour qui meurt,
L'heure triste du fond de sa vie est venue, D'un pas trainant, comme affaibli, L'heure s'en va*
and are found in *Vingt mélodies* of Ropartz.

     Rorem, Ned   ***Flight for Heaven*** (Eng.)   Presser
     (b. 1923) Am.
A interesting and challenging cycle of love songs listed for bass but because of the tessitura
more suited for mature bass-baritone with words by Robert Herrick.

879.	*To Music, to Becalm His Fever* Fast 3/4	(F#2-Eb4)	H	Mod. diff.
880.	*Cherry-Ripe* Allegretto 6/8	(G2-Db4)	MH	Mod. diff.
881.	*Upon Julia's Clothes* Con spirito 2/4	(D3-D4)	MH-H	Mod. diff.
882.	*To Daisies, Not to Shut So Soon* Very fast 4/4	(B2-D4)	MH	Diff.
883.	*Epitaph Upon a Child That Died* Andante 6/8	(C3-C4)	M-MH	Mod. diff.
884.	*Another Epitaph* Semplice 4/4	(C3-C4)	M-MH	Mod. diff.
885.	*To the Willow-Tree* Moderato 3/4	(G#2-C4)	ML-MH	Mod. diff.
886.	*Comfort to a Youth That Had Lost His Love* Melancholy 4/4	(G#2-D#4)	M-H	Mod. diff.
	(Piano Interlude)			
887.	*To Anthea, Who May Command Him Anything* Gentle 4/4	(F#2-Eb4)	MH-H	Diff.

     Rorem, Ned   ***War Scenes*** (Eng.)   B & H
This very exacting cycle suitable for mature bass-baritone with easy high notes was originally

"Designed for Gerard Souzay" (baritone) with words by Walt Whitman. This work is musically, vocally, emotionally, and interpretively challenging.

888.	*A Night Battle*			
	Frantic 2/2	(G2-Gb4)	M-VH	Very diff.
889.	*Specimen Case*			
	Simple 4/4	(Bb2-Fb4)	MH-H	Diff.
890.	*An Incident*			
	Fast 2/2	(C3-C4)	MH	Very diff.
891.	*Inauguration Ball*			
	Fast 3/4	(B2-F#4)	M-VH	Very diff.
892.	*The Real War Will Never Get in the Books*			
	Moderate 3/4	(G2-Eb4)	M-H	Very diff.

| Rossellini, Renzo | *4 Liriche* (It.) | | | Ricordi |
| (1908-1982) It. | | | | |

An interesting cycle of songs for bass and piano for left hand. It was composed for Nicola Rossi Lemeni, famous Italian basso, who also wrote the poetry. The set has moderate problems musically and vocally several songs require command of high mezza voce singing.

893.	*Sorella*			
	Lento 3/4	(D3-D4)	M-MH	Mod. diff.
894.	*Esilio*			
	Allegretto 3/4	(D3-E4)	MH	Mod. diff.
895.	*La mèta*			
	Andante 6/4	(C3-E4)	MH	Mod. diff.
896.	*Al dolore*			
	Lento 4/4	(C3-E4)	M-MH	Mod. diff.

| Rubbra, Edmund | *Three Psalms* (Eng.) | | | Lengnick |
| (1901-1986) Eng. | | | | |

These three songs for low voice require flexibility, rapid articulation, and are rhythmically complex.

897.	*Psalm VI*			
	Slow	(F#2-Eb4)	MH	Mod. diff.
898.	*Psalm XXIII*			
	Sustained	(A2-D4)	M-MH	Mod. diff.
899.	*Psalm CL*			
	Fast	(Bb2-F4)	M-H	Mod. diff.

Satie, Erik   *Trois Poèmes d'Amour* (Fr.)   Salabert
(1866-1925) Fr.
A curious cycle of three very short songs which must be approached with a light touch.
900.   No. 1
                               no tempo 4/4   (B2-B3)   M   Med.diff.

901.   No. 2
                               no tempo 4/4   (B2-B3)   M   Med. diff.

902.   No. 3
                               no tempo 4/4   (A2-A3)   M   Med. diff.

Sauguet, Henri   *Movements du Coeur* (Fr.)   Heugel
(b. 1901-1989) Fr.
An extremely interesting and important group of songs composed by six influential French
composers in memory of Frédéric Chopin at his death in 1949. Of particular significance are
the songs written by Poulenc and Milhaud. The songs were composed for Doda Conrad, French
bass.
903.   *Prèlude* (composed by Henri Sauguet)
                               Andantino 6/8, 9/8   (Bb2-Eb4)   MH   Diff.

904.   *Mazurka* (composed by Francis Poulenc)
                               Lento 3/4   (G2-Eb4)   M-MH   Diff.

905.   *Valse* (composed by Georges Auric)
                               Waltz tempo 3/4   (Bb2-Eb4)   M-MH   Diff.

906.   *Scherzo impromptu* (composed by Jean Francaix)
                               Molto allegro 3/8   (B2-E4)   MH   Diff.

907.   *Etude* (composed by Leo Preger)
                               Moderato 4/4   (A2-D4)   M   Diff.

908.   *Ballade nocturne* (composed by Darius Milhaud)
                               Animated 6/8, 9/8   (Ab2-D4)   ML-MH   Diff.

909.   *Postlude: Polonaise* (composed by Henri Sauguet)
                               Alla Polaka 3/4   (Ab2-Eb4)   MH   Diff.

Sauguet, Henri   *Visions infernales* (Fr.)   Heugel
Composed for and dedicated to Doda Conrad, French bass, this cycle of songs is somewhat
demanding musically, with vague harmony, occasional complex rhythm, and sophisticated sense
of style.
910.   *Voyage*
                               Allegro agitato 6/8 (G2-D4)   ML-MH   Diff.

911.   *Volssinage*
                               Quasi lento 4/4   (A2-E4)   M-MH   Diff.

912.   *Que penser de mon salut*
                               Allegro moderato 4/4   (Bb2-E4)   MH-H   Diff.

913.   *Règates mysterieuses*
                               Tempo Barcarola 6/8   (B2-E4)   MH-H   Diff.

914.   *Le petit paysan*
                               Allegretto, varied meter (A2-D4)   M-MH   Diff.

915.   *Exhortation*
                               Andante 2/4   (G2-Eb4)   M-MH   Diff.

Schoeck, Othmar   *Zwölf Eichendorff-Lieder* (Ger.)   Breitkopf
(1886-1957) Swiss.

Most of these twelve songs are suitable for bass, require a wide range, are musically complex, and are interpretively sophisticated.

916.   *Waldeinsamkeit*
                               Sehr breit 3/4   (Gb2-C4)   ML-M   Diff.

917.   *Kurze Fahrt*
                               Lebhaft 3/4   (F2-F4)   ML-H   Diff.

918.   *Winternacht*
                               Nicht zu breit 3/4   (F2-C4)   L-M   Diff.

919.   *Im Wandern*
                               Gemächlich 2/2   (A2-F4)   M-MH   Diff.

920.   *Sterbeglocken*
                               Sehr ruhig 2/4   (F2-A3)   L-M   Mod. diff.

921.   *Ergebung*
                               Nicht zu langsam 4/4   (G2-Eb4)   ML-MH   Diff.

922.   *Nachklang*
                               Ruhige Bewegung 4/4   (A2-D4)   M-MH   Diff.

923.   *Der verspätete Wanderer*
                               Sehr getragen 3/2, 5/4 (F2-B3)   L   Diff.

924.   *Nacht*
                               Etwas breit 6/4   (E#2-A3)   L-ML   Diff.

925.   *Lockung*
                               Nicht zu schnell 6/8   (G2-Ab3)   M-VH   Diff.

926.   *An die Lützowschen Jäger*
                               Ruhig 3/4   (F2-Bb4)   L-ML   Diff.

927.   *Auf dem Rhein*
                             Ruhige Bewegung 3/4 (G2-F4)   MH-H   Diff.

928.   Schubert, Franz   *Die Winterreise* (Ger.)   Peters+
        (1797-1828) Aus.   (see nos. 572-95)

        Schubert, Franz   *Drei Gesänge von Metastasio* (It.)   Dover
More in the framework of vocal show pieces, these three songs for bass or bass-baritone voice
require vocal agility. These songs are found in the Complete Works.
929.   *L'incanto degli occhi*
                             Allegretto 2/4   (G2-D4)   ML-MH   Mod. diff.

930.   *Il traditor deluso*
                             Allegro 4/4   (G2-E4)   M-H   Mod. diff.

931.   *Il modo di prender moglie*
                             Allegro 6/8   (Bb2-D4)   MH   Mod. diff.

932.   Schubert, Franz   *Gesänge des Harfners* (Ger.)   International+
These three songs were originally composed in a higher key, but are acceptable in any key for
male voices. In the key present here in the International low voice edition volume III. of
Schubert songs the overall range is (C3-Eb4) and tessitura is MH.

933.   Schubert, Franz   *Schwanengesang* (Ger.)   Peters+
                             (see nos. 596-609)

934.   Schumann, Robert   *Dichterliebe* (Ger.)   International+
        (1810-1856) Ger.
Sixteen songs on poems of Heinrich Heine, this true cycle of songs was originally composed for
tenor voice. It can be sung by bass, but the accompaniment sounds somewhat muddy. The
particulars below are for the entire cycle as contained in the International low voice edition.
                             Varied tempo & meter (G2-D4(G4)) M-MH   Med. diff.

        Schumann, Robert   *Vier Husarenlieder* (Ger.)   Breitkopf
These four songs are for intermediate or advanced bass.
935.   I
                             Allegro 6/8   (D3-D4)   MH   Mod. diff.

936.   II
                             Nicht schnell 2/4   (G2-Bb3)   ML-M   Mod. diff.

937.   III
                             Mit Lustigkeit 2/4   (D3-Eb4)   MH-H   Mod. diff.

938.   IV
                             Allegro 12/8   (F2-C4)   L-M   Mod. diff.

Shostakovich, Dmitri   **Five Romances** (Russ./ Ger.)   Sikorski
(1906-1975) Russ.
Shostakovich has composed many solo works for bass and bass-baritone. In addition to the
cycles listed below the interested may want to investigate Op. nos. 46, 62, 91, 98, 123, 128,
146, all solo works for bass or bass-baritone. Most all of his vocal works are considered vocally
demanding and musically complex.
939.   *Eigene Aussage*
                             Moderato 3/4, 4/4   (G2-Eb4)   ML-MH   Mod. diff.

940.   —   *Schwer erfüllbarer Wunsch*
                             Moderato 3/4, 4/4   (A2-Eb4)   M-MH   Diff.

941.   *Umsicht*
                             Largo 4/4   (Ab2-G3)   ML   Mod. diff.

942.   *Irinka und der Hirte*
                             Allegro 2/4, 9/8, 6/8   (Bb2-D4)   M   Diff.

943.   *Übertriebene Begeisterung*
                             Moderato 3/4   (D3-D4)   MH   Diff.

Shostakovich, Dmitri   **Suite on Verses of Michelangelo** (Russ./Ger.)   Sikorski
                             (see previous selection)
944.   *Wahrheit* (Truth)
                             Adagio 4/4   (B2-Eb4)   MH-H   Diff.

945.   *Morgan* (Morning)
                             Allegretto, varied meter (C3-D4)   MH   Diff.

946.   *Liebe* (Love)
                             Allegretto 4/4, 3/2   (C3-C#4)   M-MH   Diff.

947.   *Trennung* (Separation)
                             Moderato, no meter   (Db3-D4)   MH   Diff.

948.   *Zorn* (Wrath)
                             Allegro, varied meter   (E3-F4)   H   Diff.

949.   *Dante*
                             Moderato, varied meter (Bb2-Eb4)   MH   Diff.

950.   *An den Verbannten* (To the Exile)
                             Largo, varied meter   (C#3-E4)   MH   Diff.

951.   *Schaffen* (Creativity)

Moderato, varied meter	(C#3-E4)	MH-H	Diff.

952. *Nacht* (Night)
Andante, varied meter (B2-E4) MH-H Diff.

953. *Tod* (Death)
Adagio, varied meter (Bb2-D4) MH Diff.

954. *Unsterblichkeit* (Immortality)
Allegretto, varied meter (A#3-D4) ML-MH Diff.

Siegl, Otto   ***Zwei Gesänge für eine Bassstimme*** (Ger.)   Ludwig
(1896-1978) Austrian

Two musically demanding and interpretively challenging songs for bass voice and piano.

955.   *Der entlassene Knecht*
Gemessen 3/4, 4/4 (B2-Eb4) M-MH Diff.

956.   *Wanderung im Advent*
Lento, varied meter (Gb2-C4) ML Diff.

Siegmeister, Elie   ***The Face of War*** (Eng.)   C. Fischer
(b. 1909-1991) Am.

First performed by William Warfield in 1968, this philosophical and sober cycle on the effects of war is musically complex, vocally strenuous, and requires interpretive maturity.

957.   *Official Notice*
Slow, varied meter (A2-Fb4) ML-M Diff.

958.   *Listen Here, Joe*
Lively, varied meter (G2-Eb4) ML-MH Diff.

959.   Peace
Slow 3/4 (B2-D4) MH Diff.

960.   *The Dove*
Moderate, varied meter (G#2-D4) ML-M Diff.

961.   *War*
Fast, varied meter (Bb2-Eb4) M-MH Diff.

Siegmeister, Elie   ***Songs of Experience*** (Eng.)   C. Fischer

A musically complex cycle for bass voice with words by William Blake is characterized by many leaps, rhythmic intricacy, and many lower notes.

962.   *The Voice of the Bard*
Fast, varied meter (F#2-Eb4) ML-MH Diff.

963.   *Earth's Answer*
Moderato, varied meter (F#2-D#4) ML-MH Diff.

| 964. | *The Fly* | | | |
| | Lively, varied meter | (Ab2-D4) | M-MH | Diff. |

| 965. | *The Garden of Love* | | | |
| | Slow, varied meter | (G2-Bb3) | ML-MH | Diff. |

| 966. | *The Thief and the Lady* | | | |
| | Lively, varied meter | (F#2-D4) | ML-MH | Diff. |

| 967. | *The Tiger* | | | |
| | Mod. fast, varied meter | (F2-D4) | ML-MH | Diff. |

Somervell, Arthur   ***Maud*** (Eng.)   Recital Pub.
(1863-1937) Eng.

Take from Tennyson's *Maud*, this moody and sometimes oppressive cycle has several effective songs including *Birds in the High Hall-Garden* and *Come into the Garden Maud*. Originally composed for Harry Plunket Green (baritone), this set is also appropriate for bass-baritone.

| 968. | *I Hate the Dreadful Hollow* | | | |
| | Adagio 3/4 | (A2-E4) | MH | Med diff. |

| 969. | *A Voice by the Cedar Tree* | | | |
| | Moderato 9/8 | (A2-Eb4) | MH | Med. diff. |

| 970. | *She Came to the Village Church* | | | |
| | Andante 4/4 | (A2-D4) | MH | Med. diff. |

| 971. | *O Let the Solid Ground* | | | |
| | Molto allegro 6/8 | (C3-E4) | MH-H | Mod. diff. |

| 972. | *Birds in the High Hall-Garden* | | | |
| | Andante 3/4 | (Bb2-Db4) | M-MH | Mod. easy |

| 973. | *Go Not, Happy Day* | | | |
| | Allegretto 2/4 | (Bb2-Eb4) | MH | Mod. diff. |

| 974. | *I Have Led Her Home* | | | |
| | Andante 4/4 | (C3-D4) | MH | Med. diff. |

| 975. | *Come into the Garden, Maud* | | | |
| | Allegro 6/4 | (A2-Eb4) | MH | Mod. diff. |

| 976. | *The Fault Was Mine* | | | |
| | Adagio 4/4 | (Bb2-Db4) | M | Med. diff. |

| 977. | *Dead, Long Dead* | | | |
| | Allegro 6/8 | (A2-Eb4) | MH | Mod. diff. |

| 978. | *O That 'Twere Possible* | | | |
| | Lento 2/4 | (C#3-D#4) | MH | Med. diff. |

979.   *My Life Has Crept So Long*
                                 Non troppo allegro 4/4 (A2-Eb4)   MH-H   Mod. diff.

          Sowerby, Leo   **Three Psalms** (Eng.)   Novello
          (1895-1968)
A tasteful group of religious songs for bass voice with secure low notes at the intermediate to
advanced level.
980.   *Hear My Cry, O God*
                                 Slowly 4/4   (F2-Eb4)   M-MH   Mod. diff.

981.   *The Lord Is My Shepherd*
                                 Quietly 4/4   (F2-Db4)   L-M   Med. diff.

982.   *How Long Wilt Thou Forget Me*
                                 Animated 3/4   (Ab2-Eb4)   M-MH   Mod. diff.

          Stanford, C. Villiers **A Fire of Turf** (Eng.)   Musica Britannica
          (1851-1924) Br.
One of Stanford's better cycles, this one is for low voice and piano and presents few problems.
983.   *A Fire of Turf*
                                 Larghetto 3/4   (A2-D4)   M-MH   Med. diff.

984.   *The Chapel on the Hill*
                                 Andante 3/4   (A2-D4)   M-MH   Med. diff.

985.   *Cowslip Time*
                                 Allegro 2/4   (C3-Eb4)   MH   Med. diff.

986.   *Scared*
                                 Lento 3/2, 12/8   (Bb2-Eb4)   MH   Med. diff.

987.   *Blackberry Time*
                                 Allegretto 2/4   (B2-D4)   MH   Med. diff.

988.   *The Fair*
                                 Allegro 4/4   (D3-D4)   MH   Med. diff.

989.   *The West Wind*
                                 Andante 4/4   (C3-Eb4)   MH   Med. diff.

          Stanford, C. Villiers **An Irish Idyll** (Eng.)   B & H
Somewhat sentimental and dated this cycle praising Ireland was composed for Harry Plunket
Green, baritone, and is appropriate for intermediate bass-baritone. The songs present few
problems. Of particular interest is the second song, *The Fairy Lough*, which is considered one
of Stanford's best songs.
990.   *Corrymeela*
                                 Lento 4/4, 6/8   (C3-Eb4)   MH   Med. diff.

991.	*The Fairy Lough*			
	Andante 9/8	(A2-Eb4)	MH	Med. diff.
992.	*Cuttin' Rushes*			
	Allegretto 2/4	(B2-D4)	MH	Med. diff.
993.	*Johneen*			
	Allegretto 6/8	(C3-Db4)	M-MH	Med. diff.
994.	*A Broken Song*			
	Adagio 4/4	(Bb2-Db4)	M-MH	Med. diff.
995.	*Back to Ireland*			
	Allegro 4/4	(C3-Eb4)	MH	Med. diff.

Stanford, C. Villiers   *Cushendall* (Eng.)   Stainer & Bell
An Irish song cycle for low voice that is workable for the bass voice. The group presents few
musical or vocal problems.

996.	*Ireland*			
	Andante	(C3-D4)	M-MH	Mod. easy
997.	*Did You Ever?*			
	Allegretto	(Bb2-Db4)	M-MH	Mod. easy
998.	*Cushendall*			
	Adagio 4/4	(Bb2-D4)	MH	Mod. easy
999.	*The Crow*			
	Andante 4/4	(A2-D4)	M-MH	Mod. easy
1000.	*Daddy-Long-Legs*			
	Allegro 4/4	(B2-D4)	MH	Mod. easy
1001.	*How Does the Wind Blow?*			
	Allegro 6/8	(A2-Eb4)	MH	Med. diff.
1002.	*Night*			
	Larghetto 3/2	(C3-C4)	M-MH	Mod. easy

Stanford, C. Villiers   *Songs of the Sea* (Eng.)   B & H
A group of sea songs for bass-baritone and optional chorus was originally composed for Harry
Plunket Green, baritone. The first and last songs are particularly effective pieces.

1003.	*Drake's Drum*			
	Moderato 4/4	(C3-E4)	MH-H	Med. diff.
1004.	*Outward Bound*			
	Andante 3/4	(Eb3-Eb4)	MH-H	Med. diff.

| 1005. | Devon, O Devon, in Wind and Rain | | | |
| | Allegro 4/4 | (Eb3-Eb4) | MH-H | Med. diff. |

| 1006. | Homeward Bound | | | |
| | Andante 6/4 | (Db3-D4) | MH | Med. diff. |

| 1007. | The Old Superb | | | |
| | Allegro 4/4 | (Bb2-Eb4) | M-MH | Med. diff. |

Strauss, Richard   *Vier Gesänge* (Op. 87)(Ger.)   Universal
(1864-1949) Ger.

These four demanding songs labelled for bass voice are more appropriate for bass-baritone or perhaps baritone.

| 1008. | Vom künftigen Alter | | | |
| | Langsam 4/4 | (Ab2-F#4) | H | Diff. |

| 1009. | Erschaffen und Beleben | | | |
| | Breit 4/4 | (D3-F4) | H | Diff. |

| 1010. | Und dann nicht mehr | | | |
| | Moderato 4/4 | (G2-F#4) | H | Diff. |

| 1011. | Im Sonnenschein | | | |
| | Schnell 3/4 | (Ab2-F4) | H | Diff. |

Strauss, Richard   *Zwei Gesänge* (Op. 51)(Ger.)   B & H

These two songs are for low bass and orchestra but are also published for bass and piano. The songs present few problems.

| 1012. | Das Thal | | | |
| | Ruhiges Zeitmas 3/4 | (F2-D4) | ML-MH | Mod. diff. |

| 1013. | Der Einsame | | | |
| | Adagio 4/4 | (F2-C4) | L-M | Med. diff. |

Tommasini, Vincenzo   *Due Liriche Sacre* (Lat.)   Santis
(1878-1950) It.

These two songs on religious texts are published separately and contain some musical demands.

| 1014. | Salvator Mundi | | | |
| | Agitato 2/4 | (Bb2-Eb4) | M-MH | Mod. diff. |

| 1015. | O Bone Jesu | | | |
| | Andante 4/4 | (Eb2-Db4) | M-MH | Mod. diff. |

Travis, Roy   *Songs and Epilogues* (Eng.)   Oxford
(b. 1922) Am.

With words by Sappho, Lord Byron, Dante, and Edward Arlington Robinson, this unique cycle for bass alternates piano only epilogues and prologues with songs for voice and piano. The piano sections are largely atonal in approach while the voice and piano sections are mostly tonal. The work favors a lower tessitura, is musically exacting, and requires maturity in interpretation.

1016.	*Round About Me*			
	Allegro 2/4, 3/4	(B2-B3)	M	Diff.
	Round About Me: Epilogue (Piano)			
1017.	*Hesperus the Bringer*			
	Andantino 2/4	(G#2-B3)	ML	Diff.
	Hesperus the Bringer: Epilogue (piano)			
1018.	*One Girl*			
	Andantino 4/4	(G#2-D#4)	ML-MH	Diff.
	One Girl: Epilogue (piano)			
	The Dust of Timas: Prologue (piano)			
1019.	*The Dust of Timas*			
	Fast 4/8, 3/8	(G#2-C#4)	ML-M	Diff.
	Full Moon: Prologue (piano)			
1020.	*Full Moon*			
	Grave, varied meter	(A2-B3)	ML-M	Diff.

	Vaughan Williams, R. (1872-1958) Eng.	*Songs of Travel* (Eng.)		B & H

A popular cycle of songs for baritone some of which are suitable for bass including *The Vagabond*, *The Roadside Fire*, and the relatively easy *Bright Is the Ring of Words*.

1021.	*The Vagabond*			
	Allegro 4/4	(A2-Eb4)	MH	Med. diff.
1022.	*Let Beauty Awake*			
	Moderato 9/8	(E3-E4)	MH-H	Med. diff.
1023.	*The Roadside Fire*			
	Allegretto 4/4	(B2-E4)	MH	Med. diff.
	(Available in a lower key; see no. 127)			
1024.	*Youth and Love*			
	Andante 3/4	(C3-E4)	MH-H	Med. diff.

| 1025. | *In Dreams* | | | |
| | Andantino 3/4 | (D3-F4) | MH-H | Med. diff. |

| 1026. | *The Infinite Shining Heavens* | | | |
| | Andante 3/2 | (C3-Eb4) | MH-H | Med. diff. |

| 1027. | *Whither Must I Wander?* | | | |
| | Andante 4/4 | (Bb2-Eb4) | MH | Med. diff. |

| 1028. | *Bright Is the Ring of Words.* | | | |
| | Moderato 3/4 | (Ab2-Db4) | M-MH | Mod. easy |

| 1029. | *I Have Trod the Upward and the Downward Slope* | | | |
| | Andante 3/2 | (C3-D4) | MH | Med. diff. |

| Voormolen, Alexander | ***Three Songs on British Verse*** | | | Donemus |
| (1895-1980) Dutch | (Eng.) | | | |

These three songs require a wide range and are musically complex and vocally demanding.

| 1030. | *Diana and Her Darlings Deare . . .* | | | |
| | Allegretto 4/4 | (G2-E4) | MH | Diff. |

| 1031. | *I Am Confirm'd . . .* | | | |
| | Allegro 2/4 | (E2-E4) | M-H | Diff. |

| 1032. | *Grey Recumbent Tombs* | | | |
| | Lento 6/8 | (F2-Eb4) | M-H | Diff. |

| Wolf, Hugo | ***Harfenspieler Lieder*** (Ger.) | | | Peters |
| (1860-1903) Aus. | | | | |

The "Three Harper's Songs" are all sustained, with soft dynamics and should be performed by a more advanced bass or bass-baritone.

| 1033. | I | | | |
| | Slow 4/4 | (B2-F4) | MH-H | Mod. diff. |

| 1034. | II | | | |
| | Slow 4/4 | (C3-Db4) | M-MH | Med. diff. |

| 1035. | III | | | |
| | Slow 4/4 | (C3-E4) | MH | Mod. diff. |

| Wolf, Hugo | ***Michelangelo Lieder*** (Ger./ Eng.) | | | Peters |

An important cycle of songs for the intermediate or advanced bass voice. Each song is sustained and must be approached with fine legato and a keen sense of style. The first song contains a section at the end which has an arduously high tessitura. The third song is particularly agreeable.

1036.	*Wohl denk' ich oft*			
	(I Often Ponder)			
	Lento 4/4	(C3-E4)	M-H	Mod. diff.

1037.	*Alles endet, was entstehet*			
	(All Creation Once Must Perish)			
	Langsam 4/4	(F#2-C4)	L-M	Mod. diff.

1038.	*Fühlt meine Seele*			
	(Oh, Does My Spirit Feel)			
	Sehr langsam 4/4	(A2-D4)	M-MH	Mod. diff.

Wolpe, Stefan   ***Six Songs from Hebrew*** (Eng.)   McGinnis & Marx
(1902-1972) Ger./Am.

The first and last song of this musically demanding group are not appropriate for bass voice.
If they are disregarded the remaining four middle songs make a fine set for bass or
bass-baritone.

1039.	*Lilacs*			
	Allegro, varied meter	(Ab2-F#4)	VH	Diff.

1040.	*On a Mural by Diego Rivera*			
	Allegro, varied meter	(G#2-Eb4)	MH	Diff.

1041.	*David's Lament over Jonathan*			
	Quiet, varied meter	(F2-Eb4)	ML-MH	Diff.

1042.	*Lines from the Prophet Micah*			
	Allegro, varied meter	(B2-F4)	MH-H	Diff.

1043.	*Isaiah*			
	Con moto, varied meter	(Bb2-Eb4)	MH	Diff.

1044.	*Song of Songs*			
	Fast, varied meter	(B-F#4)	VH	Diff.

Wordsworth, William   ***Four Sacred Sonnets*** (Eng.)   Lengnick
(1908-1988) Eng.

These emotionally expressive songs are well-crafted with a fine melodic line and wide range.
Composed for low voice and piano and suitable for bass or bass-baritone.

1045.	*At the Round Earth's Imagin'd Corners*			
	Moderately	(G2-E4)	MH	Mod. diff.

1046.	*Batter My Heart*			
	Moderately	(G2-E4)	MH	Mod. diff.

1047.	*Death Be Not Proud*			
	Moderately	(G2-Eb4)	MH	Mod. diff.

1048.	*Thou Hast Made Me*			
	Moderately	(F#2-Eb4)	MH	Mod. diff.

Wordsworth, William   *Three Songs* (Eng.)   Lengnick
An expressive group of songs for low voice suitable for bass or bass-baritone.

1049.	*Clouds*			
	Moderately	(B2-E4)	M-H	Mod. diff.

1050.	*Red Skies*			
	Moderately	(B2-D4)	MH	Mod. diff.

1051.	*The Wind*			
	Moderately	(G#2-D4)	M-MH	Mod. diff.

Zwilich, Ellen T.   *Einsame Nacht* (Ger.)   Merion
(b. 1939) Am.
Constant changing of meter, chromaticism, large leaps to odd intervals are some of the demands
placed on the singer in this arduous work which is best suited for bass-baritone.

1052.	*Über die Felder*			
	Moderato, varied meter	(A2-D4)	ML-MH	Very diff.

1053.	*Wie sind die Tage schwer*			
	Andante, varied meter	(A2-Eb4)	M-MH	Very diff.

1054.	*Schicksal*			
	Vivace, varied meter	(A2-F4)	MH-H	Very diff.

1055.	*Elisabeth*			
	Allegretto, varied meter	(A2-E4)	ML-MH	Very diff.

1056.	*Nacht*			
	Lento, varied meter	(B2-E4)	M-H	Very diff.

1057.	*Mückenschwarm*			
	Vivace, varied meter	(Bb-E4)	MH	Very diff.

CHAPTER VII

BASS VOICE WITH INSTRUMENTS INCLUDING SOLO CANTATAS

The following chapter includes works from various style periods requiring diverse instruments.

1058. Ahrens, Sieglinde   *Drei Gesänge* (Ger.)(1963)   Muller
(three songs for bass voice and organ)
Varied tempo & meter   (G2-D4)   M-MH   Mod. diff.
Chromatic; somewhat complex musically; sustained.

1059. Amram, David   *Shakespeare Songs* (see nos. 633-5)   Peters
     (b. 1930)   (for bass voice, trombone, flute, and piano)

1060.   *Songs for America* (see nos. 636-8)   Peters
(for bass voice, woodwind quintet, and string quintet)

1061. Bach, J. S.   *Amore Traditore* (It. & Eng.)   Schott
     (1685-1750) Ger.   (Secular cantata for bass voice and harpsichord)
ed. by Tippett and Bergman
Andante 12/8, 3/4   (G2-E4)   MH   Diff.
Requires agility; flowing line.

1062.   *Ich habe genug* (Cantata no. 82)(Ger.)   Breitkopf+
(Solo cantata for bass voice, 2 violins, viola, oboe, and
continuo)
Various tempo & meter   (G2-Eb4)   MH   Mod. diff.
Important solo cantata; consists of three arias and two
recitatives; requires flexibility; sustained sections; animated
sections.

1063.   *Ich will den Kreuzstab* (Cantata no. 56)(Ger.)   Breitkopf+
(Solo cantata for bass voice, oboe, violins, viola, continuo)
Various tempo & meter   (G2-E4)   MH-H   Mod. diff.
Important solo cantata; consists of two arias and one
recitative; very florid sections; sustained sections.

1064.   *Come Blessed Cross*   Schirmer
(from "St. Matthew Passion")(Ger./ Eng.)
(for bass voice, cello, and orch.)
Larghetto 4/4   (A2-E4)   MH   Mod. diff.
Beautiful combination of voice and instrument; sustained.

1065. Biber, Heinrich   *Nisi Dominus Aedificaverit Domum* (Lat.)   Deutscher
     (1644-1704) Ger.   (for low bass voice, violin, and continuo)

Adagio/Allegro 3/4, 4/4   (D2-D4)   L-MH   Mod. diff.
Requires a wide range, agility, and a low D2.

1066. Brevi, Giovanni   *Catenae Terrenae* (Lat.)   Bieler
      (late 17th century) It.   (solo cantata for bass voice and continuo) ed. by Ewerhart
                            Various tempo 4/4   (F2-D4)   M-MH   Med. diff.
                            Flexibility required.

1067. Brossard, S. de   *O Plenus Irarum Dies* (Lat.)   Bieler
      (1655-1730)   (solo cantata for bass voice and continuo) ed. by Ewerhart
                            Various tempo & meter   (G2-Eb4)   MH   Mod. diff.
                            Flexibility required.

1068. Bruhns, Nicholaus   *De Profundis Clamavi* (Lat.)   Peters
      (1665-1697) Danish   (for bass, organ, 2 violins, cello) ed. by Stein
                            Various tempo & meter   (D2-E4)   L-MH   Mod. diff.
                            Demands flexibility.

1069.   *Der Herr hat seinen Stuhl im Himmel bereitet* (Ger.)   Peters
                            (for bass voice, bassoon, 2 violins, 2 violas, cello, organ)
                            ed. by Stein
                            Various tempo 4/4   (E2-D4)   ML-M   Mod. diff.
                            Flexibility required.

1070.   *Mein Herz ist bereit* (Ger.)   Peters
                            (solo cantata for bass voice, violin, and continuo (organ))
                            ed. by Stein.
                            Various tempo & meter   (D2-D4)   L-MH   Mod. diff.
                            Wide range and flexibility required.

1071. Burkhart, Willy   *Das ewige Brausen* (Ger.)   Schott
      (1900-1955) Swiss   (for bass and chamber group)
                            Various tempo & meter   (F2-F4)   MH-H   Diff.
                            Musically demanding.

1072. Buxtehude, Dietrich   *I Am the Resurrection* (English only)   Concordia
      (1637-1707) Danish   (for low bass, 2 violins, cello or bassoon and organ)
                            Various tempo & meter (E2-C4(D4)) L-M   Med. diff.
                            Flexibility and wide leaps to low notes.

1073.   *Mein Herz ist bereit* (Ger.)   Bärenreiter
                            (solo cantata for bass voice, 3 violins, cello, and continuo)
                            Various tempo & meter   (F#2-F4)   ML-MH Mod. diff.
                            High F4 is just touched on; requires flexibility.

1074. Campra, Andre   *Exaltabo te, Deus meus, Rex* (Lat.)   Bieler
      (1660-1744) Fr.   (solo cantata for bass and continuo) ed. by Ewerhart
                            Moderato 3/4   (A2-E4)   M-H   Med. diff.
                            Sustained; flexibility required.

1075. Carissimi, Giacomo   *O Vulnera Doloris* (Lat.)   Bieler
      (1605-1674) It.   (solo cantata for bass and continuo) ed. by Ewerhart
                            No tempo indication 6/4 (G2-D4)   M-MH   Med. diff.

1076. Cazzati, Maurizio   *Dulcis Amor* (Lat.)   Bieler
      (1620-1677) It.   (solo cantata for bass and continuo) ed. by Ewerhart
                            No tempo ind. 4/4, 3/2 (F2-D4)   ML-M   Med. diff.
                            Flexibility required.

1077.   *Factum est Praetium Magnam* (Lat.)   Bieler
                            (solo cantata for bass and basso continuo) ed. by Ewerhart
                            No tempo 6/4   (E2-E4)   M-MH   Med. diff.
                            Flexibility required.

1078.   *In Calvaria Rupe* (Lat.)   Bieler
                            (solo cantata for bass and basso continuo) ed. by Ewerhart
                            No tempo 4/4, 3/4, 3/2 (A#2-C#4)   M   Med. diff.
                            Sustained.

1079. Cimarosa, D.   *Il maestro di cappella* (It.)   Ricordi
      (1749-1801) It.   (Intermezzo burlesco for bass-bartone)
                            Various tempo & meter (C#3-F#4)   H   Diff.
                            Demanding comic piece; vocal imitation of instruments of
                            the orchestra; facile articulation and agility required with
                            high tessitura.

1080. Dallapiccola, Luigi   *Preghiere* (It.)   B & H
      (1904-1975) It.   (for bass-baritone and chamber group)
                            Various tempo & meter (F#2-F#4 (G4))   H   Very diff.
                            Avant-garde techniques; musically very challenging.

1081. Egk, Werner   *Natur, Liebe, Tod* (Ger.)   Schott's
      (1901-1983) Ger.   (for bass, chamber group)
                            Various tempo & meter (F2-E4)   L-H   Diff.
                            Musically complex; vocally demanding.

1082. El-Dabh, Halim   *The Eye of Horus* (Eng.)   Peters
      (b. 1921) Egyptian   (for bass, percussion)

1083. Erlebach, P. H.   *Wem geliebt Wein und Bier* (Ger.)   Arno
      (1657-1714)   (for bass, 2 violins, continuo)
                            Andante 4/4   (G2-E4)   ML-MH   Med. diff.
                            Contained in "The German Solo Song and the Ballad."
                            Requires agility.

1084. Geist, Christian   *Dominum* (Lat.)   Peters
      (1640-1711)   (for bass, 2 violins, cello, and organ) ed. by Lundgren

1085. Handel, G. F.   *The Trumpet Shall Sound* (from "Messiah")(Eng.) Schirmer
      (1685-1759) Ger.   (for bass voice and trumpet)

Moderato 3/4   (A2-E4)   MH-H   Mod. diff.
Big, trumpet-like sound; demanding vocally; a favorite.

1086.   *Dalla guerra amorosa* (It.)   Bärenreiter
                                    (for bass, continuo) ed. by Zenck
                                    Allegro 3/8, 4/4   (G2-F4)   MH-H   Diff.
                                    Agility required.

1087.   *Spande ancor a mio dispetto* (It.)   Bärenreiter
                                    (solo cantata for bass, 2 violins, continuo)
                                    Allegro moderato 4/4   (D2-E4)   MH   Diff.
                                    Vocally challenging; large leaps; agility required.

1088. Haydn, Michael   *Ave Regina* (Lat.)   Peters+
      (1737-1806) Austrian   (for bass, viola solo, string quartet, organ)
                                    Larghetto 3/4   (A2-D4(Eb4))   M-MH   Med. diff.
                                    Sustained with some agility required; effective work.

1089. Holst, Imogen   *Six Shakespeare Songs* (Eng.)   Faber
      (1907-1984) Br.   (for bass-baritone and three recorders)

1090. Koellreutter, H.   *Eight Haikai des Pedro Xisto* (Span.)   Modern
      (b. 1915) Ger.   (for bass, flute, piono, guitar, percussion)
                                    Various tempo & meter   (F#2-E4)   M-MH   Very diff.
                                    Musically complex.

1091. Leibowitz, René   *String Quartet No. 7* (Ger.)   Bomart
      (1913-1972) Polish/Fr.   (for bass voice, string quartet) Op. 72

1092. Leichtling, Alan   *Three Songs of Emily Dickinson* (Eng.)   Seesaw
      (b. 1947) Am.   (for bass voice and cello) (see nos. 780-2)

1093. Marx, Karl   *Vier Gesänge vom Tage* (Ger.)   Bärenreiter
      (1897-1985) Ger.   (for bass-baritone and string quartet or orchestra)
                                    (see nos. 797-800)

1094. Monteverdi, C.   *Ah aeterno ordinata sum* (Lat.)   Universal
      (1567-1643) It.   (for bass and continuo)
                                    Moderately slow   (C2-D4)   VL-MH   Diff.
                                    Contained in complete works vol. 15; musically and vocally
                                    demanding; florid; wide leaps; two sustained low C2s.

1095.   *Laudati Dominum* (Lat.)   Universal
                                    (for bass and continuo)
                                    Moderato   (F2-D4)   L-MH   Mod. diff.
                                    Contained in complete works vol. 16; flexibility required;
                                    sustained sections.

1096.   *Laudate Dominum* (Lat.)   Universal
                                    (for bass and continuo)

Moderato   (F2-D4)   ML-MH   Mod. diff.
Contained in complete works vol. 16; very sustained
sections; florid sections; excellent piece.

1097. Moore, Dorothy R.   *Weary Blues*   Hal Leonard
      (b. 1940) Am.   (for bass, cello, and piano)
                             Moderato 4/4   (B2-G4)   M-H   Diff.
                             Contained in "Anthology of Art Songs by Black American
                             Composers"; musically challenging; high G and F only
                             touched on once with relatively short notes; suitable for
                             advanced bass-baritone.

1098. Moore, Douglas   *The Ballad of William Sycamore* (Eng.)   Galaxy
      (1893-1969) Am.   (for bass voice, flute, trombone, and piano)
                             Various tempo & meter (Ab2-D#4) ML-MH   Mod. diff.
                             Vigorous, rhythmic and energetic; vocally challenging at
                             times; an excellent ballad.

1099. Mozart, W. A.   *Per questa bella mano* (It.)   International+
      (1756-1791) Austrian   (concert aria for bass, double bass/cello, and piano)
                             Andante/Allegro 6/8, 4/4 (F#2-D4) ML-MH Mod. diff.
                             Some flexibility required; an excellent piece.

1100. Peyton, Malcolm   *Two Sonnets from John Donne* (Eng.)   Bomart
      (b. 1932) Am.   (for bass-baritone, horn, trombone, viola, cello, and bass)

1101. Purcell, Henry   *Unto Thee Will I Cry* (Eng.)   Bärenreiter
      (1659-1695) Eng.   (for bass voice, strings, and continuo) ed. by Just
                             Andante 2/2   (D2-E4)   L-H   Mod. diff.
                             Wide range; rewarding piece.

1102. Rameau, J. P.   *Aquilon et Orithie* (Fr.)   Salabert
      (1683-1764) Fr.   (solo cantata for bass voice and continuo)
                             Various tempo & meter (F#2-E4)   M-H   Mod. diff.
                             Facile articulation; agility; some high, sustained passages.

1103. Redel, Martin   *Epilog* (Ger.)(1971)   Bote
      (b. 1947) Ger.   (for bass voice, guitar, and flute)
                             Allegretto 3/4   (F2-E4)   L-H   Very diff.
                             Avant-garde techniques.

1104. Reutter, Hermann   *Ein kleines Requiem* (Ger.)   Schott's
      (1900-1985) Ger.   (for bass voice, cello, and piano)
                             Various tempo & meter (F2-Eb4) M-MH   Diff.
                             Musically complex.

1105. Rosenmüller, J.   *Von den himmlischen Freuden* (Ger.)   Bärenreiter
      (1619-1684) Ger.   (Cantata for bass voice and continuo)
                             Mod./Allegro 3/4, 4/4 (C3-D4)   MH   Med. diff.
                             Requires some agility; sustained in sections.

1106. Rosetti, Francesco   *Ad festa, fideles* (Lat.)   Bieler
      (Rössler, Franz) Ger.   (solo cantata for bass and continuo) ed. by Ewerhart
      (1746-1792)   Moderato   (G2-D4)   MH   Med. diff.
                                Animated; florid sections.

1107. Scarlatti, D.   *Amenissimi Pratti* (It./Ger.)   Gerig
      (1685-1757) It.   (cantata for bass and continuo) ed. by Hautus
                                Various tempo & meter (G2-Eb4)   M-MH   Med. diff.
                                Flexibility required.

1108. Schauss-Flake, M.   *Jauchzet dem Herrn, alle Welt* (Ger.)   Hanssler
      (b. 1921) Ger.   (for bass, oboe, organ)

1109. Schoeck, Othmar   *Elégie* (op. 36)   Breitkopf
      (1886-1957) Swiss.   (for bass-baritone, chamber group)

1110. Schütz, Heinrich   *Attendite, popule meus* (Lat.)   Breitkopf
      (1585-1672) Ger.   (from "Symphoniae Sacrae" for low bass, 4 trombones, and
                                continuo/organ)
                                Moderate 4/4   (E2-C4)   L-M   Med. diff.
                                Agility required; excellent piece for intermediate or
                                advanced bass.

1111.   *Fili mi, Absalom* (Lat.)   Breitkopf
                                (from "Symphoniae Sacrae" for bass, 4 trombones, and
                                continuo/organ)
                                Moderate 3/2   (G2-D4)   ML-MH   Med. diff.
                                Sustained; excellent piece for intermediate or possibly
                                beginning bass.

1112.   *Herr, nun laessest du deinen*   Bärenreiter
                                Diener im Friede fahren - no. 1 (Ger.)
                                (from "Symphoniae Sacrae" for low bass, 2 violins, and
                                continuo/organ)
                                Moderate 4/4   (D2-C4)   L-M   Med. diff.
                                Agility required.

1113.   *Herr, nun laessest du deinen*   Bärenreiter
                                Diener im Friede fahren - no. 2 (Ger.)
                                (from "Symphoniae Sacre" for low bass, 2 violins, and
                                continuo/organ)
                                Moderate 4/4   (D2-D4)   L-M   Med. diff.
                                Agility required.

1114. Sfetsas, Kyriacos   *Artefact* (Eng.)   Transat.
      (b. 1945) Greek   (for bass-baritone, cello, double bass, and piano)

1115. Sibelius, Jean   *Der Span auf den Wellen* (Fin./Ger.)   Breitkopf
      (1865-1957) Finn.   (for bass voice, flute, clarinet, 2 horns, strings)

1116.   *Locknung* (op. 17, no. 3)(Swed./Ger.)   Breitkopf
                                (for bass voice, 2 flutes, oboe, clarinet, horn, harp, cello,
                                and strings)

1117. Stanley, John   *Welcome Death* (Eng.)   Peters
      (1713-1786)   (for bass voice, 2 violins, cello, and bass)

1118. Stradella, A.   *Exultate in deo Fideles* (Lat.)   Peters
      (1642-1682) It.   (solo cantata for bass voice, 2 violins, and continuo)
                               Various tempo & meter (E2-E4(F#)) H   Mod. diff.
                               Requires agility; wide leaps

1119. Telemann, G. P.   *Die Hoffnung ist mein Leben* (Ger.)   Bärenreiter
      (1681-1767) Ger.   (solo cantata for bass, violin, and continuo)
                               Various tempo 4/4   (A2-E4)   MH-H   Mod. diff.
                               Requires flexibility.

1120. Thomass, Eugen   *Morgue*   Modern
                               (for bass voice, percussion, and piano)

1121. Ugolini, G.   *De la Justitia e Falsita* (It.)   Sonzogno
                               (for bass voice, strings, and piano)

1122. Viadana, L. G. da   *O Jesu, Dulcis Memoria* (Lat.)   Bieler
      (1564-1645) It.   (for bass voice, and continuo) ed. by Ewerhart
                               Moderately slow   (F2-C4)   ML-M   Med, diff.
                               Contained in "Drei geistliche Konzerte" by Viadana;
                               sustained; florid sections; wide leaps; lyric.

1123.   *Salve, Regina* (Lat.)   Bieler
                               (for bass and continuo)
                               Moderately slow   (G2-C4)   M   Med. diff.
                               Contained in (see previous listing); very sustained.

1124. Werner, Gregor J.   *Salve Regina* (Lat.)   Bieler
      (1695-1766) Austrian   (for bass voice, 2 violins, and continuo)

CHAPTER VIII

OPERATIC ANTHOLOGIES, COLLECTIONS AND CONCERT ARIAS

There are several operatic anthologies available for bass voice with some overlap in contents. The various operatic anthologies are compared in contents in this chapter. The Concert Arias are found at the end of the chapter. Additional opera arias not found in these operatic anthologies are annotated in other reference books such as "Music for the Voice" by Kagen.

ARIAS FOR BASS
G. Schirmer Opera Anthology
Compiled and edited by R. Larsen
Published by G. Schirmer, 1992

This is a new edition from Schirmer of arias for bass with important new additions and changes.

1125. Bellini, Vincenzo   *Vi ravviso* (from "La Sonnambula")(It.)
       (1801-1835) It.   Andante/Allegro 4/4, 6/8 (G2-Eb4)   M-H   Mod. diff.
       First half, flowing cantabile; second half, energetic allegro.

1126. Bizet, George   *Quand la flamme de l'amour*
       (1838-1875) Fr.   (from "Le Jolie Fille de Perth")(Fr.)
       Andante 12/8   (B2-E4)   M-H   Mod. diff.
       Drinking song; requires big, sonorous sound; sustained.

1127. Donizetti, Gaetano   *Ah! Un foco insolito* (from "Don Pasquale")
       (1797-1848) It.   Vivace 3/8   (C3-E4)   MH   Med. diff.
       Lighthearted comic aria; good introductory aria of its type.

1128.   *Dalle stanza ove Lucia*
       (from "Lucia di Lammermoor")(It.)
       Various tempo & meter (A#2-E4)   M-H   Mod. diff.
       Flowing legato line.

1129. Gounod, Charles   *Le veau d'or* (from "Faust")(Fr.)
       (1818-1893) Fr.   Allegro maestoso 6/8 (C3-Eb4)   MH-H   Mod. diff.
       Vocally demanding; sonorous sound; high tessitura.

1130.   *Vous qui faites l'endormie* (from "Faust")(Fr.)
       Allegretto 3/4   (G2-E4(G4)) M-H   Mod. diff.
       Challenging style and interpretation; vocally demanding.

1131. Massenet, Jules   *Épouse quelque brave fille* (from "Manon")(Fr.)
       (1842-1912) Fr.   Andante 3/4   (C3-F4)   M-MH   Med. diff.
       Smooth flowing line; good introductory aria of its type for intermediate level bass.

1132.   *Pour les couvents c'est fini* (Piff, paff)

(from "Les Huguenots")(Fr.)
Allegretto 3/8   (F2-E4)   ML-H   Diff.
Vocally demanding; big sound; agility required.

1133. Mozart, W. A.   *Aprite un po' quegl' occhi*
      (1756-1791) Austrian   (from "Le Nozze di Figaro")(It.)
                             Andante 4/4   (Bb2-Eb4)   M-H   Mod. diff.
                             Sections of high tessitura; sections of rapid articulation.

1134.   *In diesen heil'gen Hallen* (from "Die Zauberflöte")(Ger.)
                             Larghetto 2/4   (F#2(E2)-C#4) L-M   Med. diff.
                             Sustained aria for low bass; good for beginning or
                             intermediate level.

1135.   *La vendetta* (from "Le Nozze di Figaro")(It.)
                             Allegro 4/4   (G#2-E4)   MH   Mod. diff.
                             Facile articulation in Italian required; big booming sound;
                             comic.

1136.   *Madamina!* (from "Don Giovanni")(It.)
                             Allegro/Andante 4/4, 3/4 (A2-Eb4) MH   Mod. diff.
                             Familiar aria for comic bass; some rapid articulation
                             required.

1137.   *Non più andrai* (from "Le Nozze di Figaro")(It.)
                             Vivace 4/4   (C3-E4)   MH   Mod. diff.
                             Vocally challenging at times; familiar, humorous aria with
                             some command of facile articulation required.

1138.   *O Isis und Osiris* (from "Die Zauberflöte")(Ger.)
                             Adagio 3/4   (F2-C4)   L-M   Med. diff.
                             Slow, sustained aria for low bass; good introductory aria for
                             beginning bass.

1139.   *O, wie will ich triumphiren* (Ger.)
                             (from "Die Entführung aus dem Serail")
                             Allegro vivace 2/4   (D2-D4)   VL-MH   Diff.
                             Energetic and vocally demanding; wide range; command of
                             low D2; excellent comic aria for low bass.

1140.   *Se vuol ballare* (from "Le Nozze di Figaro")(It.)
                             Allegretto/Presto 3/4, 2/4 (C3-F4) M-H   Med. diff.
                             Humorous, well-known aria with some command of facile
                             articulation required.

1141. Nicolai, Otto   *Als Büblein klein* (Ger.)
      (1810-1849) Ger.   (from "Die lustigen Weiber von Windsor")
                             Various tempo & meter (E2-E4)   ML-MH   Med. diff.
                             Drinking song with wide range.

1142. Puccini, Giacomo   *Vecchia zimarra, senti* (from "La Boheme")(It.)
      (1858-1924) It.   Allegretto 2/4   (C#3-Eb4)   M-MH   Med. diff.
                             Sustained, legato line; good introductory aria for beginning

or intermediate bass.

1143. Rossini, Gioachino   *La calunnia* (from "Il Barbiere di Siviglia")(It.)
      (1792-1868) It.   Allegro 4/4   (B2-E4)   M-H   Mod. diff.
                             Vocally demanding; requires big sound; some rapid
                             articulation; excellent to see it here in its normal
                             performance key.

1144.   *Miei rampolli femminini* (from "La Cenerentola")(It.)
                             Allegro 4/4   (A2-F#4)   MH-H   Diff.
                             Vocally challenging aria with high tessitura, rapid
                             articulation, and great agility required; excellent piece.

1145. Tchaikovsky, P. I.   *Gremin's Aria* (from "Eugene Onegin")(Russ.)
      (1840-1893) Russ.   Andante/Allegro 2/4   (Gb2-Eb4)   MH   Mod. diff.
                             Difficult language; transliteration provided in front of book;
                             sustained, flowing line.

1146. Thomson, Virgil   *What Is It* (from "The Mother of Us All")(Eng.)
      (b. 1896) Am.   Various tempo 4/4   (G2-E4)   M-MH   Mod. diff.
                             Sustained; dramatic; effective climax.

1147. Verdi, Giuseppe   *Come dal ciel precipita* (from "Macbeth")(It.)
      (1813-1901) It.   Adagio 4/4   (A2-E4)   M-H   Mod. diff.
                             Sustained; requires sonorous high E4.

1148.   *Il lacerato spirito* (from "Simon Boccanegra")(It.)
                             Various tempo & meter (F#2-D4)   M-MH   Med. diff.
                             Sustained, flowing line; good introductory aria of its type
                             for intermediate level.

1149.   *Infelice! e tuo credevi* (from "Ernani")(It.)
                             Andante 4/4   (G2-Eb4)   MH   Mod. diff.
                             Sustained, flowing line.

1150.   *O tu, Palermo* (from "I Vespri Siciliani")(It.)
                             Largo 4/4   (F2-Eb4)   MH   Mod. diff.
                             Very sustained, flowing line.

1151. Weber, C. M. von   *Schweig'! damit dich Niemand warnt*
      (1786-1826) Ger.   (from "Der Freischütz")(Ger.)
                             Mod./Allegro 4/4   (F#2-E4)   ML-H   Diff.
                             Demands big, mean sound; agility over wide range required.

1152. Weill, Kurt   *Let Things Be Like They Always Was*
      (1900-1950) Ger.   (from "Street Scene")(Eng.)
                             Various tempo 4/4   (A2-D4)   M-MH   Mod. diff.
                             Dark and menacing; long, sustained notes; dramatic.

ARIAS FOR BASS
Schirmer's Singer's Library
In Two Volumes
Compiled by Irving Brown
Published by G. Schirmer, 1977

The contents for these two volumes compiled by Brown are the same as the one volume
anthology edited by Kurt Adler except for one additional aria in the Adler edition. Both are
published by Schirmer. For the contents of the Adler edition see this edition below and no.
1275.

VOLUME I

1153. Beethoven, L. van   *Hat man nicht auch Gold daneben*
      (1770-1827) Ger.   (from "Fidelio")(Ger.)
                             Allegro 2/4, 6/8   (Bb2-D4)   M-MH   Med. diff.
                             Lighthearted comic aria.

1154. Donizetti, Gaetano   *Ah, un foco insolito* (from "Don Pasquale")(It.)
      (1797-1848) It.   Vivace 3/8   (C3-E4)   MH   Mod. diff.
                             Buffo aria requiring facile articulation.

1155.   *A tanto amor* (from "La Favorita")(It.)
                             Allegro/Andante 4/4   (C#3-E4)   MH-H   Mod. diff.
                             Flowing line.

1156.   *Dalle stanze, ove Lucia*
                             (from "Lucia di Lammermoor")(It.)
                             Moderato 4/4, 2/4, 3/8 (B2-E4)   MH-H   Mod. diff.
                             Lyric, flowing line.

1157. Gounod, Charles   *Vous qui faites l'endormie* (from "Faust")(Fr.)
      (1818-1893) Fr.   Allegretto 3/4   (G2-G4)   MH   Mod. diff.
                             Cynical and sarcastic; laugh on high G.

1158.   *Le veau d'or* (from "Faust")(Fr.)
                             Allegro 6/8   (C3-Eb4)   MH-H   Diff.
                             High tessitura with a big sound.

1159. Halévy, Jacques F.   *Si la rigueur* (from "La Juive")(Fr.)
      (1799-1862) Fr.   Andante 2/4   (E2-C4)   L-M   Med. diff.
                             Sustained; for solid, low bass voice.

1160. Meyerbeer, G.   *Piff, Paff* (from "Les Huguenots")(Fr.)
      (1791-1864) Ger.   Allegro/Allegretto 4/4,3/8 (F2-E4) MH   Diff.
                             Agility required; vocally demanding.

1161. Mozart, W. A.   *Madamina!*
      (1756-1791) Aus.   ("Don Giovanni")(It.)

Allegro/Andante 2/2, 3/4 (A2-E4)   MH   Mod. diff.
Buffo aria; some facile articulation, agility, and sostenuto.

1162. Mussorgsky, M.   *I Have Attained to Power* (from "Boris Godunov")(Russ.)
(1839-1881) Russ.   Various tempo & meter (Bb2-Gb4) MH-H   Diff.
                         Interpretively and vocally arduous. The original Boris was
                         Ivan Mel'nikov (1832-1906), who created other bass roles in
                         operas by Borodin, Rimsky-Korsakov and others.

1163.   *Pimen's Tale* (from "Boris Godunov")(Russ.)
                         Andante 4/4   (D3-E4)   MH-H   Diff.
                         Language and tessitura demands.

1164.   *Varlaam's Song* (from "Boris Godunov")(Russ.)
                         Allegro 2/4   (F3-E4)   MH-H   Diff.
                         Language and tessitura demands.

1165. Nicolai, Otto   *Als Büblein klein* ("Die lustigen Weiber von
(1810-1849) Ger.   Windsor")(Ger.)
                         Various tempo & meter (E2-E4)   ML-MH Mod. diff.
                         Comic drinking song.

1166. Rossini, Gioachino *La calunnia* (from "Il Barbiere di Siviglia")(It.)
(1792-1868) It.   Allegro 4/4   (C#3-F#4)   MH-H   Diff.
                         Traditionally this aria is performed down one whole-step in
                         the key of C. The transposed version is available in the
                         Larsen edition (see no. 1143) published by Schirmer.
                         Demanding comic aria; requires patter and big sound.

1167.   *A un dottor della mia sorte* ("Il Barbiere di Siviglia")(It.)
                         Andante 4/4   (Bb2-F4)   MH-H   Diff.
                         A very demanding buffo aria requiring considerable facile
                         articulation and agility with a high tessitura.

1168. Smetana, Bedrich   *Kezal's Aria* (from "The Bartered Bride")(Ger.)
(1824-1884) Czech.   Allegro 3/4   (D3-D4)   MH   Med. diff.
                         Comic aria with few demands.

1169. Tchaikovsky, P. I. *Gremin's Aria* (from "Eugene Onégin")(Russ.)
(1840-1893) Russ.   Andante/Allegro 2/4 (Gb2-Eb4)   MH   Mod. diff.
                         Sustained lyrical line.

1170. Verdi, Giuseppe   *Dormirò sol nel manto mio regal*
(1813-1901) It.   ("Don Carlo")(It.)
                         Andante 4/4   (G2-E4)   MH   Diff.
                         Sustained and grand.

1171.   *Infelice! e tuo credevi* (from "Ernani")(It.)
                         Andante 4/4   (G2-Eb4)   MH   Mod. diff.
                         Sustained flowing line.

1172.   *Infin che un brando vindice* (from "Ernani")(It.)
                            Allegro 4/4   (C3-F4)   MH-H   Diff.
                            Vocally demanding; sustained high notes.

1173. Wagner, Richard   *Nun hört und versteht*
      (1813-1883) Ger.   (from "Die Meistersinger von Nürnberg")(Ger.)
                            Allegro 3/4, 4/4   (A2-F4)   MH-H   Diff.
                            Declamatory; high climax.

VOLUME II

1174. Cornelius, Peter   *Mein Sohn* (from "Der Barbier von Bagdad")(Ger)
      (1824-1874) Ger.   Various tempo & meter (D2-E4)   L-H   Mod. diff.
                            Large leaps; extremes of range.

1175. Dargomyzhsky, A.   *The Miller's Song* (from "Rusalka")(Russ.)
      (1813-1869) Russ.   Allegro 2/4   (B2-E4)   M-H   Mod. diff.
                            Comic aria; requires some flexibility and facile articulation.

1176. Flotow, F. von   *Lasst mich euch fragen* (from "Martha")(Ger.)
      (1812-1883) Ger.   Andante 6/8   (G2-F4)   ML-H   Mod. diff.
                            Sustained; drinking song with wide range.

1177. Gluck, C. W. von   *De noirs pressentiments*
      (1714-1787) Ger.   ("Iphigènie en Tauride")(Fr.)
                            Andante 4/4   (C#3-Eb4)   MH-H   Mod. diff.
                            Sustained with some high tessitura.

1178. Massenet, Jules   *Épouse quelque brave fille* (from "Manon")(Fr.)
      (1842-1912) Fr.   Andante 3/4   (C3-F4)   MH   Med. diff.
                            Legato; flowing line; high F4 is not held; good aria for
                            intermediate level bass or bass-baritone.

1179. Mozart, W. A.   *In diesen heil'gen Hallen*
      (1756-1791) Austrian   (from "Die Zauberflöte")(Ger.)
                            Larghetto 2/4   (F#2(E2)-C#4) L-M   Mod. diff.
                            Sustained; good introductory aria for beginning or
                            intermediate low bass.

1180.   *Non più andrai* (from "Le Nozze di Figaro")(It.)
                            Allegro 4/4   (C3-E4)   MH   Mod. diff.
                            Comic aria; facile articulation required; good study aria for
                            bass-baritone at intermediate level.

1181.   *O Isis und Osiris* (from "Die Zauberflöte")(Ger.)
                            Adagio 3/4   (F2-C4)   L-M   Med. diff.
                            Slow and sustained; good introductory aria for the beginning
                            low bass.

1182.   *Se vuol ballare, signor contino*

(from "Le Nozze di Figaro")(It.)
Allegretto 3/4, 2/4   (C3-F4)   MH   Mod. diff.
Some facile articulation; comic aria; good study aria for
bass-baritone at intermediate level.

1183.   *Solche hergelaufne Laffen*
                         (from "Die Entführung Aus Dem Serail")(Ger.)
                         Allegro 4/4, 3/4   (F2-F4)   ML-H   Diff.
                         An extremely demanding aria vocally with facile
                         articulation, extremes of range, and agility.

1184.   *Wer ein Liebchen hat gefunden*
                         (from "Die Entführung Aus Dem Serail")(Ger.)
                         Andante 6/8   (G2-D4)   ML-MH   Med. diff.
                         Large leaps; sustained.

1185. Ponchielli, A.   *Ombre di mia prosapia* (from "La Gioconda")(It.)
      (1834-1886) It.   Allegro 6/8   (G2-F4)   M-H   Diff.
                         Dramatic and vocally demanding; some agility required.

1186. Puccini, Giacomo   *Vecchia zimarra* (from "La Boheme")(It.)
      (1856-1924) It.   Allegretto 2/4   (C#3-Eb4)   M-MH   Med. diff.
                         Smooth flowing legato line.

1187. Thomas, Ambroise   *De son coeur j'ai calmè la fièvre* (from "Mignon")(Fr.)
      (1811-1896) Fr.   Andantino 6/8   (A2-D4)   M-MH   Med. diff.
                         Good aria for beginning or intermediate bass voice; flowing
                         legato.

1188. Verdi, Giuseppe   *Come dal ciel precipita* (from "Macbeth")(It.)
      (1813-1901) It.   Adagio 4/4   (A2-E4)   M-H   Mod. diff.
                         Sustained; dramatic; requires a solid high E4.

1189.   *Di due figli vivea padre beato* (from "Il Trovatore")(It.)
                         Andante 4/4, 3/4   (B2-E4)   M-H   Diff.
                         Considerable agility required; vocally demanding.

1190.   *Il lacerato spirito* (from "Simon Boccanegra")(It.)
                         Andante 4/4, 3/4   (F#2-D4)   M-MH   Med. diff.
                         Good introductory aria of its type for intermediate level
                         bass; sustained; dramatic moments.

1191. Wagner, Richard   *Mögst du, mein Kind*
      (1813-1883) Ger.   (from "Der Fliegende Holländer")(Ger.)
                         Allegro 4/4   (A2-D4)   MH   Mod. diff.
                         Narrative; declamatory.

1192.   *Tatest du's wirklich?* (from "Tristan und Isolde")(Ger.)
                         Various tempo 4/4   (G2-E4)   ML-H   Diff.
                         Very long and demanding aria; chromatic; interpretively

difficult; sustained.

CELEBRATED OPERA ARIAS
For BASS
Edited by Max Spicker
Published by Patelson's

An excellent collection of standard bass arias and many noteworthy more obscure selections are contained in this volume. Each aria is presented in its original key and language with an English version as well.

1193. Adam, Adolphe   *Vallons de l'helvétie* (from "Le Chalet")(Fr.)
      (1803-1856) Fr.   Andante 6/8, 4/4   (Bb2-Eb4)   MH-H   Diff.
                           Requires command of agility.

1194. Apolloni, Giovanni   *Fu dio che disse* (from "Lebreo")(It.)
      (1822-1889) It.   Andante 4/4   (Db3-F4)   MH-H   Mod. diff.
                           Sustained and energetic; agility required.

1195. Bizet, Georges   *Quand la flamme de l'amour*
      (1838-1875) Fr.   (from "La Jolie Fille de Perth")(Fr.)
                           Andante 12/8   (B2-E4)   MH-H   Diff.
                           Drinking song; requires big sound.

1196. David, Félicien   *Je crois au Dieu* (from "Herculanum")(Fr.)
      (1810-1876) Fr.   Andantino 2/4   (C#3-E4)   MH   Mod. diff.
                           An aria with organ accompaniment; religious.

1197. Donizetti, Gaetano   *A tanto amor* (from "La Favorita")(It.)
      (1797-1848) It.   Andante 4/4   (C#3-E4)   MH-H   Mod. diff.
                           Flowing, cantabile style.

1198.   *Vieni! la mia vendetta* (from "Lucrezia Borgia")(It.)
                           Largo/Mod. 4/4, 3/4   (Ab2-Eb4)   MH-H   Mod. diff.
                           Secure high notes required.

1199. Flotow, F. von   *Lasst mich euch fragen* (from "Martha")(Ger.)
      (1812-1883) Ger.   Andante 6/8   (G2-F4)   ML-H   Mod. diff.
                           Requires secure high F4 and solid low G2; drinking song.

1200. Gluck, C. W. von   *De noirs pressentiments*
      (1714-1787) Ger.   (from "Iphigénie en Tauride")(Fr.)
                           Andante 4/4   (C#3-Eb4)   MH   Mod. diff.
                           Sustained with numerous high D4s and Eb4s.

1201. Gounod, Charles   *Au bruit des lourds Marteaux d'Airain*
      (1818-1893) Fr.   (from "Philémon et Baucis")(Fr.)
                           Allegro 2/4   (Ab2-Eb4)   M-MH   Mod. diff.
                           Facile articulation and agility required.

1202.   *Que les songes heureux* (from "Philémon et Baucis")(Fr.)
                                   Andante 3/4   (E2-C#3)   L-M   Med. diff.
                                   Sustained; good aria for intermediate low bass.

1203.   Sous les pieds d'une femme (from "La Reine de Saba")(Fr.)
                                   Larghetto 12/8   (E2-D4)   L-MH   Mod. diff.
                                   Sustained with some agility required.

1204.   *Vous qui faites l'endormie* (from "Faust")(Fr.)
                                   Allegretto 3/4   (G2-E4(G4)) MH   Mod. diff.
                                   Sinister and sarcastic; laugh on high G.

1205. Halévy, Jacques   *Si la rigueur* (from "La Juive")(Fr.)
      (1799-1862) Fr.   Andante 2/4   (E2-C4)   L-M   Med. diff.
                                   For low bass with solid low notes; sustained.

1206. Handel, G. F.   *Col raggio placido* (from "Agrippina")(It.)
      (1685-1759) Ger.   Allegro 3/8   (G2-E4)   ML-MH   Diff.
                                   Requires considerable agility and facile articulation.

1207. Joncières, V. de   *Le front dans la poussière* (from "Sardanapale")(Fr.)
      (1839-1903) Fr.   Andante/Allegro 3/4, 4/4 (G2-E4) M-MH   Mod. diff.
                                   Sostenuto with quick sections; facile articulation.

1208. Meyerbeer, G.   *Le jour est levé* (from "Le Pardon de Ploërmel")(Fr.)
      (1791-1864) Ger.   Allegro 6/8   (B2-E4)   MH   Mod. diff.
                                   Requires agility and facile articulation.

1209.   *Nonnes qui reposez* (from "Robert le Diable")(Fr.)
                                   Moderato 4/4   (B2-D#4)   M-MH   Med. diff.
                                   Sustained; good introductory aria of its type for intermediate
                                   bass.

1210.   *O jours heureux* (from "L'Étoile du Nord")(Fr.)
                                   Andantino 3/4   (Gb2-E4)   M-MH   Mod. diff.
                                   Expressive cantabile; some agility required.

1211. Mozart, W. A.   *In diesen heil'gen Hallen*
      (1756-1791) Austrian   (from "Die Zauberflöte")(Ger.)
                                   Larghetto 2/4   (F#2-C#4)   L-M   Mod. diff.
                                   Sustained with flowing line; excellent aria for intermediate,
                                   low bass.

1212.   *Madamina! il catalogo è questo* ("Don Giovanni")(It.)
                                   Allegro 2/2   (A2-E4)   MH   Diff.
                                   Buffo aria with agility, facile articulation, and sostenuto
                                   requirements.

1213.   *Non più andrai* (from "Le Nozze di Figaro")(It.)
                                   Allegro 4/4   (C3-E4)   MH   Mod. diff.

Good introductory aria of its type for intermediate
bass-baritone.

1214.   *O Isis und Osiris* (from "Die Zauberflöte")(Ger.)
                Adagio 3/4   (F2-C4)   L-M   Med. diff.
                Excellent introductory aria of its type for beginning or
                intermediate, low bass.

1215.   *Se vuol ballare* (from "Le Nozze di Figaro")(It.)
                Allegretto 3/4   (C3-F4)   MH   Med. diff.
                Good introductory aria of its type for intermediate
                bass-baritone.

1216. Nicolai, Otto   *Als Büblein klein*
      (1810-1849) Ger.   (from "Die lustigen Weiber von Windsor")(Ger.)
                Andante 4/8, 5/8, 3/8 (E2-E4)   ML-MH   Med. diff.
                Drinking song for comic bass with wide range.

1217. Pergolesi, G.   *Bella mia* (from "Il Maestro di Musica")(It.)
      (1710-1736) It.   Larghetto 3/8   (G3-E4)   MH-H   Med. diff.
                Sustained; lyric line.

1218. Ponchielli, A.   *Ombre di mia prosapia* (from "La Gioconda")(It.)
      (1834-1886) It.   Allegro 6/8   (G2-F4)   M-MH   Diff.
                Vocally demanding aria of vengeance; requires agility and
                vocal power.

1219. Rameau, J.   *Monstre affreux* (from "Dardanus")(Fr.)
      (1683-1764) Fr.   Lento 4/4, 3/4   (G2-Eb4)   ML-MH   Mod. diff.
                Sustained and grand.

1220. Righini, Vincenzo *Al nome tuo temuto* (from "La Selva incantata")(It.)
      (1756-1812) It.   Larghetto 4/4   (E2-D4)   L-M   Med. diff.
                Sustained with flowing line; agility required; good for low
                bass.

1221. Rossini, Gioachino *Que ton âme si noble* (from "Robert Bruce")(Fr.)
      (1792-1868) It.   Andantino 12/8   (Bb2-Eb4)   M-H   Mod. diff.
                Requires agility with flowing line.

1222. Thomas, Ambroise   *De son coeur j'ai calmé la fièvre*
      (1811-1866) Fr.   (from "Mignon")(Fr.)
                Andantino 6/8   (A2-D4)   MH   Med. diff.
                Flowing line.

1223. Verdi, Giuseppe   *Come dal ciel precipita* (from "Macbeth")(It.)
      (1813-1901) It.   Adagio 4/4   (A2-E4)   M-H   Mod. diff.
                Sustained with solid high E4 required.

1224.   *Dormirò sol nel manto mio regal* (from "Don Carlo")(It.)

Andante 4/4   (G2-E4)   MH   Diff.
Sustained with effective high climax.

1225.   *Il lacerato spirito* (from "Simon Boccanegra")(It.)
Andante 3/4   (F#2-D4)   M-MH   Med. diff.
Excellent introductory aria of its type for intermediate bass;
sustained; supplication.

1226.   *Infelice! e tuo credevi* (from "Ernani")(It.)
Andante 4/4   (G2-Eb4)   MH   Mod. diff.
Sustained lyric line.

1227.   *O tu palermo* (from "I Vespri Siciliani")(It.)
Lento 12/8   (F2-Eb4)   MH   Mod. diff.
Very sustained; lyric line.

1228.   *Tu sul labbro de' veggenti* (from "Nabucodonosor")(It.)
Andante 4/4   (G2-E4)   MH   Mod. diff.
Sustained with solid high E4.

1229. Wagner, Richard   *Pogner's Address*
(1813-1883) Ger.   (from "Die Meistersinger von Nürnberg")(Ger.)
Allegro 4/4, 3/4   (A2-F4)   M-H   Diff.
Long declamatory aria.

1230.   *Wahn! Wahn!* (from "Die Meistersinger von
Nürnberg")(Ger.)
Various tempo & meter (A2-E4)   M-H   Diff.
A long monologue requiring good interpretive skills.

1231.   *Was duftet doch der Flieder*
(from "Die Meistersinger von Nürnberg")(Ger.)
Various tempo & meter (A2-E4)   M-MH   Mod. diff.
A good introductory aria of its type for intermediate or
advanced bass; a long monologue.

1232.   *Wotans Abschied* (from "Die Walküre")(Ger.)
Various tempo 4/4   (A#2-E4)   M-H   Diff.
Well-known aria for dramatic bass-baritone; vocally
demanding and dramatically intense.

1233. Weber, C. M. von   *Schweig'! damit dich Niemand warnt*
(1786-1826) Ger.   (from "Der Freischütz")(Ger.)
Allegro 2/2   (F#2-E4)   ML-H   Diff.
Requires agility and vocal stamina.

CELEBRI ARIE D'OPERA
PER BASSO
Published by Ricordi

1234. Bellini, Vincenzo
(1801-1835) It.

Vi ravviso, o luoghi ameni
(from "La Sonnambula")(It.)
Andante/Allegro 4/4 (G2-Eb4)   MH-H   Mod. diff.
First part in flowing "cantabile" style; second part in an
energetic "bravura" style; the first part may be performed
alone.

1235. Boito, A.
(1842-1918) It.

Son lo spirito che nega (from "Mefistofele")(It.)
Allegro 6/8, 2/8, 3/8 (G2-E4)   MH-H   Diff.
Aggressive and vocally demanding.

1236. Gomes, A. C.
(1836-1896) Braz.

Di sposa... di padre...le gioie serene
(from "Salvator Rosa")(It.)
Andante 4/4   (F#2-E4)   M-MH   Med. diff.
Sustained, flowing; excellent study piece for intermediate to
advanced level.

1237. Halévy, J.
(1799-1862) Fr.

Se oppressi ognor da ria sentenza (from "La Juive")(It.)
Andantino 2/4   (E2-C4)   L-M   Med. diff.
"Si la rigueur" is normally performed in French; sustained
with solid low notes.

1238. Mozart, W. A.
(1756-1791) Austrian

Non piu andrai (from "Le Nozze di Figaro")(It.)
Allegro 4/4   (C3-E4)   MH-H   Mod. diff.
A humorous aria.

1239. Puccini, G.
(1858-1924) It.

Vecchia zimarra (from "La Bohème")(It.)
Allegretto 2/4   (C#3-Eb4)   M-MH   Med. diff.
A shorter, lyric aria.

1240. Rossini, G.
(1792-1868) It.

La calunnia (from "Il Barbiere di Siviglia")(It.)
Allegro 4/4   (C#3-F#4)   MH-VH   Diff.
See no. 1143 for traditional lower key; comic aria requiring
facile articulation and a big sound.

1241. Verdi, G.
(1813-1901) It.

Ella giammai m'amò (from "Don Carlo")(It.)
Andante 4/4   (G2-E4)   MH   Mod. diff.
Sustained with high climax.

1242.

Il lacerato spirito (from "Simon Boccanegra")(It.)
Andante 4/4, 3/4   (F#2-D4)   M-MH   Med. diff.
Sustained; excellent beginning study aria of its type.

1243.

Infelice.....e tuo credevi (from "Ernani")(It.)
Allegro/Andante 4/4 (G2-Eb4)   MH   Mod. diff.
Sustained, lyric sound.

1244.

O tu, Palermo, terra adorata ("I Vespri Siciliani")(It.)
Andante/Largo 6/8, 12/8 (A2-Eb4)   MH   Mod. diff.
Very sustained, flowing style.

TEN MOZART ARIAS FOR BASS
Edited by S. Kagen
Published by International

A useful collection of Mozart arias for bass voice, particularly low bass with half the selections
for this category.

1245.   *Ihr Mächtigen, seht ungerührt* (from "Zaide")
               Allegretto/Mod. 2/2, 3/8 (A2-F4)   M-F   Mod. diff.
               Sustained.

1246.   *In diesen heil'gen Hallen* (from "Die Zauberflöte")
               Larghetto 2/4   (F#2(E2)-C#4)   L-MH   Med. diff.
               Slow sustained aria suitable for beginning or intermediate
               low bass.

1247.   *La vendetta* (from "Le Nozze di Figaro")
               Allegro con spirito 4/4 (A2-E4)   M-MH   Mod. diff.
               Buffo aria of vengeance; facile articulation and booming
               sound required.

1248.   *Madamina, il catalogo* (from "Don Giovanni")
               Allegro/Andante 2/2, 3/4 (A2-E4)   MH   Mod. diff.
               Buffo aria; agility, facile articulation, and sostenuto.

1249.   *O Isis und Osiris* (from "Die Zauberflöte")
               Adagio 3/4   (F2-C3)   L-M   Med. diff.
               Slow sustained aria for beginning or intermediate low bass.
               The two arias from "Die Zauberflöte" were written for
               Franz Gerl, the original Sarastro.

1250.   *O, wie will ich triumphieren* (from "Die Entführung")
               Allegro vivace 2/4   (D2-D4)   VL-MH   Diff.
               Sustained low D; extremes of range; agility; facile
               articulation; vocally arduous.

1251.   *Solche hergelaufne Laffen* (from "Die Entführung")
               Allegro 4/4, 3/4   (F2-F4)   L-MH   Diff.
               Facile articulation; agility; vocal power, extremes of range.

1252.   *Tardi s'avvede* (from "La Clemenza di Tito")
               Allegretto 3/4   (B2-D4)   MH   Med. diff.
               Flowing, legato line; some agility required.

1253.   *Wer ein Liebchen hat gefunden* (from "Die Entführung")
               Andante 6/8   (G2-D4)   M-MH   Med. diff.
               The three arias from "Die Entführung" were written for
               Karl Ludwig Fischer, the original Osmin. Flowing legato

line.

1254.   *Wer hungrig bei der Tafel sitzt* (from "Zaide")
                         Allegro assai 6/8   (C3-F4)   M-H   Mod. diff.
                         Facile articulation; agility.

TWENTY MOZART ARIAS
FOR BASS/BARITONE
In Two Volumes
Edited by S. Kagen
Published by International

This two volume collection contains a number of suitable arias for bass and bass-baritone.

VOLUME I

1255.   *A forza di martelli* (from "La Finta Giardiniera")
                         For baritone.

1256.   *Deh vieni alla finestra* (from "Don Giovanni")
                         Allegretto 6/8   (D3-E4)   MH   Med. diff.
                         Flowing legato; love song.

1257.   *Donne mie* (from "Così fan tutte")
                         For baritone.

1258.   *Ella vuople ed io torrei* (from "La Finta Semplice")
                         Moderato 2/2   (C3-D4)   MH   Med. diff.
                         Buffo aria.

1259.   *Finch' han dal vino* (from "Don Giovanni")
                         Presto 2/4   (D3-Eb4)   MH-H   Mod. diff.
                         Requires facile articulation; agility required; ability to
                         handle a high tessitura.

1260.   *Ho capito, signor, sì* (from "Don Giovanni")
                         Allegro molto 2/2   (C3-C4)   M-MH   Mod. easy
                         Has few demands; usually performed by a lighter voice for
                         proper character delineation.

1261.   *Non c'è al mondo altro che donne* ("La Finta Semplice")
                         Allegro 6/8   (A2-E4)   M-MH   Med. diff.
                         Buffo aria.

1262.   *Nur mutig, mein Herze* (from "Zaide")
                         For baritone.

1263.   *Un marito, o Dio, vorresti* (from "La Finta Giardiniera")

For baritone.

1264.   *Vieni, vieni, o mia ninetta* (from "La Finta Semplice")
                         For baritone.

VOLUME II

1265.   *Aprite un po' quegl' occhi* (from "Le Nozze di Figaro")
                         Moderato 4/4   (Bb2-Eb4)   M-H   Mod. diff.
                         Sarcastic and witty aria about women.

1266.   *Con certe persone* (from "La Finta Semplice")
                         For baritone

1267.   *Con un vezzo all'Italiana* (from "La Finta Giardiniera")
                         For baritone.

1268.   *Der Vogelfänger bin ich* (from "Die Zauberflöte")
                         For baritone.

1269.   *Ein Mädchen oder Weibchen* (from "Die Zauberflöte")
                         For baritone.

1270.   *Non più andrai* (from "Le Nozze di Figaro")
                         Allegro vivace 4/4   (C3-E4)   MH   Mod. diff.
                         Excellent aria for intermediate level bass.

1271.   *Se vuol ballare* (from "Le Nozze di Figaro")
                         Allegretto 3/4   (C3-F4)   M-H   Mod. diff.
                         Excellent aria for intermediate level bass.

1272.   *Troppa briga a prender moglie* ("La Finta Semplice")
                         For baritone.

1273.   *Ubriaco non son io* (from "La Finta Semplice")
                         Allegro 4/4   (C3-D4)   MH   Med. diff.

1274.   *Vedrò mentr' io sospiro* (from "Le Nozze di Figaro")
                         For baritone.

OPERATIC ANTHOLOGY
Bass Voice Volume
Edited by Kurt Adler
Published by G. Schirmer

Except for the following aria the contents in this single volume are the same as the two volume
edition by Schirmer edited by Brown. (for contents see Brown anthology nos. 1153-1192)
1275. Wagner, Richard   *Mein Herr und Gott* (from "Lohengren")(Ger.)

(1813-1883) Ger.   Adagio 3/4   (F2-Eb4)   M-MH   Med. diff.
                        Sustained; prayer.

CONCERT ARIAS FOR BASS

1276. Beethoven, L. Van   *Two Concert Arias* (see nos. 645-6)   International
       (1770-1827) Ger.

CONCERT ARIAS FOR BASS
By Mozart
Published by Breitkopf and also International

The great Concert Arias by Mozart for bass are generally characterized as long, with wide ranges, high and low tessitura, large leaps, as well as requiring agility and facile articulation. Originally for bass voice and orchestra these piano reductions are uneven, the International edition being the better of the two. Not listed below but of interest is the concert aria "Io ti lascio" (K. 621a) for bass voice and strings where only the violin parts are attributed to Mozart and the rest to Jacquin. (see the New Groves Dictionary)

1277.   *Alcandro, lo confesso*
                        Andante/Allegretto 2/2,6/8 (E2-Eb4) L-MH   Diff.
                        Sustained.

1278.   *Cosi dunque tradisci*
                        Allegro 4/4   (D2-F4)   ML-MH   Diff.
                        It is thought that this demanding aria was composed for Karl
                        Ludwig Fischer, the original Osmin.

1279.   *Männer suchen stets zu naschen*
                        Allegretto 2/4   (C3-D4)   MH   Med. diff.
                        This piece is not included in the International edition.

1280.   *Mentre ti lascio o figlia*
                        Larghetto/Allegro 2/4, 2/2 (A2-Eb4) M-H   Mod. diff.
                        Sustained; effective climax.

1281.   *Per questa bella mano*
                        (For bass voice, double bass or cello and piano)
                        Andante/Allegro 6/8, 4/4 (F#2-D4) ML-MH   Mod. diff.
                        In the International edition this aria is also available for bass
                        voice and piano only. This unusual aria was written in
                        March, 1791 for Franz Gerl who later was the first Sarastro
                        in "Die Zauberflöte." Sustained sections; animated sections;
                        a very effective piece.

1282.   *Rivolgete a lui lo sguardo*
                        Allegro 4/4, 2/2   (G2-F4)   MH-H   Diff.

This aria was originally conceived for the opera "Così fan tutte" to be performed by Guilielmo.

1283.   *Un baccio di mano*
                        Allegretto 2/4   (B2-E4)   **MH**   Med. diff.

CHAPTER IX

ANTHOLOGIES AND COLLECTIONS OF ARIAS FROM CANTATAS AND ORATORIOS

It should be noted that many "bass" solo parts or roles in oratorios and cantatas are for bass-baritone or baritone with a general range of A2 or Bb2 - E4 or F4 and a high tessitura.

ANTHOLOGY OF SACRED SONG
CELEBRATED ARIAS SELECTED FROM ORATORIOS
Volume IV (Bass)
Edited by Max Spicker
Published by G. Schirmer, 1929

All selections in this well conceived anthology are in English.

1284. Bach, J. S. *Mighty Lord and King*
(1685-1750) Ger. (from "Christmas Oratorio")
Moderato 2/4 (A2-E4) M-H Mod. diff.
Agility required; stately.

1285. *O Lord, My Darken'd Heart Enlighten*
(from "Christmas Oratorio")
Andante 2/4 (B2-E4) M-H Mod. diff.
Sustained; agility also required in sections.

1286. Barnby, Joseph *The Daughters of the City*
(1838-1896) Eng. (from "Rebekah")
Andante 3/4 (F2-Eb4) MH Med. diff.
Sustained.

1287. Benedict, Sir Julius *How Great, O Lord, Is Thy Goodness*
(1804-1885) Ger./Eng. (from "St. Peter")
Andante 4/4 (C3-F4) H Med. diff.
Sustained.

1288. Blumner, Martin *Despoiled Is Thy Crown of Honor*
(1827-1901) Ger. (from "The Fall of Jerusalem")
Various tempo & meter (A#2-E4) M-H Mod. diff.

1289. Dubois, Théodore *God, My Father*
(1837-1924) Fr. (from "The Seven Last Words")
Andante maestoso 4/4 (B2-F4) H Med. diff.
Sustained.

1290. Dvorák, Anton *Give Ear, Ye People!*
(1841-1904) Bohem. (from "St. Ludmilla")

Various tempo 3/4   (G2-E4)   M-H   Mod. diff.
Sustained section; somewhat animated section.

1291. Gaul, Alfred   *Glory Be to Thee, O Lord!*
      (1837-1913) Eng.   (from "Ruth")
                            Moderato 4/4   (C3-D4)   MH   Med. diff.

1292. Handel, G. F.   *Arm, Ye Brave!*
      (1685-1759) Ger./Eng. (from "Judas Maccabaeus")
                            Allegro 4/4   (B2-E4)   MH   Med. diff.
                            Energetic; some agility required.

1293.   *But Who May Abide*
                            (from "Messiah")
                            Various tempo 4/4, 3/8 (G2-E4)   MH   Mod. diff.
                            Sustained sections; animated sections requiring agility.

1294.   *His Sceptre Is the Rod of Righteousness*
                            (from "Occasional Oratorio")
                            Allegro moderato 4/4   (F#2-E4)   M-H   Diff.
                            Requires agility.

1295.   *Honor and Arms*
                            (from "Samson")
                            Allegro 4/4   (G2-Eb4)   M-H   Mod. diff.
                            Agility required.

1296.   *My Father, Look upon My Anguish*
                            (from "The Passion")
                            Adagio 4/4   (Bb2-Eb4)   MH   Med. diff.
                            Sustained.

1297.   *Tears, Such as Tender Fathers Shed*
                            (from "Deborah")
                            Largo 4/4   (Bb2-Eb4)   MH   Med. diff.
                            Sustained.

1298.   *The People That Walked in Darkness*
                            (from "Messiah")
                            Larghetto 4/4   (F#2-E4)   MH   Med. diff.
                            Sustained.

1299.   *The Trumpet Shall Sound*
                            (from "Messiah")
                            Pomposo, 3/4   (A2-E4)   M-H   Diff.
                            Energetic; some flexibility required.

1300.   *Why Do the Nations*
                            (from "Messiah")
                            Allegro 4/4   (B2-E4)   M-H   Diff.

Requires considerable agility and vocal energy.

1301. Haydn, Joseph   *Behold, Along the Dewy Grass*
    (1732-1809) Austrian   (from "The Seasons")
                Allegro 4/4   (G2-F4)   MH   Diff.
                Agility required; large leaps.

1302.   *Now Heav'n in Fullest Glory*
                (from "The Creation")
                Maestoso 3/4   (F2-D4)   ML-MH Med. diff.
                Recit. has alternate low D2; some agility required.

1303.   *Rolling in Foaming Billows*
                (from "The Creation")
                Allegro 4/4   (G2-F4)   M-H   Mod. diff.
                Energetic section; flowing legato section.

1304.   *With Joy th' Impatient Husbandman*
                (from "The Seasons")
                Allegretto 2/4   (Bb2-E4)   M-H   Mod. diff.
                Agility required.

1305. Hiller, Ferdinand   *Jeremiah's Lament*
    (1811-1885) Ger.   (from "The Destruction of Jerusalem")
                Various tempo 4/4   (B2-Eb4)   MH   Med. diff.
                Sustained section; animated section.

1306.   *Obedience 'Tis, the Lord of Hosts Demandeth* (from "Saul")
                Allegro con fuoco 4/4 (A#2-E4)   M-H   Mod. diff.
                Energetic.

1307. Klughardt, August   *Holy One, Dying for Mortals*
    (1847-1902) Ger.   (from "The Burial of Christ")
                Larghetto 3/4   (A2-F4)   M-H   Mod. diff.
                Sustained.

1308. Lange, Samuel de   *God Is Eternal*
    (1840-1911) Dutch   (from "Moses")
                Various tempo & meter (G2-E4)   ML-H   Mod. diff.
                Sustained sections; animated sections.

1309. MacKenzie, A.   *The Wilderness Shall Be*
    (1847-1935) Scottish   (from "The Rose of Sharon")
                Moderato 3/4, 4/4   (E2-D4)   L-MH   Med. diff.
                Sustained.

1310. Maréchal, Henri   *O My Home*
    (1842-1924) Fr.   (from "The Nativity")
                Various tempo & meter (Bb2-F4)   H   Diff.
                Sustained sections; animated sections.

1311. Massenet, Jules   *The Days Are All Sunshine*
      (1842-1912) Fr.   (from "Mary Magdalen")
                           Allegro con spirito 3/4 (G2-F4)   M-H   Med. diff.
                           Energetic.

1312. Mendelssohn, Felix *Consume Them All*
      (1809-1847) Ger.   (from "St. Paul")
                           Allegro molto 2/2   (B2-D4)   MH   Med. diff.

1313.   *For Know Ye Not*
                           (from "St. Paul")
                           Allegro moderato 4/4 (A2-D4)   MH   Med. diff.
                           Energetic.

1314.   *Is Not His Word Like a Fire?*
                           (from "Elijah")
                           Allegro con fuoco 4/4 (C3-F4)   M-H   Mod. diff.
                           Energetic.

1315.   *It Is Enough*
                           (from "Elijah")
                           Adagio/Allegro 3/4, 2/4 (A2-E4)   M-H   Mod. diff.
                           Sustained section; animated section.

1316.   *Lord God of Abraham*
                           (from "Elijah")
                           Adagio 4/4   (Bb2-Eb4)   MH   Med. diff.
                           Sustained.

1317.   *O God, Have Mercy*
                           (from "St. Paul")
                           Various tempo 4/4   (B2-D4)   MH   Med. diff.
                           Sustained sections; animated sections.

1318. Molique, G.   *Lead Me, O Lord*
                           (from "Abraham")
                           Andante 4/4   (D3-E4)   M-H   Med. diff.
                           Sustained.

1319. Raff, Joseph   *Lord, Hear My Voice*
      (1822-1882) Swiss.   (from "The World's End")
                           Larghetto 3/4   (D3- Eb4)   MH   Med. diff.
                           Sustained.

1320. Rubinstein, Anton   *Wake, Ye Spirits*
      (1829-1894) Russ.   (from "Paradise Lost")
                           Allegro 3/4   (A2-D4)   MH   Mod. diff.
                           Spirited; agitated; some agility required.

1321. Spohr, Ludwig   *Tears of Sorrow*

(1784-1859) Ger.	(from "Calvary")			
	Larghetto 4/4	(Bb2-C4)	M	Med. diff.
	Sustained.			

1322. Sullivan, Sir Arthur
(1842-1900) Eng.

Daughters of Jerusalem
(from "The Light of the World")
Andante 3/4   (B2-F#4)   H   Med. diff.
Sustained.

BACH SONGS AND AIRS
For Bass
Book I & II
Edited by E. Prout
Published by Augener, 1909

The Bach arias in this helpful collection are in English and German.

VOLUME I

1323.   *Awake, Awake Ye Sheep That Wander*
                                    (from "O Ewigkeit, du Donnerwort")
                                    Andante maestoso 4/4 (G2-E4)   M-H   Mod. diff.
                                    Sustained; some flexibility required.

1324.   *Away Then, Ye Cares That So Vainly Beset Me*
                                    (from "Liebster Gott, wann werd' ich sterben")
                                    Andante con moto 12/8 (A2-E4)   M-H   Mod. diff.
                                    Agility required.

1325.   *Despisest Thou the Riches of His Goodness?*
                                    (from "Herr, deine Augen sehen nach dem Glauben")
                                    Vivace 3/8   (G2-Eb4)   M-H   Mod. diff.
                                    Requires considerable agility.

1326.   *Fare Thee Well, Thou Worldly Tumult*
                                    (from "Wer weiss wie nahe mir mein Ende")
                                    Largo 3/4   (G2-Eb4)   MH   Med. diff.
                                    Sustained.

1327.   *Lord, As Thou Wilt*
                                    (from "Herr, wie du willt, so schick's mit mir")
                                    Larghetto 3/4   (G2-Eb4)   MH   Med. diff.
                                    Sustained.

1328.   *Mark, O My Heart, Evermore Only This*
                                    (from "So du mi deinem Munde bekennest Jesum")
                                    Allegro maestoso 3/8   (A2-E4)   M-H   Mod. diff.
                                    Agility required.

1329.   *O Most Holy Three in One*
                 (from "Erschallet, ihr Lieder")
                 Maestoso 4/4   (G2-D4)   M   Med. diff.
                 Sustained; some agility required.

1330.   *Peace, Thou Unruly Sea!*
                 (from "Jesus schläft, was ich hoffen?")
                 Allegro 4/4   (B2-E4)   M-H   Mod. diff.
                 Agility required.

1331.   *The End Is Come, The Pain Is Over*
                 (from "Sehet, wir geh'n hinauf gen Jerusalem")
                 Larghetto 4/4   (G2-Eb4)   MH   Med. diff.
                 Flowing legato.

1332.   *Thou Most Blest, All Quickening Day*
                 (from "Wachet, betet")
                 Various tempo & meter (G2-F4)   M-H   Diff.
                 Requires considerable agility.

1333.   *Ye Happy Flock, The Sheep of Jesus*
                 (from "Du Hirte Israel, höre")
                 Andante 12/8   (F#2-D4)   ML-MH   Med. diff.
                 Sustained; flowing legato.

VOLUME II

1334.   *Awake, My Powers and All Within Me*
                 (from "Unser Mund sei voll Lachens")
                 Allegro maestoso 4/4 (F#2-E4)   M-H   Mod. diff.
                 Agility required.

1335.   *Be Silent, Hosts of Hell*
                 (from "Wo soll ich fliehen hin")
                 Vivace 4/4   (Bb2-D4)   MH   Med. diff.
                 Some agility required.

1336.   *Have Not People with Their Children*
                 (from "Schweigt stille, plaudert nicht")
                 Allegro moderato 4/4 (B2-E4)   M-H   Mod. diff.
                 Rapid articulation; agility required.

1337.   *Hence, All Ye Evil-Doers!*
                 (from "Ach Herr, mich armen Sünder")
                 Allegro 2/2   (A2-E4)   M-H   Mod. diff.
                 Agility required.

1338.   *Here, Within My Father's Mansions*
                 (from "Liebster Jesu, mein Verlangen")
                 Andante 3/8   (G2-E4)   M-H   Med. diff.

Sustained.

1339. *I Will Cross with Gladness Carry*
(from "Ich will den Kreuzstab gerne iragen")
Adagio 3/4   (G2-Eb4)   MH   Med. diff.
Sustained; flowing line.

1340. *Slumber Now, Ye Weary Eyelids*
(from "Ich habe genug")
Larghetto 4/4   (Bb2-Eb4)   MH   Med. diff.
Flowing legato.

1341. *Therefore Be Ye Not Anxious*
(from "Es wartet Alles auf dich")
Allegro 2/2   (G2-Eb4)   MH   Med. diff.
Some agility required.

1342. *Up, Up, with Trumpet Tone*
(from "Auf Christi Himmelfahrt allein")
Allegro maestoso 3/4   (F#2-E4)   MH   Med. diff.
Agility required.

1343. *With Desiring*
(from "Der Streit swischen Phoebus und Pan")
Largo 3/8   (B2-F#4)   H   Mod. diff.
Sustained; agility required.

1344. *Yes, Yes, Thy Foes I Soon Will Conquer*
(from "Selig ist der Mann")
Vivace 3/4   (G2-Eb4)   MH   Mod. diff.
Agility required.

BASS ARIAS FROM ORATORIOS
Schirmer's Singer's Library
Volume I & II
Compiled by Irving Brown
Published by G.Schirmer, 1977

This anthology in two volumes has the same contents as *Anthology of Sacred Song* in one volume edited by Max Spicker and published by Schirmer. (for contents see nos. 1284-1322)

ORATORIO SONGS
Volume IV
For BASS
Published by John Church

This volume is sufficiently different in contents from other volumes presented to warrant annotation. All selections are in English except where they are otherwise indicated.

1346. Bach, J. S.   *Bring Me Cross and Cup*
      (1685-1750) Ger.   (from "The St. Matthew Passion")
                                Andantino 3/8   (G2-Eb4)   MH   Med. diff.
                                Somewhat sustained.

1347.   *Consider, O My Soul*
                                (from "The St. John Passion")
                                Adagio 4/4   (Bb2-E4)   M-H   Med. diff.
                                Sustained.

1348.   *Give Me Jesus, I Implore You*
                                (from "The St. Matthew Passion")
                                Moderato 4/4   (G2-E4)   M-H   Mod. diff.
                                Sustained.

1349.   *Mighty Lord and King*
                                (from "Christmas Oratorio")
                                Moderato 2/4   (A2-E4)   M-H   Mod. diff.
                                Agility required; stately.

1350. Barnby, Joseph   *The Daughters of the City*
      (1838-1896) Eng.   (from "Rebekah")
                                Andante 3/4   (F2-Eb4)   MH   Med. diff.
                                Sustained.

1351. Benedict, Sir Julius   *How Great, O Lord, Is Thy Goodness*
      (1804-1885) Ger./Eng.   (from "St. Peter")
                                Andante 4/4   (C3-F4)   H   Med. diff.
                                Sustained.

1352. Bennett, Sterndale   *Whosoever Drinketh*
      (1816-1875) Eng.   (from "Woman of Samaria")
                                Larghetto 4/4   (B2-E4)   M-H   Med. diff.
                                Sustained.

1353. Costa, Michael   *Although My House Be Not with God*
      (1808-1884) It./Eng.   (from "Eli")
                                Andante agitato 4/4 (Db2-E4)   ML-MH   Mod. diff.
                                Energetic; sustained sections.

1354.   *Arise, O Lord*
                                (from "Naaman")
                                Moderato 2/2   (C3-E4)   M-H   Med. diff.
                                Sustained.

1355.   *If Thou Should'st Mark Iniquities*
                                (from "Eli")
                                Cantabile 3/4   (Eb2-Eb4)   M-MH   Med. diff.

Sustained.

1356. Dvorak, Anton	*I Was Not Deceived*			
(1841-1904) Bohem.	(from "Saint Ludmila")			
	Poco adagio 2/4	(F#2-D4)	L-MH	Med. diff.

1357. Handel, George F.	*Arm, Ye Brave!*			
(1685-1759) Ger./Eng.	(from "Judas Maccabaeus")			
	Allegro 4/4	(B2-E4)	MH	Med. diff.
	Energetic; some agility required.			

1358.	*But Who May Abide*			
	(from "Messiah")			
	Various tempo 4/4, 3/8	(G2-E4)	MH	Mod. diff.
	Sustained sections; animated sections requiring agility.			

1359.	*His Sceptre Is the Rod of Righteousness*			
	(from "Occasional Oratorio")			
	Allegro moderato 4/4	(F#2-E4)	M-H	Diff.
	Requires agility.			

1360.	*Honor and Arms*			
	(from "Samson")			
	Allegro 4/4	(G2-Eb4)	M-H	Mod. diff.
	Agility required.			

1361.	*Why Do the Nations*			
	(from "Messiah")			
	Allegro 4/4	(B2-E4)	M-H	Diff.
	Requires considerable agility and vocal energy.			

1362.	*With Pious Hearts*			
	(from "Judas Maccabaeus")			
	Larghetto 3/4	(G2-Eb4)	MH	Med. diff.
	Sustained.			

1363. Haydn, Joseph	*With Joy th' Impatient Husbandman*			
(1732-1809) Austrian	(from "The Seasons")			
	Allegretto 2/4	(Bb2-E4)	M-H	Mod. diff.
	Agility required.			

1364.	*Behold, Along the Dewy Grass*			
	(from "The Seasons")			
	Allegro 4/4	(G2-F4)	MH	Mod. diff.
	Agility required; large leaps.			

1365.	*Rolling in Foaming Billows*			
	(from "The Creation")			
	Allegro 4/4	(G2-F4)	M-H	Mod. diff.
	Energetic section; flowing legato section.			

1366. Liszt, Franz   *Through the Mist of the Valley*
      (1811-1886) Hung.   (from "St. Elizabeth")
                            Allegro con brio 3/4   (C3-F4)   H   Mod. diff.
                            Energetic.

1367. MacKenzie, A.   *Unto My Charger*
      (1847-1935) Scottish (from "The Rose of Sharon")
                            Allegro 4/4   (A2-Gb4)   H   Mod. diff.
                            Energetic.

1368. Massenet, Jules   *Judas*
      (1842-1912) Fr.   (from "Mary Magdalen")
                            Allegro 3/4   (G2-E4)   M-H   Med. diff.
                            Energetic.

1369. Mendelssohn, Felix   *Lord God of Abraham*
      (1809-1847) Ger.   (from "Elijah")
                            Adagio 4/4   (Bb2-Eb4)   MH   Med. diff.
                            Sustained.

1370.   *It Is Enough*
                            (from "Elijah")
                            Adagio/Allegro 3/4, 2/4 (A2-E4)   M-H   Mod. diff.
                            Sustained section; animated section.

1371.   *O God, Have Mercy*
                            (from "St. Paul")
                            Various tempo 4/4   (B2-D4)   MH   Med. diff.
                            Sustained sections; animated sections.

1372. Molique, G.   *Lead Me, O Lord*
                            (from "Abraham")
                            Andante 4/4   (D3-E4)   M-H   Med. diff.
                            Sustained.

1373. Rossini, Gioachino   *Lord Preserve Me Uncomplaining*
      (1792-1868) It.   (from "Stabat Mater")(Eng./Lat.)
                            Allegretto 3/4   (A2-E4)   M-H   Mod. diff.
                            Agility required.

1374. Rubinstein, Anton   *From My Soul's Depths*
      (1829-1894) Russ.   (from "Paradise Lost")
                            Allegro 3/4   (A2-D4)   MH   Med. diff.
                            Requires agility.

1375. Spohr, Ludwig   *Oh What Is Man*
      (1784-1859) Ger.   (from "Fall of Babylon")
                            Allegro moderato 4/4   (Db3-E4)   MH   Med. diff.

1376.   *Tears of Sorrow, Pain and Anguish*

	(from "Calvary")			
	Larghetto con moto 4/4	(Bb2-C4)	M	Med. diff.
	Sustained.			

1377. Sullivan, Sir Arthur *When the Son of Man*
(1842-1900) Eng.   (from "Light of the World")
Various tempo 4/4   (C3-E4)   M-H   Mod. diff.
Sustained sections; animated sections.

1378. Verdi, Giuseppe   *From the Accursed*
(1813-1901) It.   (from "Requiem")(Eng./Lat.)
Andante 4/4   (A2-E4)   M-H   Diff.
Sustained and vocally demanding.

CHAPTER X

SACRED SONGS

This chapter contains a sampling of those religious, inspirational, and Christmas songs of the type most often presented at churches of various denominations. Though not always of the highest caliber, the songs listed here will give the student a resource for selecting sacred sheet music that has more general appeal. Also included at the end of this chapter is one anthology of sacred songs. Generally not included in this chapter are songs and arias from cantatas and oratorios. (see the previous chapter.)

INDIVIDUAL SELECTIONS

1379. Adam, A.	*O Holy Night*			Schirmer
	Andante 12/8	(A2-D4(F4))	MH	Med. diff.
	A popular Christmas song.			
1380. Adams, S.	*The Holy City*			B & H
	Andante 4/4	(C3-E4)	MH	Med. diff.
	A favorite.			
1381. Allitson, F.	*The Lord Is My Light*			Schirmer
	Allegro 4/4	(A2-Eb4)	M-MH	Mod. diff.
	Exuberant; demands a mature sound.			
1382. Bach, J. S.	*If Thou Be Near* (Eng./Ger.)			Schirmer
	Lento 3/4	(A2-Eb4)	M-MH	Med. diff.
	Sustained.			
1383.	*Hallelujah*			Paterson
	Allegro 4/4	(A2-D4)	M-MH	Mod. diff.
	Agility required; from "Cantata 29."			
1384.	*Jesus, Shepherd, Be Thou Near Me*			Concordia
	Andante	(Bb2-Db4)	M-MH	Med. diff.
	General and wedding; sustained; setting of "Sheep May Safely Graze."			
1385. Banks, H.	*O Brother Man*			H. W. Gray
	Andante 4/4	(F2-C4)	ML-M	Mod. easy.
	Expressive; sustained.			
1386. Bitgood, R.	*Be Still and Know That I Am God*			H. W. Gray
	Andante 2/2	(B2-D4)	M-MH	Mod. easy
	Dramatically varied.			
1387. Brahe, M.	*Bless This House*			B & H
	Moderato 4/4	(A2-Eb4)	M-MH	Mod. easy
	Popular old favorite; sustained.			

1388. Burleigh, H.   *Deep River*   Belwin
                            Slow 4/4   (G2-E4)   ML-MH   Med. diff.
                            Favorite spiritual; one important high E4.

1389.   *Nobody Knows the Trouble I've Seen*   Belwin
                            Slow 4/4   (C3-C4)   M-MH   Mod. easy
                            Good for beginners; spiritual.

1390.   *Sometimes I Feel Like a Motherless Child*   Belwin
                            Slow 2/4   (A2-A3)   ML   Mod. easy
                            Good for beginners; spiritual.

1391.   *Were You There?*   Belwin
                            Slow 4/4   (Bb2-Eb4) M-MH   Mod. easy
                            Sustained; a favorite spiritual.

1392. Calder, L.   *God Is My Salvation*   Galaxy
                            Larghetto 4/4   (C3-D4)   M-MH   Mod. easy
                            Sustained.

1393. Clarke, R.   *The Blind Ploughman*   Chappel
                            Moderato 4/4   (C3-D4)   M-MH   Mod. easy
                            A favorite; effective climax.

1394. Dawson, W.   *There Is a Balm in Gilead*   Music Press
                            Slow 4/4   (C3-C4)   M-MH   Mod. easy
                            Familiar spiritual.

1395. Dvorak, A.   *God Is My Shepherd*   C. Fischer
                            Andante 4/4   (B2-C#4)   M-MH   Mod. easy
                            Sustained; see "Biblical Songs" in Chapter Six for additional
                            selections.

1396. Edmunds, J.   *Jesus, Jesus, Rest Your Head*   Row
                            Andante 2/4   (G2-C4)   M   Mod. easy
                            An American Christmas folk song arrangement.

1397. Franck, C.   *O Lord Most Holy* (Panis Angelicus)   C. Fischer
                            Moderato 4/4   (Db3-Bb3) M   Mod. easy
                            Narrow range; sustained.

1398. Freudenthal, J.   *The Earth Is the Lord's*   Transcontinental
                            Majestic 4/4   (B2-D4)   M-MH   Mod. easy

1399. Harker, F.   *How Beautiful upon the Mountains*   Schirmer
                            Moderato 4/4   (Bb2-Eb4) M-MH   Mod. easy
                            Requires a mature sound for this old favorite.

1400. Hazelhurst, C.   *O Leave Your Sheep*   B & H
                            Allegro 2/2   (Bb2-Eb4) M-MH   Med. diff.

Flowing legato line; Christmas song.

1401. Johnson, H.   *Ride On, King Jesus*   C. Fischer
                        Alla marcia 4/4   (Ab2-F4)   M-H   Mod. diff.
                        Exuberant with excellent climax; spiritual.

1402. LaForge, F.   *Before the Crucifix*   Schirmer
                        Slow 4/4   (Bb2-Eb4)   M-MH   Mod. easy
                        Effective climax.

1403. Liddle, S.   *How Lovely Are Thy Dwellings*   B & H
                        Andante 4/4   (Bb2-Eb4)   M-MH   Mod. easy
                        Popular old favorite; dramatic moments.

1404.   *The Lord Is My Shepherd*   B & H
                        Moving 3/4   (B2-C4)   M   Mod. easy
                        Mature sound for this favorite.

1405. MacDermid, J.   *God So Loved the World*   Forster
                        Allegro 4/4   (Bb2-Eb4)   M-MH   Mod. easy
                        Dramatic sections.

1406. MacGimsey, R.   *Sweet Little Jesus Boy*   C. Fischer
                        Slowly 4/4   (D3-D4)   M   Med. diff.
                        Rather unique and appealing Christmas song in recitative
                        style.

1407. Malotte, A.   *The Beatitudes*   Schirmer
                        Adagio 6/8   (C3-Eb4)   M-MH   Mod. easy
                        Sustained; effective climax.

1408.   *The Lord's Prayer*   Schirmer
                        Slow 4/4   (G2-D4)   ML-MH   Med. diff.
                        Very sustained; old favorite.

1409.   *The Twenty-Third Psalm*   Schirmer
                        Slow 3/4   (Bb2-Eb4)   M-MH   Med. diff.
                        Dramatically variable; interpretively somewhat demanding.

1410. Mendelssohn, F.   *Lord God of Abraham*   Schirmer
                        Andante 4/4   (Bb2-Eb4)   M-MH   Mod. diff.
                        Sustained and commanding; strong opening phrase
                        From "Elijah."

1411.   *O God, Have Mercy*   Schirmer
                        (from "St. Paul")
                                             (B2-D4)   M-MH   Med. diff.

1412. Morgan, O.   *At Christmas Tide*   Ashdown
                        Andante 2/4   (Bb2-Db4)   M   Mod. easy

A lyrical Christmas song.

1413. Niles, J. J.

I Wonder As I Wander   Schirmer
Moderato 6/8   (Bb2-D4)   M   Mod. easy
Appalachian folk song for Christmas or Easter.

1414.

Jesus, Jesus, Rest Your Head   Schirmer
Moderato 2/4   (A2-D4)   M-MH   Mod. easy
Kentucky folk song suitable for Christmas.

1415. O'Hara, G.

Art Thou the Christ   Schirmer
Moderately 4/4   (A2-D4)   M-MH   Mod. easy
Sustained.

1416.

Come to the Stable with Jesus   Schirmer
Moderate 3/4   (B2-C4)   M   Mod. easy
Sentimental Christmas song.

1417.

I Walked Today Where Jesus Walked   Schirmer
Moderato 4/4   (G#2-C4)   M   Mod. easy
Sentimental favorite.

1418. Owen, W.

Laudamus   Boston
Moderato 3/4   (Ab2-D4)   M-MH   Med. diff.
A Welsh melody; song of adoration.

1419. Peeters, F.

The Lord's Prayer   Peters
Adagio 3/2   (C3-D4)   MH   Med. diff.
Sustained; refined setting.

1420.

Wedding Song   Peters
Andante 2/2   (C3-E4)   MH   Med. diff.
Song of Ruth.

1421. Purcell, H.

An Evening Hymn   Novello
Moderato 3/2   (Bb2-Eb4)   M-MH   Mod. diff.
More demanding.

1422. Quilter, R.

An Old Carol   B & H
Andante 2/4   (C3-D4)   M-MH   Mod. easy
A peaceful Christmas song with 15th-century text.

1423. Rogers, J.

Great Peace Have They   Schirmer
Moderato 4/4   (Bb2-C4)   M-MH   Med. diff.
Mature sound; dramatic in places.

1424. Sanderson, W.

Green Pastures   B & H
Moderato 3/4   (Bb2-Eb4)   MH   Mod. easy
Old favorite.

1425. Schubert, F.   *Ave Maria*   C. Fischer
                             Slow   (D3-D4)   MH   Med. diff.
                             Sustained with some rhythmic difficulties.

1426. Schütz, H.   *Wedding Song*   Chantry
                             Slowly   (D3-D4)   MH   Mod. diff.
                             Baroque style period.

1427. Scott, J.   *Come Ye Blessed*   Schirmer
                             Moderato 3/4   (Bb2-Eb4)   M-MH   Mod. easy
                             Ardent, flowing line; popular.

1428. Speaks, O.   *Thou Wilt Keep Him in Perfect Peace*   Schirmer
                             Andante 4/4   (B2-D4)   M-MH   Mod. easy
                             Legato flowing line; dramatic section.

1429. Tchaikovsky, P. I.   *Pilgrim's Song*   Schirmer
                             Andante 4/4   (A2-D4)   M-MH   Med. diff.
                             Sustained; melodious; effective climax.

1430. Thiman, E.   *The God of Love My Shepherd Is*   Novello
                             Allegretto 3/4   (Ab2-Db4)   M-MH   Med. diff.
                             Flowing legato line.

1431.   *Jesus the Very Thought of Thee*   Novello
                             Moderato 3/2   (Bb2-D4)   M-MH   Mod. easy
                             Expressive legato line.

1432.   *Thou Wilt Keep Him in Perfect Peace*   Gray
                             Andante 5/4   (Bb2-Eb4)   M-MH   Med. diff.
                             Meter is unusual but not complex.

1433. Van de Water, B.   *The Publican*   Presser
                             Maestoso 4/4   (C3(G2)-E4) M-H   Mod. diff.
                             Requires a mature sound; strong climax.

1434. Williams, D.   *Jesus the Very Thought of Thee*   J. Fischer
                             Moderato 6/8   (A2-E4)   M-H   Mod. easy
                             Flowing legato line.

1435.   *A Wedding Prayer*   Gray
                             Andante   (C3-D4)   M-MH   Mod. easy
                             Tastefully written.

1436. Work, J.   *Go Tell It on the Mountain*   Galaxy
                             Moderato 4/4   (C3-D4)   MH   Mod. easy
                             Traditional spiritual for Christmas.

SACRED SONGS
Volume IV
For Bass
Edited by W. J. Henderson
Published by John Church

Although many of the songs in this anthology are more suited for baritone voice sufficient songs
appropriate for bass are contained here to warrant the book's inclusion.

1437. Abt, Franz   *Far O'er the Stars There Is Rest* (Eng./Ger.)
      (1819-1885) Ger.   Andante 3/4   (C3-Db4)   MH   Med. diff.
                          Sustained.

1438. Adam, Adolphe   *Christmas Song* (Eng./Fr.)
      (1803-1856) Fr.   Andante 4/4   (C3-E4)   M-H   Med. diff.
                          Sustained.

1439. Adams, Stephen   *The Pilgrim* (Eng.)
      (1844-1913) Eng.   Andante 4/4   (C3-E4)   M-H   Med. diff.
                          Sustained.

1440. Barri, Odoardo   *Come unto Me* (Eng.)
      (1844-1920) Irish   Moderato 4/4   (B2-E4)   MH   Med. diff.
                          Sustained.

1441.   *The Good Shepherd* (Eng.)
                          Various tempo & meter (A2-D4)   M-MH   Med. diff.
                          Sustained.

1442. Beethoven, L. van   *Nature's Adoration* (Eng.)
      (1770-1827) Ger.   Andante 2/2   (Ab2-Eb4)   MH   Med. diff.
                          Sustained.

1443. Benedict, Julius   *He Giveth His Beloved Sheep* (Eng.)
      (1804-1885) Ger./Eng. Andante 4/4   (C3-D4)   MH   Med. diff.
                          Sustained.

1444. Bizet, Georges   *O Lamb of God* (Eng./Fr.)
      (1838-1875) Fr.   Allegro moderato 4/4 (B2-G4)   H-VH   Med. diff.
                          Energetic.

1445. Blumenthal, J.   *Life* (Eng.)
      (1829-1908) Ger.   Allegro/Lento 4/4   (G2-D4)   M-MH   Med. diff.
                          Sustained.

1446. Brandts-Buys, J.   *The Remorse of Peter* (Eng./Ger.)
      (1868-1933) Neth.   Various tempo & meter (B2-F4)   H   Med. diff.
                          Energetic.

1447. Costa, Michael   *David's Prayer* (Eng.)
      (1808-1884) It./Eng. Larghetto 2/4   (D3-E4)   M-H   Med. diff.

Sustained.

1448. Coward, J. M.   *Weary of Earth* (Eng.)
      (1824-1880) Eng.   Andante 4/4   (Ab2-Eb4)   M-MH   Med. diff.
                            Sustained.

1449. Cowen, Frederic   *The Pilgrims* (Eng.)
      (1852-1935) Eng.   Moderato 4/4   (A2-D4)   M-MH   Med. diff.
                            Sustained.

1450.   *The Watchman and the Child* (Eng.)
                            Moderato 4/4   (A2-E4)   MH   Med. diff.
                            Sustained.

1451.   *With Thee There Is Forgiveness*
                            Andante 2/4   (A2-F4)   H   Med. diff.
                            Sustained.

1452. Dvorak, Antonin   *Come unto Me* (Eng./Ger.)
      (1841-1904) Bohem.   Andante 3/4   (C#3-D4)   M-MH   Med. diff.
                            Sustained.

1453. Faure, Jean   *The Palms* (Eng./Fr.)
      (1830-1914) Fr.   Andante 2/2   (C3-Eb4)   MH   Med. diff
                            Sustained.

1454. Gounod, Charles   *Adore and Quiet Be* (Eng./Fr.)
      (1818-1893) Fr.   Adagio/Andante 4/4   (D3-F4)   H   Med. diff.
                            Sustained.

1455.   *Forever with the Lord* (Eng.)
                            Moderato 4/4   (C3-D4)   MH   Med. diff.
                            Sustained.

1456.   *Jerusalem* (Eng./Fr.)
                            Andante 4/4   (C3-F4)   M-H   Med. diff.
                            Sustained.

1457.   *Nazareth* (Eng.)
                            Moderato 6/4   (G2-C#4)   M   Med. diff.
                            Sustained.

1458.   *Power and Love* (Eng.)
                            Moderato 4/4   (C3-D4)   MH   Med. diff.
                            Sustained.

1459.   *The King of Love My Shepherd Is* (Eng.)
                            Moderato 4/4   (B2-D4)   MH   Med. diff.
                            Sustained.

1460. Gray, Hamilton   *The Golden Pathway* (Eng.)
                               Andante 4/4   (B2-D4)   MH   Med. diff.
                               Sustained.

1461.   *The Heavenly Song* (Eng.)
                               Andante 4/4   (B2-D4)   M-H   Med. diff.
                               Sustained.

1462. Handel, G. F.   *Lord Remember Me in My Trouble* (Eng.)
      (1685-1759) Ger./Eng.   Larghetto 3/4   (C#3-E4)   M-H   Med. diff.
                               Sustained.

1463. Haydn, F. J.   *O Thou Who Dryest the Mourner's Tears* (Eng.)
      (1732-1809) Austrian   Larghetto 4/4   (D3-E4)   M-H   Med. diff.
                               Sustained.

1464. Hiller, Ferdinand   *Lord of My Inmost Heart's Recesses* (Eng./Ger.)
      (1811-1885) Ger.   Moderato 2/4   (B2-D4)   M   Med. diff.
                               Sustained.

1465. Himmel, F. H.   *Battle Prayer* (Eng.)
      (1765-1814) Ger.   Slow 4/4   (A2(D2)-D4) M-MH   Mod. easy
                               Strophic song.

1466. Jude, W. H.   *Behold I Stand at the Door* (Eng.)
                               Moderato 3/4   (A2-D4)   M-MH   Med. diff.
                               Sustained.

1467. Leslie, Henry   *Come unto Him* (Eng.)
      (1822-1896) Eng.   Cantabile 6/8   (C3-D4)   MH   Med. diff.
                               Sustained.

1468. Liszt, Franz   *Peace* (Eng.)
      (1811-1886) Hung.   Lento 4/4   (B2-D4)   MH   Med. diff.
                               Sustained.

1469. Mariani, Angelo   *Invocation* (Eng./It.)
      (1822-1873) It.   Andante grave 4/4   (A2-Eb4)   M-H   Med. diff.
                               Sustained.

1470. Mendelssohn, F.   *Lord at All Times I Will Bless Thee* (Eng.)
      (1809-1847) Ger.   Andante 3/4   (B2-E4)   MH   Med. diff.
                               Sustained.

1471. Molique, W. B.   *Commit Thy Ways unto the Lord* (Eng./Ger.)
      (1802-1869) Ger.   Andante con moto 2/4 (F3-F4)   H   Med. diff.
                               Flowing legato.

1472. Mozart, W. A.   *Jesu, Word of God Incarnate* (Eng./Lat.)
      (1756-1791) Austrian   Largo 4/4   (D3-E4)   M-H   Med. diff.

Sustained.

1473. Parker, Henry   *Jerusalem* (Eng.)
      (1867-1934) Am.   Various tempo & meter (Bb2-Db4)   M-MH   Med. diff.
                               Sustained.

1474.   *Where the Wicked Cease from Troubling* (Eng.)
                               Andante 4/4   (B2-E4)   H   Med. diff.
                               Sustained.

1475. Pergolesi, G.   *O Lord Have Mercy* (Eng.)
      (1710-1736) It.   Largo/Allegretto 4/4, 3/8 (Bb2-F4) M-H   Med. diff.
                               Some agility required.

1476. Piccolomini, Maria   *Ecce Homo* (Eng.)
      (1834-1899) It.   Various tempo 4/4   (A2-D4)   M-MH   Med. diff.
                               Largely sustained.

1477.   *Pardoned* (Eng.)
                               Various tempo 4/4   (C3-Eb4)   M-H   Med. diff.
                               Largely sustained.

1478. Pinsuti, Ciro   *Lead, Kindly Light* (Eng.)
      (1829-1888) It.   Larghetto 2/4   (A2-D4)   M   Med. diff.
                               Sustained.

1479.   *The Land Beyond* (Eng.)
                               Andante 3/4   (D3-Eb4)   MH   Med. diff.
                               Sustained.

1480. Rodney, Paul   *Calvary* (Eng.)
                               Various tempo & meter (A2-C#4)   M   Med. diff.
                               Sustained.

1481.   *Emmanuel* (Eng.)
                               Various tempo & meter (Bb2-Db4)   M-MH   Med. diff.
                               Sustained.

1482.   *Sion* (Eng.)
                               Andantino 4/4   (Bb2-Eb4) MH   Med. diff.
                               Sustained.

1483. Roeckel, Joseph   *Arise, He Calleth Thee* (Eng.)
      (1838-1923) Eng.   Andantino 6/8   (Eb3-Eb4) H   Med. diff.
                               Sustained.

1484.   *Thou Art the Way* (Eng.)
                               Andante 4/4   (Bb2-Eb4) MH   Med. diff.
                               Sustained.

1485. Rossini, Gioachino   *In Memoriam* (Eng.)
     (1792-1868) It.   Andante 3/4   (A2-C4)   M   Med. diff.
      Sustained.

1486. Schubert, Franz   *Litany for the Feast of All Souls* (Eng./Ger.)
     (1797-1828) Austrian   Andante 4/4   (Bb2-Db4) M-MH Med. diff.
      Sustained.

1487. St. Saëns, Camille   *Father in Heaven* (Eng./Lat.)
     (1835-1921) Fr.   Andantino 2/4   (Bb2-Db4) MH   Med. diff.
      Flowing legato.

1488. Sullivan, Arthur   *Lead, Kindly Light*
     (1842-1900) Eng.   Moderato 4/4   (C3-Eb4) MH   Med. diff.
      Sustained.

1489. Tosti, Paolo   *When with Doubting and Dreading* (Eng./It.)
     (1846-1916) It.   Moderato 4/4   (C3-E4) MH   Med. diff.
      Sustained.

1490. Tours, Berthold   *The Gate of Heaven* (Eng.)
     (1838-1897) Dutch   Andante 6/8   (C3-Eb4) H   Med. diff.
      Sustained.

1491.   *The New Kingdom* (Eng.)
      Andante 4/4   (Bb2-D4) M-MH Med. diff.
      Sustained.

1492. Watson, Michael   *Babylon* (Eng.)
      Andante 4/4   (Bb2-Eb4) M-H   Med. diff.
      Sustained.

CHAPTER XI

MUSICAL THEATRE ANTHOLOGIES

Many songs for young basses are appropiate in the musical theatre repertory. Presented here are three of the more available musical theatre anthologies.

BROADWAY REPERTOIRE
For Baritone/Bass
Published by Hal Leonard

Most of the songs contained in this volume are from well-known musical productions.

1493. Gershwin, George   *I Got Plenty o' Nuttin'* (from "Porgy and Bess")
                                      Moderato 2/2   (B2-D4)   MH   Mod. diff.
                                        Operatic in voice production; dramatic ending.

1494. Kern, Jerome   *Ol' Man River* (from "Showboat")
                                        Moderato 4/4   (G2-E4)   L-H   Med. diff.
                                        Requires mature tone with command of low and high notes.

1495. Lane, Burton   *On a Clear Day* (from "On a Clear Day You Can See Forever")
                                        Moderato 2/2   (B2-E4)   MH   Mod. easy
                                        Flowing and lyrical.

1496. Loewe, Frederick   *If Ever I Would Leave You* (from "Camelot")
                                        Moderato 4/4   (Ab2-D4)   M-MH   Mod. easy
                                        Sustained with big climax.

1497.   *I've Grown Accustomed to Her Face* (from "My Fair Lady")
                                        Moderato 4/4   (A2-B3)   M   Mod. easy
                                        Speech like voice production; reflective love song.

1498.   *They Call the Wind Maria* (from "Paint Your Wagon")
                                        Moderato 2/2   (C3-E4)   MH-H   Mod. easy
                                        Sustained, dreamy song.

1499. Rodgers, Richard   *Lonely Room* (from "Oklahoma")
                                        Moderato 4/4   (D3-C#4)   M   Mod. easy
                                        Dreamy narrative.

1500.   *Some Enchanted Evening* (from "South Pacific")
                                        Moderato 4/4   (C3-E4)   M-MH   Mod. easy
                                        Sustained love song

1501. Rosenthal, L.   *Imagine That* (from "Sherry")
                                        Slow 2/2   (Bb2-Db4)   M-MH   Mod. easy

Presents few problems.

1502. Schmidt, Harvey   *Gonna Be Another Hot Day*
                                (from "110 in the Shade")
                                Slow 4/4   (D3-F#4)   MH-VH   Mod. easy
                                For baritone.

1503.   *My Cup Runneth Over* (from "I Do, I Do")
                                Andante 3/4   (G2-C4)   ML-M   Mod. easy
                                Narrative; lyric love song.

1504.   *Soon It's Gonna Rain* (from "The Fantasticks")
                                Moderato 4/4   (B2-D4)   M-MH   Mod. easy
                                Relaxed, crooning love song.

1505. Sondheim, Stephen   *Everybody Says Don't* (from "Side by Side")
                                Allegro moderato 4/4   (G2-E4)   ML-H   Mod. diff.
                                Demanding patter and sustained high tessitura in places;
                                effective piece.

1506. Styne, Jules   *Just in Time* (from "Bells Are Ringing")
                                Andante 2/2   (C#3-D4)   M-MH   Mod. easy
                                Lyric love song.

1507. Weill, Kurt   *Lost in the Stars* (from "Lost in the Stars")
                                Andante espressivo 4/4 (Ab2-D4)   M-MH   Med. diff.
                                Narrative with dramatic moments.

MUSICAL THEATRE CLASSICS
For Baritone/Bass
With Cassette
Published by Hal Leonard

This anthology of musical theatre classics comes with a cassette of piano accompaniments.

1508. Kern, Jerome   *Ol' Man River* (from "Showboat")
                                Moderato 4/4   (G2-E4)   L-H   Med. diff.
                                Requires mature tone with command of low and high notes.

1509. Lane, Burton   *On a Clear Day* (from "On a Clear Day You Can See
                                Forever")
                                Moderato 2/2   (B2-E4)   MH   Mod. easy
                                Flowing and lyrical.

1510. Loewe, Frederick   *C'est Moi* (from "Camelot")
                                Moderato 2/2   (C3-D4)   MH   Mod. easy
                                Vigorous; energetic.

1511.   *If Ever I Would Leave You* (from "Camelot")

Moderato 4/4   (Ab2-D4)   M-MH   Mod. easy
Sustained with big climax.

1512. Rodgers, Richard   *Do I Love You Because You're Beautiful?*
                             (from "Cinderella")
                             Moderato 2/2   (E3-E4)   H   Mod. easy
                             More appropriate for baritone.

1513.   *If I Loved You* (from "Carousel")
                             Moderato 4/4   (Db3-Gb4)   H   Mod. easy
                             More suited to baritone.

1514.   *Oh, What a Beautiful Mornin'* (from "Oklahoma")
                             Allegretto 3/4   (D3-E4)   M-H   Mod. easy
                             More suited to baritone.

1515.   *Some Enchanted Evening* (from "South Pacific")
                             Moderato 4/4   (C3-E4)   M-MH   Mod. easy
                             Sustained love song.

1516. Schmidt, Harvey   *Try to Remember* (from "The Fantasticks")
                             Moderato 3/4   (A2-C4)   ML-MH   Mod. easy
                             Flowing melodic line.

1517. Sondheim, Stephen   *Sorry-Grateful* (from "Company")
                             Andante 6/4, 4/4   (B2-E4)   M-H   Med. diff.
                             Rhythmically tricky.

THE SINGER'S MUSICAL THEATRE ANTHOLOGY
For Baritone/Bass
Published by Hal Leonard

This anthology of musical theatre is the most comprehensive volume available.
1518. Geld, Gary   *I've Heard It All Before* (from "Shenandoah")
                             Allegro 6/4   (D3-E4)   H   Med. diff.
                             More appropriate for baritone.

1519.   *Meditation I* (from "Shenandoah")
                             Moderato 2/2   (Bb2-F4)   H   Med. diff.
                             For baritone.

1520.   *Meditation II* (from "Shenandoah")
                             Various tempo & meter (C3-Eb4)   H   Med. diff.
                             More appropriate for baritone.

1521. Gershwin, George   *A Red Headed Woman* (from "Porgy and Bess")
                             Allegretto 4/4, 2/4 (D3-F4)   H   Mod. diff.
                             For baritone.

1522.   *I Got Plenty o' Nuttin'* (from "Porgy and Bess")
                              Moderato 2/2   (B2-D4)   MH   Mod. diff.
                              Operatic voice production; dramatic ending.

1523. Kern, Jerome   *Ol' Man River* (from "Showboat")
                              Moderato 4/4   (G2-E4)   L-H   Med. diff.
                              Requires mature tone with command of low and high notes.

1524. Lane, Burton   *Come Back to Me*
                              (from "On A Clear Day You Can See Forever")
                              Lively 4/4   (D3-E4)   M-H   Med. diff.
                              More appropriate for baritone.

1525.   *On a Clear Day*
                              (from "On a Clear Day You Can See Forever")
                              Moderato 2/2   (B2-E4)   MH   Mod. easy
                              Flowing and lyrical.

1526. Leigh, Mitch   *Dulcinea* (from "Man of La Mancha")
                              Moderately 6/8, 3/4   (B2-E4)   M-H   Med. diff.
                              Somewhat tricky rhythmically.

1527.   *The Impossible Dream* (from "Man of La Mancha")
                              Moderato 9/8   (D3-Eb4)   M-H   Med. diff.
                              Sustained; vocally demanding.

1528.   *The Man of La Mancha* (from "Man of La Mancha")
                              Moderato 3/4   (C3-E4)   M-H   Med. diff.
                              Rhythmical.

1529. Loewe, Frederick   *Camelot* (from "Camelot")
                              Moderato 2/2   (C3-D4)   MH   Mod. easy
                              Speech-like simplicity.

1530.   *C'est Moi* (from "Camelot")
                              Moderato 2/2   (C3-D4)   MH   Mod. easy
                              Vigorous; energetic.

1531.   *How to Handle a Woman* (from "Camelot")
                              Moderato 4/4   (A2-D4)   MH   Mod. easy
                              Speech-like simplicity.

1532.   *If Ever I Would Leave You* (from "Camelot")
                              Moderato 4/4   (Ab2-D4)   M-MH   Mod. easy
                              Sustained with big climax.

1533.   *I Still See Elisa* (from "Paint Your Wagon")
                              Lento espressivo 3/4 (G2-C4)   ML-MH   Mod. easy
                              Flowing melodic line.

1534.		*They Call the Wind Maria* (from "Paint Your Wagon") Moderato 2/2 (C3-E4) MH-H Mod. easy Sustained, dreamy song.

1535.		*Wand'rin' Star* (from "Paint Your Wagon") Moderato 4/4 (Eb3-Eb4) MH Med. diff. Rhythmical.

1536.	Porter, Cole	*Were Thine That Special Face* (from "Kiss Me, Kate") Andantino 2/2 (C3-F4) M-H Mod. easy More appropriate for baritone.

1537.		*Where Is the Life That Late I Led?* (from "Kiss Me, Kate") Allegro con fuoco 6/8 (B2-F4) M-H Med. diff. More appropriate for baritone.

1538.	Rodgers, Richard	*Do I Love You Because You're Beautiful?* (from "Cinderella") Moderato 2/2 (E3-E4) H Mod. easy More appropriate for baritone.

1539.		*If I Loved You* (from "Carousel") Moderato 4/4 (Db3-Gb4) H Mod. easy More appropriate for baritone.

1540.		*Lonely Room* (from "Oklahoma") Moderato 4/4 (D3-C#4) M Mod. easy Dreamy narrative.

1541.		*Oh, What a Beautiful Mornin'* (from "Oklahoma") Allegretto 3/4 (D3-E4) M-H Mod. easy More appropriate for baritone.

1542.		*Soliloquy* (from "Carousel") Varied tempo & meter (B2-G4) M-VH Med. diff. Monologue for baritone.

1543.		*Some Enchanted Evening* (from "South Pacific") Moderato 4/4 (C3-E4) M-MH Med. diff. Sustained love song.

1544.		*This Nearly Was Mine* (from "South Pacific") Tempo di Waltz 3/4 (B2-D4) M-MH Mod. easy Flowing melodic line; warm full sound.

1545.	Schmidt, Harvey	*Try to Remember* (from "The Fantasticks") Moderato 3/4 (A2-C4) ML-MH Mod. easy

Flowing melodic line.

1546. Sondheim, Stephen   *Everybody Says Don't*
(from "Anyone Can Whistle")
Allegro 4/4, 2/4   (G2-E4)   L-MH   Med. diff.
Rhythmic; energetic.

1547.   *Johanna* (from "Sweeney Todd")
Slowly 4/4   (C3-Eb4)   M-H   Med. diff.
More appropriate for baritone.

1548.   *Sorry-Grateful* (from "Company")
Andante 6/4, 4/4   (B2-E4)   M-H   Med. diff.
Rhythmically tricky.

1549.   *The Road You Didn't Take* (from "Follies")
Allegro moderato 3/4   (A2-E4)   ML-MH   Med. diff.
Rhythmically tricky.

1550. Weill, Kurt   *Lost in the Stars* (from "Lost in the Stars")
Andante espressivo 4/4 (Ab2-D4)   M-MH   Med. diff.
Narrative with dramatic moments.

1551.   *Mack the Knife* (from "The Threepenny Opera")
Moderato 2/2   (D3-D4)   MH   Mod. easy
Rhythmical.

1552.   *September Song* (from "Knickerbocker Holiday")
Moderato assai 4/4   (C3-Eb4)   M-H   Med. diff.
Presents few problems.

1553.   *This Is the Life* (from "Love Life")
Allegro assai 4/4   (A2-Eb4)   ML-H   Mod. diff.
Some demands musically and interpretively.

1554.   *Thousands of Miles* (from "Lost in the Stars")
Moderato assai 2/2   (A2-C4)   M   Med. diff.
Smooth flowing line.

CHAPTER XII

SONG ANTHOLOGIES OF SPIRITUALS, RUSSIAN FOLK SONGS, AND SEA SHANTIES

Burleigh, Harry (arr.)   *The Spirituals of Harry T. Burleigh*   Belwin
(1866-1949) Am.

This is an important collection of spirituals arranged by a champion of the genre. Many of the songs are suitable for bass and present few problems. Also of interest but not included here is the out-of-print "Seventy Negro Spirituals" for low voice edited by William A. Fisher and published by Oliver Ditson with arrangements by Boatner, Johnson, Robinson, and others in ranges suitable for bass.

1555.	*Ain't Goin' to Study War No Mo'*			
	Lento 4/4	(Eb3-Db4)	MH	Mod. easy
1556.	*Balm in Gilead*			
	Andante 4/4	(G3-D4)	MH-H	Mod. easy
1557.	*Behold That Star*			
	Andante 4/4	(B2-E4)	MH-H	Mod. easy
1558.	*By an' By*			
	Andante 4/4	(C3-D4)	MH-H	Mod. easy
1559.	*Couldn't Hear Nobody Pray*			
	Andante 4/4	(Bb2-Db4)	M-MH	Mod. easy
1560.	*De Blin' Man Stood on de Road an' Cried*			
	Lento 4/4	(Db3-Db4)	MH	Mod. easy
1561.	*De Gospel Train*			
	Moderato 2/4	(Bb2-C4)	MH	Mod. easy
1562.	*Deep River*			
	Lento 4/4	(G2-E4)	L-MH	Med. diff.
1563.	*Didn't My Lord Deliver Daniel*			
	Andante 4/8	(F3-D4)	MH-H	Med. diff.
1564.	*Don't Be Weary Traveler*			
	Andante 2/2	(A#2-D4)	M-MH	Mod. easy
1565.	*Don't You Weep When I'm Gone*			
	Andante 4/4	(Fb3-Eb4)	H	Mod. easy

1566.	*Ev'ry Time I Feel the Spirit*			
	Slowly 4/4	(B2-D4)	M-MH	Mod. easy
1567.	*Give Me Jesus*			
	Andante 2/2	(C3-E4)	MH	Mod. easy
1568.	*Go Down in the Lonesome Valley*			
	Poco adagio 4/4	(G2-C4)	ML-M	Mod. easy
1569.	*Go Down Moses*			
	Lento 4/4	(D3-D4)	MH	Mod. easy
1570.	*Go Tell It on de Mountains*			
	Slowly 4/4	(D3-E4)	MH-H	Mod. easy
1571.	*Hard Trials*			
	Moderato 2/4	(Eb3-Eb4)	MH	Mod. easy
1572.	*Hear de Lambs A-Cryin'*			
	Andante 4/4	(E3-D4)	MH	Mod. easy
1573.	*Heav'n Heav'n*			
	Joyful 2/4	(Eb3-C4)	MH	Mod. easy
1574.	*He's Just de Same Today*			
	Moderato 4/4	(D3-D4)	M-MH	Mod. easy
1575.	*I Don't Feel No-Ways Tired*			
	Moderato 2/4	(A2-E4)	M-H	Mod. easy
1576.	*I Got a Home in A-Dat Rock*			
	Moderato 4/4	(C3-Eb4)	M-H	Mod. easy
1577.	*I Know de Lord's Laid His Hands on Me*			
	Moderato 4/4	(Bb2-Eb4)	MH	Mod. easy
1578.	*I Stood on de Ribber ob Jerdon*			
	Andante 4/4	(C3-C4)	M-MH	Mod. easy
1579.	*I've Been in de Storm So Long*			
	Moderato 4/4	(D3-D4)	MH	Mod. easy
1580.	*I Want to Be Ready*			
	Andante 2/4	(Bb2-Eb4)	M-MH	Mod. easy
1581.	*John's Gone Down on de Island*			
	Andante 4/4	(Eb3-F4)	MH-H	Med. diff.
1582.	*Joshua Fit de Battle ob Jericho*			
	Allegretto 4/4	(D#3-E4)	M-MH	Mod. easy

1583.	*Let Us Cheer the Weary Traveler*			
	Adagio 4/4	(Db3-F4)	MH-H	Mod. easy
1584.	*Little David Play on Your Harp*			
	Andante 2/4	(C3-D4)	MH	Mod. easy
1585.	*My Lord What a Mornin'*			
	Adagio 4/4	(Db3-Db4)	M-MH	Mod. easy
1586.	*My Way's Cloudy*			
	Lento 4/4	(Db3-Eb4)	MH	Mod. easy
1587.	*Nobody Knows de Trouble I've Seen*			
	Poco adagio 4/4	(C3-C4)	M	Easy
1588.	*Oh Didn't It Rain*			
	Moderato 4/4	(D3-D4)	MH-H	Mod. easy
1589.	*Oh Wasn't Dat a Wide Ribber*			
	Larghetto 2/4	(Eb3-Eb4)	MH	Med. diff.
1590.	*Oh Peter Go Ring dem Bells*			
	Andante 2/4	(C3-F4)	MH-H	Mod. easy
1591.	*O Rocks Don't Fall on Me*			
	Moderato 4/4	(D3-E4)	M-MH	Mod. easy
1592.	*Ride on King Jesus*			
	Maestoso 4/4	(D3-D4)	MH	Med. diff.
1593.	*Sinner Please Doon Let Dis Harves' Pass*			
	Andante 2/4	(E3-E4)	M-H	Mod. easy
1594.	*Sometimes I Feel Like a Motherless Child*			
	Lamentoso 2/4	(A2-A3)	M	Easy
1595.	*Stan' Still Jordan*			
	Lento 4/4	(C3-D4)	M-MH	Med. diff.
1596.	*Steal Away*			
	Adagio 4/4	(F3-D4)	MH	Mod. easy
1597.	*Swing Low, Sweet Chariot*			
	Slow 4/4	(C3-Cb4)	MH	Mod. easy
1598.	*Tis Me O Lord*			
	Moderato 4/4	(Ab3-Eb4)	H	Mod. easy
1599.	*Wade in de Water*			
	Andante 4/4	(A2-F4)	M-H	Med. diff.

1600.	*Weepin' Mary* Andante 4/4	(D3-D4)	M-MH	Mod. easy
1601.	*Were You There* Largo 4/4	(Bb2-Eb4)	M-MH	Mod. easy
1602.	*You May Bury Me in de Eas'* Lento 4/4	(F3-F4)	H	Med. diff.

Rubin, Rose   *A Russian Song Book* (Russ./Eng.)   Dover
Stillman, Michael (arr.)

A number of prominent Russian basses over the years have recorded favorite Russian folk songs and romances. This volume contains many of these popular favourites often in usable keys for bass.

PART I: FOLK SONGS

1603.	*Down the Volga River* Broadly 3/4	(D3-F4)	H	Mod. easy
1604.	*Oh, You Dear Little Night* Slowly 2/4	(D3-D4)	MH	Mod. easy
1605.	*Down Along the Mother Volga* Slowly 4/4	(D3-D4)	M-MH	Mod. easy
1606.	*Dubinushka* Moderately 4/4, 2/2	(D3-D4)	MH	Mod. easy
1607.	*The Slender Mountain Ash* Moderate 3/4	(E3-E4)	H	Mod. easy
1608.	*Farewell to Happiness* Slowly 4/4	(B2-D4)	M	Mod. easy
1609.	*The Little Bell* Calmly 6/8	(B2-E4)	MH	Mod. easy
1610.	*Do Not Scold Me and Do Not Reproach Me* Calmly 2/4	(E3-F4)	H	Mod. easy
1611.	*No Sounds from the City Are Heard* Slowly 4/4	(C3-E4)	MH	Mod. easy
1612.	*My Sweetheart* Not hasty 5/4	(F3-F4)	VH	Mod. easy
1613.	*All Throughout the Great Wide World I Wandered*			

		bounce 2/4	(C3-C4)	M-MH	Mod. easy

With bounce 2/4   (C3-C4)   M-MH   Mod. easy

1614.   *The Story of the Coachman*
               Calmly 4/4   (D3-F4)   H   Mod. easy

1615.   *In the Meadow Stood a Little Birch Tree*
               Moderately fast 4/4, 3/4 (E3-E4)   M-H   Mod. easy

1616.   *The Boundless Expanse of the Sea*
               Calmly 6/8   (E3-E4)   H   Mod. easy

1617.   *The Cliff on the Volga*
               Broadly 3/4, 2/4   (D3-F4)   H   Mod. easy

1618.   *Snow Flurries*
               Moderately 2/4   (B2-E4)   MH   Mod. easy

1619.   *Stenka Razin*
               Calmly 3/4   (B2-C#4)   MH   Mod. easy

1620.   *Troika Rushing*
               Lively 2/4   (B2-E4)   H   Mod. easy

1621.   *Do Not Awaken My Memories*
               Expressively 12/8   (B2-E4)   H   Mod. easy

1622.   *Along the Peterskaya Road*
               Broadly 2/4   (A2-D4)   MH   Mod. easy

1623.   *In the Valley*
               Moderately 6/8   (B2-D4)   MH   Mod. easy

1624.   *The Village on the Road*
               Moderately 6/8   (B2-E4)   M-H   Mod. easy

1625.   *Kalinka* (Little Snowball Bush)
               Slowly, grad. faster 2/4 (D3-D4)   MH   Mod. easy

1626.   *Why Do You Gaze at the Road?*
               Not fast 4/4   (B2-E4)   M-H   Mod. easy

1627.   *Song of the Volga Boatmen*
               Slowly 4/4   (C3-E4)   M-H   Mod. easy

PART II: POPULAR SONGS

1628.   *Moscow Nights*
               Moderately 2/4   (D3-E4)   M-H   Mod. easy

1629.   *Lonely Accordion*

	Waltz tempo 3/4	(B2-D4)	MH	Mod. easy
1630.	*Katiusha* Not fast 2/4	(B2-E4)	M-H	Mod. easy
1631.	*Wait for Me* Moderately 4/4	(B2-E4)	M-H	Mod. easy
1632.	*Silently* Moderately 4/4	(C#3-F4)	H	Mod. easy
1633.	*Dark Is the Night* Not fast 2/2	(A2-C4)	M	Mod. easy
1634.	*Strains of Guitar* (On The River) Calmly 4/4	(D3-D4)	MH	Mod. easy
1635.	*The Light* Moderately 4/4	(D3-F4)	H	Mod. easy
1636.	*Wait for Your Soldier* March tempo 2/4	(D3-F4)	H	Mod. easy
1637.	*Meadowland* March tempo 4/4	(D3-E4)	MH	Mod. easy
1638.	*Regimental Polka* Not fast 2/4	(A2-F4)	H	Mod. easy
1639.	*My Heart* Moderately 4/4	(B2-F#4)	VH	Mod. easy
1640.	*Far Away, Far Away* With movement 6/8	(C3-E4)	H	Mod. easy
1641.	*Should the Volga's Banks Be Flooded* Moderately 4/4	(B2-D4)	MH	Mod. easy
1642.	*Strolling Home* Calmly 2/4	(C3-D4)	MH	Mod. easy
1643.	*Who Knows Why* Slowly 2/4, 3/4	(B2-E4)	M-H	Mod. easy
1644.	*Through the Village* Lively 3/4, 4/4, 2/4	(B2-C#4)	MH	Mod. easy
1645.	*Clouds Have Risen over the City* Moderately 3/4	(D3-F4)	H	Mod. easy

1646.   *Song of Greeting*
                        With movement 2/4 (A2-D4)   M-MH   Mod. easy

         Terry, R. (arr.)   ***The Shanty Book***, Vol. 1 & 2 (Eng.)   Curwen
         (1865-1938) Eng.
The sea shanty is an important category for the bass voice. This collection of sea shanties in two
volumes contains a number of useful songs in the appropriate range and tessitura. The overall
range for the entire two volumes is (Bb2-E4) with the average tessitura of MH. The
arrangements are straightforward with a degree of difficulty being easy to moderately easy.

VOLUME ONE

1647.   *Billy Boy*
1648.   *Blow, My Bully Boys*
1649.   *Blow the Man Down*
1650.   *Boney Was a Warrior*
1651.   *Bound for the Rio Grande*
1652.   *Cheerily Men*
1653.   *Clear the Track, Let the Bullgine Run*
1654.   *The Dead Horse*
1655.   *Goodbye, Fare Ye Well*
1656.   *Good Morning, Ladies All*
1657.   *Hanging Johnny*
1658.   *Haul Away, Joe* (1)
1659.   *Hilo Somebody*
1660.   *The Hog's-Eye Man*
1661.   *Johnny Boker*
1662.   *Johnny Come Down to Hilo*
1663.   *Lowlands Away*
1664.   *Oh, Run, Let the Bullgine Run!*
1665.   *Paddy Doyle's Boots*
1666.   *Reuben Ranzo*
1667.   *Sally Brown*
1668.   *Santy Anna*
1669.   *Shenandoah*
1670.   *Stormalong John*
1671.   *Tom's Gone to Hilo*
1672.   *We'll Haul the Bowlin'*
1673.   *We're All Bound to Go*
1674.   *What Shall We Do with the Drunken Sailor?*
1675.   *Whiskey Johnny*
1676.   *The Wild Goose Shanty*

VOLUME TWO

1677.   *A-Roving* (I)
1678.   *A-Roving* (2)

1679.	*The Banks of Sacramento*
1680.	*The Black Bail Line*
1681.	*Blow Ye Winds of Morning*
1682.	*The Bully Boat*
1683.	*Can't You Dance the Polka?*
1684.	*Do Let Me Go*
1685.	*The Drummer and the Cook*
1686.	*Fire Down Below*
1687.	*Haul Away, Joe* (2)
1688.	*Hilo, John Brown*
1689.	*Hilonday*
1690.	*A Hundred Years Ago*
1691.	*John Brown's Body*
1692.	*Lizer Lee*
1693.	*A Long Time Ago*
1694.	*Miss Lucy Long*
1695.	*My Johnny*
1696.	*My Tommy's Gone Away*
1697.	*O Billy Riley*
1698.	*One More Day*
1699.	*Paddy Works on the Railway*
1700.	*Roll the Cotton Down*
1701.	*The Sailor Likes His Bottle, O*
1702.	*Shallow Brown*
1703.	*The Shaver*
1704.	*Sing Fare You Well*
1705.	*So Handy, Me Gels*
1706.	*Stormalong John*
1707.	*Time For Us to Leave Her*
1708.	*Walk Him Along, Johnny*
1709.	*Whoop Jamboree*
1710.	*Won't You Go My Way?*

CHAPTER XIII

ADDITIONAL SONGS

This chapter contains additional noteworthy songs and arias that are not included elsewhere in this book. The entries are organized by composer according to language, and are largely confined to songs in their original keys composed specifically for bass voice, songs for low voice that are suited to the bass voice, or transposed songs suitable for bass voice. For a complete list of songs by composer consult the Composer Index.

SONGS IN ENGLISH

1711. Andrews, Mark   *Sea Fever*   Schirmer
       (1875-1939) Am.   Animato 6/8   (A2-D4)   MH   Med. diff.
                            Rhythmic; strong ending. (see Ireland version no. 1779)

1712. Arne, Thomas A.   *Blow, Blow, Thou Winter Wind*   Brown
       (1710-1778) Eng.   Andante 4/4   (Bb2-Eb4)   M-MH   Med. diff.
                            Contained in "Expressive Singing Song Anthology," vol. II, for low voice, by Van Christy; requires some flexibility.

1713.   *Now Phoebus Sinketh in the West*   Novello
                        Allegro 6/8   (G2-Eb4)   M-MH   Mod. easy
                        Requires flexibility.

1714.   *Should You Ever Find Her Complying*   Elkin
                        Minuet 3/4   (A2-D4)   M-MH   Mod. easy
                        Somewhat dramatically expressive.

1715.   *The Lass with the Delicate Air*   Brown
                        Allegretto 3/4   (A2-D4(F4))   M-MH   Med. diff.
                        Contained in "Expressive Singing Song Anthology," vol. II, for low voice, by Van Christy; some flexibility required.

1716.   *Why So Pale and Wan*   Schirmer
                        Andante 4/4   (G2-D4)   M-MH   Med. diff.
                        Found in "Reliquary of English Songs," vol. II.

1717. Attey, John   *On a Time the Amorous Silvy*   Stainer
       (died c.1640) Eng.   Graceful   (A2-D4)   M-MH   Mod. easy
                        Found in "Forty Elizabethan Songs," vol. IV, ed. by Fellows.

1718. Bacon, Ernst   *A Clear Midnight*   Stainer
       (b. 1898) Am.   Slow   (G#2-C#4)   M   Med. diff.
                        Sustained; subdued.

1719.

Brady   B & H
Andante 2/4   (A2-Fb4)   ML-MH   Med. diff.
Humorous story about a gambler; for beginning or
intermediate bass.

1720. Barton, Gerard
(1861-?) Am.

It Was a Lover and His Lass   Dover
Allegro 4/4   (G2-D4)   M   Mod. easy
Contained in "American Art Songs of the Turn of the
Century."

1721. Binkerd, Gordon
(b. 1916)

Her Definition   B & H
Moderato 4/4, 5/8, 7/8 (G2-Eb4)   MH   Diff.
Unique love song; for more advanced.

1722. Birch, Robert
Am.

The Philosophist   Presser
Allegretto 2/4   (B2-Eb4)   M-MH   Med. diff.
A humorous satire; dedicated to Alexander Kipnis, Met.
bass.

1723. Bliss, Arthur
(1891-1975) Eng.

Feast   B & H
Moderately slow   (A2-D#4)   MH   Mod. diff.
From "Seven American Poems" for low voice by Bliss;
sustained; generally subdued.

1724.

Gone, Gone Again Is Summer   B & H
Moderately slow   (Bb2-Eb4)   MH   Mod. diff.
From (see previous listing); sustained; subdued.

1725. Blow, John
(1649-1708) Eng.

Arms, Arms, Arms He Delights In   Arno
Moderato 2/2   (E2-E4)   L-MH   Med. diff.
Found in "The Solo Song Outside German Speaking
Countries"; requires flexibility; has several low E2's.

1726.

Rise, Mighty Monarch   Gregg
Moderato   (D2-E4)   L-MH   Med. diff.
Contained in "6 Songs from Amphion Angelicus," ed. by
Arkwright; wide range; two octave descending leap; agility
required.

1727. Boatner, Edward
(1898-?) Am.

On Ma Journey   Ricordi
Spirited   (C3-C4)   MH   Mod. easy
Spiritual; rhythmical.

1728. Bowles, Paul
(b. 1910) Am.

Cabin   Schirmer
Moderato 6/8, 9/8   (C#3-C#4)   M-MH   Med. diff.
From the cycle "Blue Mountain Ballads"; flowing legato.

1729.

Lonesome Man   Schirmer
Fast 4/8   (Eb3-Eb4)   MH   Mod. diff.
From the cycle "Blue Mountain Ballads"; very energetic and

rhythmical; some tricky meter changes.

1730. Bristow, George F.   *Alas! They Know Me Not*   Norton
      (1825-1898) Am.   Moderately slow   (E2-E4)   MH   Med. diff.
                              Contained in "Music in America"; sustained; dramatic
                              sections; animated sections; ends on low E2.

1731. Britten, Benjamin   *The Plough Boy*   B & H
      (1913-1976) Eng.   Allegretto 2/2   (A2-D4)   M-MH   Med. diff.
                              Requires agility.

1732. Brown, Charles   *A Song Without Words*   Marks
      (b. 1940) Am.   Slow, not strict 4/4   (Ab2-Db4) M-MH   Med. diff.
                              Found in "Anthology of Art Songs by Black American
                              Composers"; vocalise; improvisatory; very effective.

1733. Bullard, Fredrick   *The Indifferent Mariner*   Ditson
      (1864-1904) Am.   Andante 4/4   (G2-Eb4)   M-MH   Med. diff.
                              Crusty old sailor's song; agility required.

1734. Campian, Thomas   *Fair, If You Expect Admiring*   Stainer
      (1567-1620) Br.   Animated   (B2-C#4)   M-MH   Mod. easy
                              Found in "Forty Elizabethan Songs," vol. IV.

1735. Chadwick, George   *Drake's Drum*   Ditson
      (1854-1931) Am.   Moderato   (A2-Eb4)   MH   Med. diff.
                              Animated.

1736. Chanler, Theodore   *The Policeman in the Park*   Schirmer
      (1902-1961) Am.   Andante 2/2   (Ab2-D4)   ML-MH Med. diff.
                              Humorous narrative; some maturity in interpretation
                              required.

1737. Dello Joio, Norman   *The Assassination*   C. Fischer
      (b. 1913) Am.   Andante 6/4, 3/4 5/4 (Bb2-D4)   M-MH   Mod. diff.
                              Two fates discuss the assassination of hope; dramatic.

1738.   *Ballad of Thomas Jefferson*   Weaner-Levant
                              Spirited 4/4   (A2-D4)   MH   Mod. diff.
                              Narrative; tricky rhythmically.

1739. Dett, R. Nathaniel   *Sit Down, Servant, Sit Down*   Schirmer
      (1882-1943) Can./Am.   Spirited   (C3-Db4)   MH   Mod. easy
                              Spiritual; rhythmical.

1740. Dibdin, Charles   *Blow High, Blow Low*   Schirmer
      (1745-1814) Eng.   Lively   (G2-C4)   M   Mod. easy
                              Found in "Reliquary of English Song," vol. II.

1741.   *The Lass That Loves a Sailor*   Schirmer

Lively 4/4   (C3-F4)   H   Mod. easy
Contained in (see previous listing); an engaging song;
energetic; may need transposing.

1742.   *Tom Bowling*   Schirmer
                         Andante 2/4   (Bb2-D4)   M-MH   Mod. easy
                         Found in (see previous listing); sustained; ballad; effective.

1743. Dowland, John   *Weep No More, Sad Fountains*   Stainer
      (1563-1626) Eng.   Slowly   (A2-D4)   MH   Mod. easy
                         Found in "Forty Elizabethan Songs," vol. III.

1744. Duke, John   *Give Me Your Hand*   Southern
      (1899-1984) Am.   Lento 6/4   (A2-Eb4)   M-MH   Mod. diff.
                         Quiet mood; found in "Songs by John Duke," vol. II.

1745.   *In the Fields*   C. Fischer
                         Slow, varied meter (A2-E4)   M-H   Med. diff.
                         Sustained, prayerful song of spring.

1746.   *Silver*   Schirmer
                         Slow 3/4   (A2-D4)   M-MH   Med. diff.
                         Found in "20th Century Art Songs"; requires control of soft
                         singing.

1747. Elgar, Edward (Sir) *Sea Slumber Song*   B & H
      (1857-1934) Eng.   Andantino 4/4   (G2-D4)   M-MH   Med. diff.
                          From "Sea Pictures"; flowing legato line.

1748. Finzi, Gerald   *Rollicum-Rorum*   B & H
      (1901-1956) Eng.   Allegro 2/4   (A2-E4)   M-MH   Med. diff.
                         Satirical; humorous; E4 on two short notes.

1749. Fisher, William A. *Sigh No More, Ladies*   Dover
      (1861-1948) Am.   Con brio 2/4   (C3-D4)   MH   Med. diff.
                         Contained in "American Art Songs of the Turn of the
                         Century"; for bass voice; facile articulation and agility
                         required.

1750. Ford, Thomas   *Not Full Twelve Years*   Stainer
      (1580-1646) Eng.   Slowly   (A2-E4)   MH   Mod. easy
                         Found in "Forty Elizabethan Songs," vol. IV.

1751. German, Edward   *Big Steamers*   Cramer
      (1862-1936) Eng.   Allegretto 6/8   (B2-E4)   H   Med. diff.
                         Humorous; effective piece.

1752. Gibbs, C. Armstrong *The Ballad of Semmerwater*   Curwen
      (1889-1960) Eng.   Andante 3/4   (Gb2-Eb4) ML-MH   Med. diff.
                          Poem by William Watson on the curse of a beggar.

1753.   *Sailing Homeward*   Rogers
                          Lento 3/4   (Bb2-E4)   M-MH   Med. diff.
                          An effective song of the sea.

1754. Gottschalk, L. F.   *At the Sign of the Three Black Crows*   White-Smith
      (1868-1934) Am.   Animato 6/8   (A2-D4)   MH   Med. diff.
                          Rousing drinking song.

1755. Griffes, Charles T. *Song of the Dagger*   Peters
      (1884-1920) Am.   Various tempo & meter (Ab2-F4)   M-H   Mod. diff.
                          Ballad; dramatic.

1756.   *Two Kings Sat Together at Orkadal*   Schirmer
                          Moderato 2/4   (Bb2-E4)   MH   Mod. diff.
                          Ballad; dramatic.

1757. Hageman, Richard   *The Rich Man*   Galaxy
      (1882-1966) Am.   Moderato 4/4   (B2-D4)   MH   Med. diff.
                          A humorous, colorful song; perhaps for encore.

1758. Hancock, E. W.   *Absalom*   Marks
      (b. 1929) Am.   Slow, varied meter   (F#2-Eb4)   ML-MH   Diff.
                          Found in "Anthology of Art Songs by Black American
                          Composers"; sustained; requires good low notes.

1759.   *Nunc Dimittis* (Eng.)   Marks
                          Andante 5/4   (G2-D4)   ML-MH   Med. diff.
                          Found in same volume as previous; religious text; smooth
                          legato line.

      Handel, George F.   International
      (1685-1759) Ger./Eng.
Outlined below are a few of the many songs composed by this prolific composer. All are
contained in "45 arias" for low voice in three volumes published by International and are in their
original keys. Other songs and arias by Handel are in the Italian section of this chapter and are
found elsewhere by consulting the Composer Index.

1760.   *Honor and Arms* (from "Samson")
                          Allegro 4/4   (G2-Eb4)   MH   Mod. diff.
                          Found in vol. III; agility required; wide leaps; effective
                          piece.

1761.   *How Willing My Paternal Love* (from "Samson")
                          Larghetto 4/4   (B2-E4)   MH   Med. diff.
                          Found in vol. II; sustained.

1762.   *O Ruddier Than the Cherry* (from "Acis and Galatea")
                          Allegro 4/4   (F2-F4)   ML-H   Mod. diff.
                          Found in vol. I; wide range; wide leaps; agility required;
                          very effective piece.

1763.   *Revenge, Timoetheus Cries* (from "Alexander's Feast")
                          Andante allegro 4/4   (A2-E4)   MH   Mod. diff.
                          Found in vol. II; flexibility required.

1764.   *See the Raging Flames* (from "Joshua")
                          Allegro 4/4   (A2-E4)   MH-H   Mod. diff.
                          Found in vol. I; energetic; agility required.

1765. Harty, Hamilton   *Homeward*   Novello
      (1879-1941) Eng.   Vigorous   (C3-E4)   ML-MH Med. diff.
                          Spirited sailors song; wide range, original key.

1766.   *Sea Wrack*   B & H
                          Lento 4/4   (Bb2-Eb4) MH   Med. diff.
                        Found in "Contralto Songs"; originally composed for
                        contralto; works well for bass; dramatic ballad.

1767. Hawley, Charles B. *Noon and Night*   Ditson
      (1858-1915) Am.   Moderato 2/4, 3/4, 4/4 (A2-C4)   ML-M Mod. easy
                        Lyric love song for beginning bass; found in "The
                        Clippinger Class-Method of Voice Culture."

1768. Head, Michael   *A Dog's Life*   B & H
      (1900-1976) Eng.   Allegro 4/4, 2/4   (A2-D4)   M-MH Med. diff.
                        Energetic song of the sea; from "Six Sea Songs."

1769.   *Lone Dog*   B & H
                          Allegro vigoroso 4/4 (C3-Eb4) M-MH Med. diff.
                        Contained in "Michael Head Song Album," vol. III;
                        humorous; energetic; rhythmical.

1770.   *Ships of Arcady*   B & H
                        Moderato 3/2   (Bb2-Eb4) M-MH Med. diff.
                        From the cycle "Over the Rim of the Moon"; lyric;
                        subdued; good song of the sea.

1771.   *The Matron's Cat*   B & H
                      Various tempo & meter (A2-D4) M-MH Med. diff.
                      Found in "Michael Head Song Album for Male Voices";
                      humorous; rapid articulation.

1772. Holst, Gustav   *The Sergeant's Song*   Ashdown
      (1874-1934) Eng.   Allegro 2/2   (G2-D4)   M-MH Med. diff.
                      (see Finzi version no. 1748)

1773. Homer, Sidney   *The Country of the Camisards*   Schirmer
      (1864-1953) Am.   Moderato 2/4   (Bb2-Bb3) M   Mod. easy
                      Good song for teaching; pensive; sustained.

1774. Hovhaness, Alan   *O World*   Peters

(b. 1911) Am·   No tempo or meter   (F#2-E4)   ML-MH   Mod. diff.
                     Long melismatic sections over held chords; chant-like.

1775. Howard, Samuel   *Love in thy Youth*   C. Fischer
      (1710-1782) Eng. Allegretto 4/4   (G#2-D#4)   ML-M   Med. diff.
                        Contained in "The Hundred Best Short Songs," vol. IV;
                        some flexibility required.

1776. Huhn, Bruno   *Cato's Advise*   Schirmer
      (1871-1950) Eng./Am. Spirited   (G2-C4(D4)   M   Med. diff.
                        Vigorous drinking song.

1777.   *Invictus*   Schirmer
                        Energetic   (Bb2-Db4)   M-MH   Med. diff.
                        Very vigorous; somewhat declamatory.

1778. Hume, Tobias   *Fain Would I Change That Note*   Stainer
      (d. 1645) Eng.   Moderately   (A2-D4)   M-MH   Mod. easy
                        Found in "Forty Elizabethan Songs," vol. III.

1779. Ireland, John   *Sea Fever*   Stainer
      (1879-1962) Eng. Lento 4/4   (B2-D4)   M-MH   Med. diff.
                        Contained in "The Complete Works for Voice and Piano,"
                        vol. II; flowing line; his most popular song; effective.

      Ives, Charles
      (1874-1954) Am.
Entered below are a few of the excellent songs suitable for bass voice by Charles Ives. In
addition to the publishers cited, Presser has published *114 Songs* by Charles Ives.
1780.   *Charlie Rutlage*   Associated+
                        Various tempo 4/4   (D3-D4)   MH   Mod. diff.
                        Found in "Seven Songs."

1781.   *Evidence*   Peer+
                        Moderately slow   (Bb2-Eb4)   MH   Med. diff.
                        Contained in "Nine Songs," sustained; subdued.

1782.   *Incantation*   Presser+
                        Various tempo & meter (Eb3-D4) MH   Mod. diff.
                        Found in "Thirty-Four Songs."

1783.   *Songs My Mother Taught Me*   Peer+
                        Slow   (Bb2-C4(D4)) M-MH Med. diff.
                        Contained in "Fourteen Songs"; sustained; subdued.

1784. Jeffries, George *Praise the Lord O My Soul*   Norton
      (d. 1685) Eng.   Moderately   (D3-D4)   M   Mod. easy
                        Found in "The Solo Song," ed. by C. MacClintock.

1785. Johnson, R.   *I'm Troubled in My Mind*   Viking

Slow   (C3-C4)   MH   Mod. easy
Found in "The Book of American Negro Spirituals";
sustained.

1786. Kagen, Sergius   *Drum*   Mercury
      (1909-1964) Am.   Fast   (Bb2-Eb4)   M-MH   Med. diff.
                              Rhythmical; generally sustained.

1787.   *I Think I Could Turn*   Mercury
                              Slowly   (A2-D4)   M-MH   Med. diff.
                              Sustained; somber; command of soft dynamics required.

1788. Kalmanoff, Martin   *Twentieth Century*   Alfred
      (b. 1920) Am.   Various tempo & meter (C3-Eb4)   MH   Med. diff.
                              Contained in "Contemporary American Songs," for low
                              voice; rapid articulation, sustained middle section.

1789. Keel, Frederick   *A Sea Burthen*   Cramer
      (1871-1950) Eng.

1790. Kreutz, Robert   *December Lark*   Alfred
      (b. 1922) Am.   Slowly 3/4   (C3-Eb4)   MH   Med. diff.
                              Contained in "Contemporary American Songs," for low
                              voice; flowing legato.

1791. Leveridge, Richard   *Love Is a Bauble*   Warner
      (1670-1758) Eng.   Allegretto 4/4 (B2-E4)   MH   Mod. easy
                              Humorous. Leveridge, a bass, took part in many important
                              concerts and operas, particularly those of Purcell.

1792.   *The Beggar's Song*   B & H
                              Gaily 2/2   (G2-D4)   ML-MH   Mod. easy
                              Found in "Old English Melodies," ed. and arr. by Wilson;
                              energetic.

1793. Linley, Thomas   *While the Foaming Billows Roll*   B & H
      (1732-1795) Eng.   Boldly 4/4   (Ab2-Eb4)   MH   Mod. easy
                              Found in "Old English Melodies," ed. and arr. by Wilson;
                              vocally energetic.

1794. Mason, Daniel   *A Grain of Salt*   Schirmer
      (1873-1953) Am.   Animated   (A2-D4)   MH   Med. diff.
                              Humorous.

1795.   *A Sea Dirge*   Witmark
                              Animated   (D3-Eb4)   MH   Med. diff.
                              Vigorous.

1796.   *I Ain't Afeared of the Admiral*   Schirmer
                              Animated   (A2-E4)   MH   Med. diff.

Humorous.

1797. McGill, Josephine (1877-1919) Am.	*O Sleep* Slowly 3/4 (A2-C#4) M-MH Sustained, quiet song; effective.			Schirmer Med. diff.

1798. Morley, Thomas
(1557-1602) Eng.

It Was a Lover and His Lass   Brown
Allegro 4/4   (C3-C4)   M-MH   Mod. easy
Contained in "Expressive Singing Song Anthology," vol. II,
for low voice, by Van Christy; lively.

1799. Naginski, Charles
(1909-1940) Am.

Richard Cory   Schirmer
Allegretto 4/4   (A2-E4(G4)) M-H   Diff.
Declamatory style with some spoken words.

1800.

The Ship Starting   Schirmer
Slower   (Bb2-Bb3)   M   Med. diff.
Sustained.

1801. Nelhybel, Vaclav
(b. 1919) Czech.

The History of the House That Jack Built   General
Allegretto 2/4   (Bb2-C3(D4)) M-MH   Med. Diff.
Patter song; humorous; nursery rhyme.

1802. O'Hara, Geofrey
(1882-1967) Can./Am.

A Real Low Down Basso Am I   Boston
Moderate 3/4   (C2-C4)   LM-M   Mod. easy
Humorous encore song.

1803.

Tomasso Rotundo   Harms
Moderato   (C2-C4)   L-M   Mod. easy
Humorous encore song.

1804.

The Ballad of Little Billee   Harms
Vigorous 2/2   (Bb2-D4)   M-MH   Med. diff.
Humorous song of the sea for beginning and intermediate
bass.

1805. Pasatieri, Thomas
(b. 1945) Am.

To Music Bent Is My Retired Mind   Belwin-Mills
Andante 4/4   (G#2-D4)   M-MH   Mod. diff.
Found in "Songs," vol. II.

1806. Payne, John (arr.)

Crucifixion   Schirmer
Slow   (B2-B3)   M   Mod. easy
Sustained; sorrowful.

1807. Pinkham, Daniel
(b. 1924) Am.

Slow, Slow, Fresh Fount   Peters
Andantino 3/4, 4/4   (C3-C4)   M-MH   Med. diff.
Subdued.

1808. Porter, Quincy

Music, When Soft Voices Die   Mercury

(1897-1966) Am.	Slow 4/4	(D3-C4)	M-MH	Med. diff.

Subdued impressionistic feeling.

1809. Purcell, Henry   *The Fatal Hour Comes On*   Schott
(1659-1695) Br.   Adagio 4/4; Mod. 3/4 (A#2-D4) ML-MH Mod. diff.
Excellent edition by M. Tippett and W. Bergman; one half-
step lower than most editions.

1810.   *I Attempt from Love's Sickness to Fly*   Brown
Andante 3/4   (A#2-C#4) M-MH   Med. diff.
Contained in "Expressive Singing Song Anthology," vol. II,
for low voice, by Van Christy; some flexibility required.

1811.   *Let the Dreadful Engines of Eternal Will*   Schott
Allegro 2/2, 6/8   (Bb-F4)   M-H   Mod. diff.
A show piece; one of the then popular "mad songs," for
bass-baritone; edited by Tippett and Bergman.

Quilter, Roger
(1877-1953) Eng.
Quilter composed a number of songs that are available for "low voice." These "low voice"
renditions generally are, unfortunately, more suited to baritone. The following is one of a few
that have been transposed down for bass.

1813.   *Now Sleeps the Crimson Petal*   Brown
Moderato 3/4, 5/4   (Bb2-Db4) MH   Med. diff.
Contained in "Expressive Singing Song Anthology," vol. II,
for low voice, by Van Christy; flowing legato.

1814. Raphling, Sam   *Fog*   Musicus
(b. 1910) Am.   Slowly, 3/4   (C3-C4)   M   Mod. easy
Poem by Carl Sandberg; mysterious quality.

1815.   *Fugue on "Money"*   Alfred
Mod. lively, various meter (Bb2-E4) M-MH Mod. diff.
Contained in "Contemporary American Songs," for low
voice; humorous; somewhat rhythmically complex.

1816.   *Mag*   Musicus
Moderately, 5/4, 4/4, 6/4 (Bb2-D4) M-MH Mod. diff.
Bitter poem about life by Carl Sandberg.

1817. Reed, H. Owen   *The Passing of John Blackfeather*   Mills
(b. 1910) Am.   Slower 7/4   (G2-E4)   M-MH   Mod. diff.
Somber and sustained narrative.

1818. Reeve, William   *The Tar's Sheet Anchor*   Schirmer
(1757-1815) Eng.   Lively   (G2-D4)   MH   Med. diff.
Found in "Reliquary of English Song," vol. II.

1819. Robinson, A. (arr.)   *Water Boy*   B & H

    (1878-1965) Am.   Andante 6/4   (B2-D4)   M-H   Mod. easy
                                 A spiritual; sustained.

1820. Siegmeister, Elie   *Blind Man*   Knopf
      (b. 1909) Am.   Slow   (C3-C4)   M-MH   Med. diff.
                                 Found in "A Treasury of American Song"; sustained; an
                               effective arrangement of this spiritual.

1821.   *Evil*   Alfred
                       Moderato, varied meter (Ab2-Eb4) M-MH   Very diff.
                       Found in "Songs of Elie Siegmeister"; musically complex.

1822.   *The Strange Funeral in Braddock*   Presser
                       Andante, Varied meter (G#2-E4)   L-M   Very diff.
                       Requires dramatic and interpretive depth; musically
                       complex.

1823.   *This Is a Sin-Tryin' World*   Knopf
                       Animated   (E3-B3)   M   Med. diff.
                       Found in "A Treasury of American Song"; a spiritual;
                       rhythmical.

1824. Sowerby, Leo   *The Adventurer*   Gray
      (1895-1968) Am.   Moderato   (B2-D4)   MH   Mod. diff.
                       From "The Edge of Dreams," a set of five songs for
                       medium voice; sustained; gentle.

1825. Starer, Robert   *My Sweet Old Etcetera*   Leeds
      (b. 1924)   Briskly 4/4   (A2-Eb4)   M-MH   Mod. diff.
                       Performed first by Mack Harrell; light-hearted, cynical
                       narrative.

1826. Storace, Stephen   *A Sailor Loved a Lass*   B & H
      (1763-1796) Eng.   Gaily 6/8   (C3-Eb4(F4))   MH   Mod. easy
                       Contained in "Old English Melodies," ed. and arr. by
                       Wilson; energetic and rhythmic.

1827. Sullivan, A. (Sir)   *If Doughty Deeds My Lady Please*   B & H
      (1842-1900) Eng.   Allegro 4/4   (Bb2-Eb4)   MH   Med. diff.
                       Contained in "Baritone Songs"; energetic; spirited.

1828.   *Orpheus with His Lute*   Brown
                       Allegro moderato 3/4 (A2-C4(F4))   M-MH   Med. diff.
                       Contained in "Expressive Singing Song Anthology," vol. II,
                       for low voice, by Van Christy; flowing legato.

1829. Swanson, Howard   *Cahoots*   Weintraub
      (1909-1978) Am.   Moderately 4/4   (Bb2-Db4)   M-MH   Diff.
                       Dedicated to William Warfield, bass-baritone; dramatically
                       and interpretively demanding.

| 1830. | | *Pierrot* | | | Weintraub |

1830.   *Pierrot*   Weintraub
                        Allegro-Andante 4/4   (Bb2-D4)   M-MH   Mod. diff.
                        Wide range of dynamics.

1831.   *Saw a Grave upon a Hill*   Weintraub
                        Grave 3/4, 4/4, 5/4   (D2-Bb3)   L-M   Med. diff.
                        Solemn, moving song; low D2 required.

1832.   *The Negro Speaks of Rivers*   Marks
                        Moderato 2/2   (G2-E4)   L-MH   Mod. diff.
                        Contained in "Anthology of Art Songs by Black American
                        Composers"; a number of low notes; deeply felt.

1833. Thomson, Virgil   *Consider, Lord*   Southern
      (1896-1989) Am.   Slow 3/2, 2/2   (Bb2-D4)   MH   Med. diff.
                        Majestic with big climax.

1834. Van Camp, L. (arr.)   *Down among the Dead Men*   C. Fischer
                        Andante 4/4   (A2(G2)-C4)   M   Mod. easy
                        Contained in "Songs for Low Voice in a Comfortable
                        Range"; drinking song.

1835.   *The Coasts of High Barbary*   C. Fischer
                        Moderato 6/8   (B2-C3)   M   Mod. easy
                        Contained in "Songs for Low Voice in a Comfortable
                        Range"; sea shanty.

1836. Vaughan Williams, R.   *The Twilight People*   Oxford
      (1872-1958) Eng.   Moderato   (Bb2-Eb4)   M-MH   Mod. diff.
                        Interpretively demanding; quasi-recitative; restrained.

1837.   *Tired*   Oxford
                        Moderately slow   (Bb2-Db4)   M-MH   Med. diff.
                        Contained in "Four Last Songs"; sustained; quiet ending.

1838. Walthew, Richard   *The Splendour Falls*   B & H
      (1872-1951) Eng.   Poco allegretto 6/8   (Bb2(Eb2)-Eb4)   MH   Mod. diff.
                        Contained in "A Heritage of 20th Century British Song,"
                        vol. I, part B; flowing legato.

1839. Waring, Tom   *I Shall Be a Wanderer*   Shawnee
      (1902-1960) Am.   Moderato 2/2   (A#2-B4)   M   Mod. easy
                        Found in "Songs by Tom Waring"; good song for bass with
                        limited range.

1840. Warlock, Peter   *Captain Stranton's Fancy*   Stainer
      (1894-1930) Br.   Allegro   (A2-D4)   M-MH   Mod. diff.
                        Energetic drinking song.

1841.   *My Own Country*   Oxford

Andante 3/8, 4/8, 5/8   (C3-E4)   M-H   Med. diff.
Sustained; subdued; descriptive.

1842.   *The Bayly Berith the Bell Away*   B & H
                         Quasi andantino 3/8   (G2-Eb4)   MH   Med. diff.
                         Sustained; subdued.

1843.   *The Droll Lover*   Stainer
                         Allegro 2/4   (B2-Eb4)   M-MH   Med. diff.
                         Animated; humorous.

1844.   *Yarmouth Fair*   Oxford
                         Fast   (A2-D4)   M-MH   Mod. diff.
                         Gay, Norfolk folk song.

1845. Weisgall, Hugo   *I Looked Back Suddenly*   Ditson
      (b. 1912)   Varied tempo   (A2-E4)   MH   Med. diff.
                         Found in "Contemporary American Art Songs."

1846. Whelply, Benjamin *I Know a Hill*   Boston
      (1864-1964) Am.   Andante 3/4   (C#3-C#4)   MH   Med. diff.
                         Sentimental longing for home.

1847. White, Maude   *Crabbed Age and Youth*   B & H
      (1855-1937) Eng.   Allegro con brio 2/4 (A2(G2)-D4) MH   Mod. easy
                         Contained in "A Heritage of 20th Century British Song,"
                         vol. I, part A; energetic; humorous.

1848.   *King Charles*   B & H
                         Tempo di Marcia 4/4 (C3-C4)   MH   Med. diff.
                         Contained in "Baritone Songs"; energetic; vigorous; high
                         tessitura at times.

1849. Wilson, H. L. (arr.) *Ah! Willow*   B & H
                         Lento 3/4   (Bb2-C4)   M-MH   Mod. easy
                         Found in "Old English Melodies"; graceful, flowing line;
                         some command of soft dynamics required.

1850.   *Come, Let's Be Merry*   B & H
                         Gaily 3/4   (Bb2-Eb4)   MH   Mod. easy
                         Found in "Old English Melodies," ed. and arr. by Wilson;
                         energetic; requires some flexibility.

1851.   *The Happy Lover*   B & H
                         Tenderly 2/4   (Bb2-Eb4)   MH   Mod. easy
                         Found in "Old English Melodies," ed. and arr. by Wilson;
                         lyric; gently flowing melody.

1852.   *The Sailor's Life*   B & H

Cheerfully 6/8   (B2-E4)   MH   Mod. easy
Found in "Old English Melodies," ed. and arr. by Wilson;
spirited and gay song of the sea.

SONGS IN FRENCH

Unfortunately, other than the song cycles and sets annotated in Chapter Six, few songs by French composers are composed specifically for bass voice or are available in a key low enough for bass. Some of the French literature has been transposed for "low voice" by International and other publishers, but much of it is still too high or is inappropriate.

1853. Bruneau, Alfred   *L'heureux vagabond*   International
      (1857-1934) Fr.   Largamente 3/4   (Bb2-D4)   M-MH   Med. diff.
                           Contained in "40 French Songs," vol. II; sustained.

1854. Chabrier, E.   *Ballade des gros Dindons*   Schirmer
      (1841-1894) Fr.   Moderato 3/4, 6/8   (B2-F4)   M-H   Med. diff.
                           Humorous.

1855.   *Chanson pour Jeanne*
                           Andantino 3/4   (C#3-D4)   MH   Med. diff.
                           Flowing legato.

1856. Chausson, Ernest   *Cantique à l'épouse*   International
      (1855-1899) Fr.   Très calme 4/4   (Bb2-Eb4)   MH   Med. diff.
                           Contained in "20 Songs"; sustained.

1857.   *Chanson de clown*
                           Grave   (D3-Eb4)   MH   Med. diff.
                           Sustained.

1858. Debussy, Claude   *Beau soir* (Eng./Fr.)   Brown
      (1862-1918) Fr.   Andante 3/4   (Ab2-D4)   M-MH   Mod. diff.
                           Contained in "Expressive Singing Song Anthology," vol. II,
                           for low voice, by Van Christy; not original key.

1859. D'Indy, Vincent   *Lied maritime*   International
      (1851-1931) Fr.   Various tempo & meter (G2-Eb4) M-MH   Med. diff.
                           Contained in "40 French Songs," vol. II.; sea song.

1860. Duparc, Henri   *Extase*   International
      (1848-1933) Fr.   Lent et calme 3/4   (D3-E4)   MH   Med. diff.
                           Contained in "12 Songs" by Duparc for low voice;
                           sustained.

1861.   *La vague et la cloche*   International
                           Assez vite 3/4, 9/8 (Ab2-E4)   M-H   Mod. diff.
                           Contained in "12 Songs" by Duparc for low voice;
                           energetic; demanding.

1862.   *Lamento*   International
                    Lent/Animé 4/4   (Bb2-Db4)   M-MH   Med. diff.
                    Contained in "12 Songs" by Duparc for low voice; sustained
                    section; animated section.

1863.   *Le manoir de Rosemonde*   International
                    Assez vif 9/8   (Bb2- Fb4)   MH   Mod. diff.
                    Contained in "12 Songs" by Duparc for low voice;
                    energetic; sustained section.

1864. Faurè, Gabriel   *Après un rève* (Eng./Fr.)   Brown
      (1845-1924) Fr.   Andantino 3/4   (A2-D4)   M-MH   Med. diff.
                        Contained in "Expressive Singing Song Anthology," vol. II,
                        for low voice, by Van Christy; not original key; flowing
                        legato line.

1865.   *Automne*   International
                    Andante 12/8   (C3-E4)   MH   Med. diff.
                    Contained in "30 Songs"; low voice vol.; sustained; flowing
                    legato line.

1866.   *Les Berceaux* (Eng./Fr.)   Brown
                    Andantino 12/8   (G2(F2)-D4)   ML-MH   Med. diff.
                    Contained in "Expressive Singing Song Anthology"; not
                    original key; flowing legato.

1867. Ferrari, Gustave   *Le miroir*   International
      (1872-1948)   Assez lent 2/4   (C#3-D4)   M-MH   Med. diff.
                         Contained in "40 French Songs," vol. II; sustained.

1868. Flègier, Ange   *Le cor*   International
      (1846-1927) Fr.   Various tempo & meter (D2-D4)   L-MH   Med. diff.
                         Contained in "40 French Songs," vol. II; sostenuto; original
                         key; wide range.

1869. Godard, Benjamin   *Chanson Arabe*   Durand
      (1849-1895) Fr.   Contained in "Album of Twelve Songs" by Godard; requires
                         flexibility.

1870. Gounod, Charles   *Ma belle amie est morte*   Choudens
      (1818-1893) Fr.   Sustained and dramatic.

1871. Hahn, Reynaldo   *La nuit*   Heugel
      (1874-1947) Fr.   Contained in "Melodies," vol. I, by Hahn.

1872.   *L'heure exquise* (Eng./Fr.)   Brown
                    Molto tranquillo 6/8   (Bb2-D4)   M-MH   Med. diff.
                    Found in "Expressive Singing Song Anthology," vol. II, for
                    low voice, by Van Christy; one half-step lower than original
                    key.

1873.   *Offrande*   International
                               Pas trop lent 4/4   (C3-C4)   M-MH   Med. diff.
                               Contained in "40 French Songs," vol. II; sustained.

1874. Honegger, Arthur   *A la 'Santé'*   Salabert
      (1892-1955) Swiss.   (from "Six poèmes de G. Apollinaire")
                               Lent 4/4   (D3-D4)   M-MH   Mod. diff.
                               Contained in "Melodies et chansons" of Arthur Honegger.

1875.   *Automne*   Salabert
                               (from "Six poèmes de G. Apollinaire")
                               Très modéré 4/4   (C3-D4)   M-MH   Mod. diff.
                               (see previous listing)

1876. Hüe, Georges   *J'ai pleuré en rêve* (Eng./Fr.)   Brown
      (1858-1948) Fr.   Lento 4/4   (B2-Db4)   MH   Med. diff.
                               Contained in "Expressive Singing Song Anthology," vol. II,
                               for low voice, by Van Christy; not original key.

1877. Koechlin, Charles   *Villanelle*   Hachette
      (1867-1950) Fr.   Slowly   (A2-D#4)   MH   Med. diff.
                               Subdued; flowing line.

1878. Liszt, Franz   *La tombe et la rose*   Kalmus
      (1811-1886) Hung.   Lento 3/4   (A2-E4)   MH   Mod. diff.
                               Found in "Franz Liszt Songs," vol. I (part of complete
                               works); sustained.

1879.   *Le vieux vagabond*   Kalmus
                               Allegro 3/4   (E2-F4)   MH-H   Mod. diff.
                               Found in "Franz Liszt Songs," vol. I; wide range; vocally
                               demanding; low E2 at the end.

1880.   *Tristesse* (J'ai perdu ma force et ma vie)   Kalmus
                               Lent 4/4   (C3-Eb4)   M-MH   Mod. diff.
                               Found in "Franz Liszt Songs," vol. V; flowing legato.

1881. Lully, Jean Baptiste   *Il faut passer tôt ou tard*   Lemoine
      (1632-1687) Fr.   Moderately slow   (G2-D4)   MH   Med. diff.
                               Contained in "Le Chant Classique," vol. 12A; somewhat
                               animated.

1882. Massenet, Jules   *Elegy* (Eng./Fr.)   Brown
      (1842-1912) Fr.   Slowly 4/4   (A2-Eb4)   MH   Med. diff.
                               Contained in "Expressive Singing Song Anthology," vol. II,
                               for low voice, by Van Christy; not original key.

1883. Poulenc, Francis   *Chanson à boire*   Heugel
      (1899-1963) Fr.   Adagio 3/4   (B2-E4)   M-MH   Mod. diff.
                               From "Chansons Gaillardes"; song of drinking; original key.

1884.	*Epitaphe*			Salabert
	Calmement 3/4	(C3-D4)	M-MH	Mod. diff.
	Some command of soft dynamics; sustained.			

1885.	*Hymne*			Salabert
	Largo 4/4	(Gb2-D#4)	ML-MH	Diff.
	Dedicated to Doda Conrad, noted French bass; original key.			

1886. Ropartz, G.	*En mai*	Rouart
(1864-1955)	Contained in "Vingt melodies pour chant et piano" by Ropartz	

1887.	*Le temps des saintes*	Rouart
	(see previous listing)	

1888. Saint-Saëns, C.	*Chanson triste*	Durand
(1835-1921) Fr.		

1889.	*Danse macabre*			International
	Waltz 3/4	(Bb2-Eb4)	M-MH	Mod. diff.
	Contained in "40 French Songs," vol. I; demands rapid articulation; dramatic; effective song.			

1890.	*Le pas d'armes du roi Jean* (Eng./Fr.)			Durand
	Allegro 2/4	(D2-Eb4)	L-MH	Med. diff.
	Energetic.			

SONGS IN GERMAN

Songs in German for the bass voice are more numerous and are more readily available than any other foreign language. Admittedly, the few songs listed below are only a sampling of the songs composed with German texts for low voice or bass voice.

1891. Bach, J. S.	*Bist du bei mir*			Brown
(1685-1750) Ger.	Poco lento 3/4	(A2-Eb4)	M-MH	Med. diff.
	Contained in "Expressive Singing Song Anthology," vol. II, for low voice, by Van Christy; sustained.			

Brahms, Johannes
(1833-1897) Ger.

Brahms wrote very few songs specifically for bass voice, but did write a number of excellent songs for low voice many of which are appropriate for the bass voice in their original key. It is important to realize there are many songs by Brahms originally composed in higher keys which are very well-suited to the bass voice in an appropriately transposed key. Only a few of his songs are listed here. Other songs by Brahms are found elsewhere in this book by consulting the Composer Index.

1892.	*An die Nachtigall*			Peters+
	Ziemlich langsam 4/4	(B2-Eb4)	MH	Mod. diff.
	In "Brahms Album," Band I; requires control of soft			

dynamics; transposed key.

1893. *Auf dem Kirchhofe* Peters+
Andante 3/4 (B2-Eb4) M-MH Mod. diff.
In "Brahms Album," Band I; some command of dynamics
required; original key.

1894. *Der Strom, der Neben mir verrauschte* Peters+
Moderato 4/4 (C#3-E4) M-H Diff.
In "Brahms Album," Band III; agitated and intense;
original key; may need transposition.

1895. *Die Mainacht* Peters+
Sehr langsam 4/4 (Bb2-Fb4) MH-H Diff.
In "Brahms Album," Band II; Long, high phrases;
expressive maturity required; original key; may require
transposition.

1896. *Ich schleich umher betrübt* Peters+
Mässig 3/4 (D3-D4) MH Med. diff.
In "Brahms Album," Band III; original key.

1897. *Mit vierzig Jahren* Peters+
Langsam 4/4 (F#2-D4) M Med. diff.
In "Brahms Album," Band I; slow and sustained; grave;
original key.

1898. *Sapphische Ode* Peters+
Slow 2/2 (A2-D4) M Med. diff.
In "Brahms Album," Band I; sustained, flowing line;
original key.

1899. *Sonntag* Peters+
Nicht zu langsam 3/4 (Bb2-Eb4) M Med. diff.
In "Brahms Album," Band I; youthful song of love;
transposed key.

1900. *Wie Melodien zieht es mir* Peters+
Zart 2/2 (A2-E4) MH Med. diff.
In "Brahms Album," Band I; flowing melodic line; warm
tone; original key.

1901. *Verrat* Peters+
Con moto 4/4 (F#2-Eb4) ML-MH Diff.
Found in "Brahms Album," Band IV; a dark and powerful
song of vengeance; an excellent song for bass voice.

1902. Fortner, Wolfgang   *Der Totengräber* (Ger./Eng.) Arno
(1907-1987) Ger.   Very slow (A2-C4) M Mod. diff.
Contained in "The German Solo Songs and the Ballad."

Sustained.

1903. Liszt, Franz   *Der alte Vagabund*   Breitkopf
       (1811-1886) Hung.   Allegro 4/4   (E2-E4)   MH   Med. diff.
                            Found in "Musikalische Werke."

1904.   *Die Vätergruft*   Breitkopf
                            Lento 4/4   (F2-E4)   MH   Med. diff.
                            One of his best; ballad; found in (see previous listing).

1905.   *Ein Fichtenbaum steht einsam*   Breitkopf
                            Lento 3/4, 4/4   (G2-D4)   MH   Med. diff.
                            Found in (see previous listing).

1906.   *Gastibelza*   Breitkopf
                            Allegro 3/4   (F#2-E4)   M-H Med. diff.
                            Found in (see previous listing).

1907.   *Weimars Toten*   Breitkopf
                            Andante 4/4   (F#2-F4)   M-H Med. diff.
                            Found in (see previous listing).

       Loewe, Carl
       (1796-1869) Ger.
The following excellent songs of Loewe are contained in "Carl Loewes Werke," a seventeen
volume collection published by Breitkopf. They were composed specifically for bass voice and
are in their original keys. (see also Chapter Five)

1908.   *Das Geheimnis*
                            Allegretto 6/8   (F2-E4)   MH   Med. diff.
                            Found in Band II.

1909.   *Das Vaterland*
                            Allegro/Larghetto 4/4 (E2-D4) M   Med. diff.
                            Found in Band X.

1910.   *Der alte Schiffsherr*
                            Andante/Allegro 3/4, 4/4 (F2-E4) MH Med. diff.
                            Found in Band X.

1911.   *Der Feind*
                            Andante 4/4   (D2-D4)   M   Med. diff.
                            Found in Band IX.

1912.   *Ich bin ein guter Hirte*
                            Andantino 12/8   (Bb2-E4)   M-H Med. diff.
                            Found in Band XVI.

1913.   *Ihr Thoren wollt das Glück*
                            Adagio 4/4   (E2-E4)   MH   Med. diff.
                            Found in Band II.

1914.	*Lazarus ward auferwecket* Allegro maestoso (E2-C4) Found in Band XIV.	ML-M	Med. diff.

1915. *Sang des Moses*
Grave 6/4 (E2-E4) ML-MH Med. diff.
Found in Band II.

1916. Wachtpostenlied
Andante 4/4 (G2-C4) ML-M Med. diff.
Found in Band XVI.

1917. *Wer möchte noch einmal*
Larghetto 4/4 (G2-Eb4) MH Med. diff.
Found in Band II.

1918. Schönberg, Arnold *Der Mai tritt ein mit Freuden* Peters
(1874-1951) Aus./Am. Nicht langsam (C3-C4) MH Mod. diff.
Found in "Deutsche Volkslieder."

1919. *Es gingen zwei Gespielen gut* Peters
Leicht bewegt (D3-D4) MH Mod. diff.
Found in "Deutsche Volkslieder."

1920. *Mein Herz in steten Treuen* Peters
Schnell (C3-D4) MH Mod. diff.
Found in "Deutsche Volkslieder."

1921. *Mein Herz ist mir gemenget* Peters
Nicht zu langsam (D3-E4) MH Mod. diff.
Found in "Deutsche Volkslieder."

1922. *Warnung* (Op. 3, no. 3.) Universal+
Animato (Bb2-Eb4) MH Diff.
Interpretively and musically demanding.

Schubert, Franz
(1797-1828) Austrian
Most of the following sampling of excellent lieder by Franz Schubert are in their original keys and all are well-suited for bass voice. Complete works refers to "Neue Schubert-Ausgabe" published by Bärenreiter.

1923. *An den Tod* Bärenreiter
Langsam 2/2 (Bb2-C#4) M Mod. diff.
Found in complete works; sostenuto.

1924. *Auf der Donau* International
Langsam, 2/4 (F#2-Db4) M-MH Mod. diff.
Found in "200 Songs," vol. II, for low voice by Schubert; sustained; flowing legato line.

1925.   *Das Abendrot*   Bärenreiter
         Various tempo & meter   (E2-E4)   ML-H   Diff.
         Found in complete works; wide range; large leaps.

1926.   *Der Kampf*   Bärenreiter
         Animated   (D2-E4)   ML-H   Diff.
         Found in complete works; energetic; dramatic; slow middle
         section.

1927.   *Der Sieg*   Bärenreiter
         Mässig langsam 2/2   (F2-D4)   M-MH   Mod. diff.
         Found in complete works; very sustained; dramatic sections.

1928.   *Der Strom*   Bärenreiter
         Fast 2/4   (A2-Eb4)   M-MH   Diff.
         Found in complete works; dramatic and demanding; facile
         articulation required.

1929.   *Der zürnende Barde*   Bärenreiter
         Geschwind 6/8   (A2-E4)   MH-H   Diff.
         Found in complete works; declamatory; demanding.

1930.   *Fahrt zum Hades*   International
         Langsam 2/2   (G2(F2)-D4)   M-MH   Mod. diff.
         Found in "200 Songs," vol. III, for low voice by Schubert;
         very sustained and legato; optional low ending.

1931.   *Grenzen der Menschheit*   International
         Nicht zu langsam 2/2   (E2-Eb4)   L-MH   Mod. diff.
         Found in "200 Songs," vol. II, for low voice by Schubert;
         low tessitura with dark sound. (see Wolf version no. 1961)

1932.   *Gruppe aus dem Tartarus*   International
         Allegro 12/8   (C3-Eb4)   MH   Diff.
         Found in "200 Songs," vol. II, for low voice by Schubert;
         energetic and demanding vocally.

1933.   *Heliopolis II*   International
         Geschwind, 4/4   (G2-D4)   MH   Mod. diff.
         Found in "200 Songs," vol. III, for low voice by Schubert;
         energetic; last section is strenuous.

1934.   *Sehnsucht* (Op. 39)   Bärenreiter
         Ziemlich geschwind 4/4   (Ab2-E4)   MH-H   Diff.
         Found in complete works; sustained.

1935.   *Selige Welt*   Bärenreiter
         Nicht zu schnell 4/4   (C3-Eb4)   MH   Diff.
         Found in complete works; energetic.

1936.   *Wie Ulfru fischt*   Bärenreiter
         Mässig 2/2   (C3-C4)   M-MH   Mod. diff.
         Found in complete works; spirited; requires facile
         articulation.

1937.   *Dithyrambe*   Schirmer
         Geschwind 6/8   (A2-D4)   MH   Mod. diff.
         Found in "Schubert Songs," vol. II; spirited.

1938.   *Lied eines Schiffers an die Dioskuren*   International
         Langsam 3/4   (A#2-C#4)   M-MH   Mod. diff.
         Found in "200 Songs," vol. I, for low voice by Schubert;
         sustained legato.

1939.   *Prometheus*   International
         Moderato 4/4   (Ab2-C#4)   ML-MH   Diff.
         Found in "200 Songs," vol. II, for low voice by Schubert;
         poem by Goethe concerning the legend of Prometheus;
         requires vocal and interpretive maturity.

1940.   *Der Schiffer* (op. 21, no. 2)   International
         Geschwind 2/4   (Bb2-Eb4)   MH   Mod. diff.
         Found in "200 Songs," vol. II, for low voice by Schubert;
         spirited sailor's song.

Schumann, Robert
(1810-1856) Ger.
Other than the few listed below, additional songs of Schumann can be found in the chapter on
song cycles, and by consulting the Composer Index.

1941.   *Auf das Trinkglas eines verstorbenen*   Peters
         Lento   (Ab2-Eb4)   MH   Med. diff.
         Contained in "Sämliche Lieder," vol. II; sustained; subdued;
         command of soft dynamics required.

1942.   *Da liegt der Feinde gestreckte* Schar   International
         Grave 12/8   (F2-C4)   M   Med. diff.
         Contained in "90 Songs," low voice edition; dramatic;
         sustained; original key.

1943.   *Der leidige Frieden*   Peters
         Allegretto   (G2-Bb3)   M   Med. diff.
         Contained in "Sämliche Lieder"; somewhat animated;
         quasi-recitative style.

1944.   *Die beiden Grenadiere*   International
         Mässig 4/4   (Bb2-D4)   MH   Med. diff.
         Contained in "90 Songs," low voice edition; a favorite;
         demanding ending.

1945.   *Die rote Hanne*   Peters

Moderato   (G2-D4)   M-MH   Med. diff.
Contained in "Sämliche Lieder"; sustained; serious; optional
chorus.

1946.   *Wer nie sein Brot mit Tränen ass*   International
             Slow 4/4   (F2-Eb4)   MH   Med. diff.
             Contained in "90 Songs," low voice vol.; from his "Wilhelm
             Meister"; sustained; dramatic.

Strauss, Richard
(1864-1949) Ger.

With one exception, the following songs by Strauss are not in their original keys but are suitable
for bass in the keys listed. Additional songs for bass by Strauss can be found by consulting the
Composer Index.

1947.   *Allerseelen* (Eng./Fr.)   Brown
             Tranquillo 4/4   (A2-Eb4)   MH   Med. diff.
             Contained in "Expressive Singing Song Anthology," vol. II,
             for low voice, by Van Christy; flowing legato.

1948.   *Heimliche Aufforderung*   International
             Lebhaft 6/8   (A2-D4)   M-MH   Mod. diff.
             Found in "27 Songs"; vigorous; sustained.

1949.   *Ich trage meine Minne*   International
             Andante con moto 2/4   (Ab2-E4) ML-MH   Mod. diff.
             Found in (see previous selection); dramatic sections.

1950.   *Im Spätboot*   Masters+
             Langsam 4/4   (Db2-Db4)   ML-MH   Mod. diff.
             Contained in "Richard Strauss Collected Songs," vol. X,
             for low bass; sustained; excellent song; original key.

1951.   *Traum durch die Dämmerung*   International
             Sehr ruhig 2/4   (Bb2-Eb4)   M-MH   Mod. diff.
             Found in "27 Songs"; soft; sustained; requires command of
             high soft dynamics.

1952.   *Zueignung* (Eng./Ger.)   Brown
             Moderato 4/4   (A2-D4)   M-MH   Med. diff.
             Contained in "Expressive Singing Song Anthology," vol. II,
             for low voice, by Van Christy; sustained.

1953. Wagner, Richard   *Les deux grenadiers* (Fr.)   Church+
      (1813-1883) Ger.   Moderato 4/4   (A2-F#4)   MH-VH   Mod. diff.
                            Contained in "Famous Songs for Bass"; vocally demanding;
                            for bass-baritone with secure top. (see Schumann setting no.
                            1944)

1954. Webern, Anton von   *Tief von Fern*   C. Fischer
      (1883-1945) Aus.   Langsam 4/4   (G2-E4)   M-H   Mod. diff.

Found in "Eight Early Songs"; not as difficult as some of
his later works.

1955.   *Der Tod*   C. Fischer
                      Langsam 2/2   (Bb2-Eb4)   MH   Mod. diff.
                      Found in (see previous work).

1956. Wolf, Hugo   *Anakreons Grab*   International
      (1860-1903) Austrian   Sehr langsam 12/8 (D3-D4) MH   Mod. diff.
                      Contained in "65 Songs," low voice edition; sustained;
                      requires command of soft dynamics; original key.

1957.   *Biterolf*   Peters
                      Slowly 3/2   (D3-F4)   H   Mod. diff.
                      Contained in "35 Männerliedern" for baritone (bass);
                      sustained; original key.

1958.   *Cophtisches Lied I*   Peters
                      Sehr gemessen 4/4 (C3-E4)   M-H   Mod. diff.
                      Contained in "35 Männerliedern" for baritone (bass);
                      measured; interpretively demanding; original key.

1959.   *Der Musikant*   Brown
                      Moderately 2/4   (B2-C4)   M   Med. diff.
                      Contained in "Expressive Singing Song Anthology," third
                      edition, for low voice; the song of a vagabond; not original
                      key.

1960.   *Fussreise*   Peters+
                      Ziemlich bewegt 4/4 (C#3-E4) MH-H Med. diff.
                      Contained in "35 Männerliedern" for baritone (bass);
                      energetic; original key.

1961.   *Grenzen der Menschheit*   Peters
                      Slow 2/2   (F2-Eb4)   MH   Mod. diff.
                      Contained in "35 Männerliedern" for baritone (bass);
                      interpretively demanding; sustained; original key; compare
                      Schubert version. (see no. 1931)

1962.   *Prometheus*   Peters
                      Broad 4/4   (B2-E4)   H   Diff.
                      Found in "35 Männerliedern" for baritone (bass); dramatic;
                      vocally demanding; original key.

1963.   *Um Mitternacht*   International
                      Calmly 12/8   (G#2-E4)   ML-H   Mod. diff.
                      Contained in "65 Songs," low voice edition; sustained;
                      original key.

1964.   *Verborgenheit*   Brown

Slowly 4/4   (A2-D4)   M-MH   Med. diff.
Contained in "Expressive Singing Song Anthology," vol. II,
for low voice, by Van Christy; not original key.

1965. Zelter, Carl   *Berglied*   Schott's
      (1758-1832) Ger.   Moderato 6/4   (E2-C#4)   ML-M   Med. diff.
                            Found in "Fünfzig Lieder für eine Singstimme und Klavier";
                            sustained; has a sustained E2.

1966.   *Klage*   Schott's
                            Moderato   (E2-C4)   M   Med. diff.
                            Found in (same as previous).

1967.   *Der König von Thule*   Arno
                            Moderato 6/4   (A2-A3)   ML   Mod. easy
                            Contained in "The German Solo Song and the Ballad," by
                            H. J. Moser; simple, strophic ballad.

SONGS IN ITALIAN

In addition to appropriate songs contained in the recommended "26 Italian Songs and Arias"
edited by Paton and published by Alfred Publishing Co. the following songs are listed. The
more familiar songs are listed for their unusually low key. (See also the Italian anthology of
songs for bass annotated in Chapter II)

1968. Beethoven, L. van   *In questa tomba*   G.Schirmer
      (1770-1827) Ger.   Lento 2/4   (A2-C#4)   M   Med. diff.
                            Sustained; lower key than original; a favorite.

1969. Cimarosa, D.   *Mio signor* (from "Il falegname")   Zerboni
      (1749-1801) It.   Allegro moderato 4/4 (C3-E4) M-H   Mod. diff.
                            Rapid articulation; high tessitura in sections; contained in
                            "Cimarosa; dieci arie inedite."

1970.   *Se lo specchio* (from "Il falegnome") Zerboni
                            Allegro 4/4   (C3-E4)   MH   Med. diff.
                            Rapid articulation and agility required; contained in (see
                            previous selection).

1971. Davico, Vincenzo   *Come un cipresso*   Ricordi
      (1889-1969) It.   Slow   (Db3-C4)   MH   Mod. diff.
                            From "Tre liriche"; sustained.

1972. Falconieri, Andrea   *O bellissimi capelli*   Ditson
      (1585-1656) It.   Andante 3/4   (B2-D4)   MH   Med. diff.
                            Contained in "Classic Italian Songs," vol. II, for low voice;
                            flowing legato.

Handel, G. F.
(1685-1759) Ger./Eng.
Handel composed a number of Italian operas. Included here are a few of the more important arias from those operas in their original key and are found in "45 Arias" for low voice in three volumes published by International. Additional works by Handel are listed in the Composer Index.

1973.   *Cara sposa* (from "Rinaldo")
                       Largo/Allegro 3/4, 4/4   (A2-D4)   M-MH   Med. diff.
                       Found in vol. I; sustained section; animated section; agility
                       required.

1974.   *Dove sei, amato bene?* (from "Rodelinda")
                       Largo 3/8   (B2-E4)   MH   Med. diff.
                       Found in vol. III; sustained.

1975.   *Sorge infausta una procella* (from "Orlando")
                       Allegro 4/4   (G2-Eb4)   MH   Mod. diff.
                       Found in vol. III; flexibility required.

1976. Landi, Stefano   *Superbi colli*   Norton
      (1586-1639) It. Moderato   (C2-E4)   VL-MH   Mod. diff.
                       Contained in "The Solo Song 1580-1730"; majestic; florid
                       sections; several low C2's and D2's; original key.

1977. Legrenzi, Giovanni   *Che fiero costume* (It./Eng.)   Brown
      (1626-1690) It. Allegretto 12/8   (B2-C#4(E))   M-MH   Med. diff.
                       Found in "Expressive Singing Song Anthology," vol. II. by
                       Christy; rapid articulation.

1978. Monteverdi, C.   *Ben che severo* (from "La favola d'Orfeo")   Universal
      (1567-1643) It. Moderately slow   (A2-A3)   ML   Med. diff.
                       Contained in complete works, vol. 11; sustained; tranquil.

1979.   *Ecco la sconsolata donna* (from "Poppea")   Universal
                       Moderato   (G2-D4)   MH   Med. diff.
                       Contained in complete works, vol. 13; sustained; requires
                       agility in sections.

1980.   *Io che nell'otio nacqui*   Universal
                       Slow   (D2-D4)   L-MH   Diff.
                       Contained in complete works, vol. 7; sustained sections;
                       florid sections; wide leaps; wide range; challenging.

1981.   *O tu che innanzi morte*   Universal
                       (from "La favola d'Orfeo")
                       Moderato   (F2-Bb3)   L-M   Med. diff.
                       Contained in complete works, vol. 11; somewhat animated.

1982. Pergolesi, G.   *Nina* (It./Eng)   Brown
      (1710-1736) It. Andante 4/4   (Bb2-C4)   M-MH   Mod. easy

Contained in "Expressive Singing Song Anthology," vol. II,
for low voice by Christy; flowing legato.

1983. Scarlatti, A. (1660-1725) It.	*Toglietemi la vita ancor* Andante 4/4 (C#3-Eb4) MH Found in "Aria Antiche," vol. III; passionate.	Ricordi Med. diff.
1984. Tosti, F. Paolo (1846-1916) It./Eng.	*L'ultima canzone* Allegro 4/4 (C3-Eb4) MH Energetic Neopolitan song.	Ricordi Mod. easy
1985.	*Serenata* Andantino 4/4 (C3-C4) M-MH Flowing legato; Neopolitan song.	Schirmer Mod. easy
1986. Stravinsky, Igor (1882-1971) Russ./Am.	*Con queste paroline* (It.) Lively (G2-E4) M-H Animated arietta after Pergolesi.	Chester Diff.
1987. Torelli, Giuseppe (1658-1709) It.	*Tu lo sai* (It./Eng.) Andante 3/4 (G2-C4(D4)) M-MH Contained in "Expressive Singing Song Anthology," vol. II; for low voice by Christy.	Brown Med. diff.

SONGS IN RUSSIAN

Russian and bass are two words that are closely associated. Despite this association the bass is
limited in finding suitable songs in original keys or in appropriate transposed keys and in
acceptable English translations. Most of the songs listed below are in an English translation and
in their original key or in a suitable transposed key. (for additional Russian songs see nos. 228-
240)(Boris Christoff has recorded numerous by songs by Glinka, Cui, Borodin, and others.)

1988. Balakirev, Mily (1837-1910) Russ.	*Burning Out Is the Sunset's Red Flame* Slow (A#2-D#4) MH Contained in "Modern Russian Songs," vol. I; sustained.	Ditson Mod. diff.
1989. Borodin, A. (arr.) (1833-1887) Russ.	*Ah, No Stormy Wind* Moderato 4/4 (C3-D4) M-MH Contained in "Pathways of Song," vol. IV; folk song; deeply felt; tragic; interpretively demanding.	Warner Med. diff.
1990.	*The Jailer's Slumber Song* Andante 4/4 (Bb2-Db4) M-MH Contained in (see previous listing); folk song; poignant; emotionally expressive.	Warner Med. diff.
1991. Cui, Cesar (1835-1918) Russ.	*If I Only Could Forget* Moderato (B2-D4) MH Contained in "Six Songs."	Boston Mod. diff.

1992.	*Oh, Gentle Wind*			Boston
	Moderato	(B2-E4)	MH	Mod. diff.
	Contained in "Six Songs."			

1993.	*The Statue at Tsarskoe Selo*			Leeds
	Slowly	(Db3-Eb4)	MH	Mod. diff.
	Found in "50 Russian Art Songs"; sustained.			

1994.	*Three Birds*			Boston
	Moderato	(A2-F4)	M-MH	Mod. diff.
	Contained in "Six Songs."			

1995. Dargomyzhsky, A.	*An Eastern Song*			Novello
(1813-1869) Russ.	Slow	(C#3-D4)	MH	Mod. diff.
	Found in "Six Russian Songs"; sustained.			

1996.	*The Old Corporal* (Russ./Eng.)	Breitkopf
	Available from Classical Vocal Reprints.	

1997. Glinka, Michael	*The Midnight Review* (Russ.)			Classical
(1804-1857) Russ.	Alla marcia 4/4	(Bb2(F2)-Db4)	M-MH	Med. diff.
	A ballad; original key; one of Glinka's more important songs; available from Classical Vocal Reprints.			

1998. Gretchaninoff, A.	*My Native Land*			Schirmer
(1864-1956) Russ.	Moderato	(C3-Eb4)	MH	Med. diff.
	Sustained.			

1999.	*Wounded Birch*			Schirmer
	Moderato	(B2-Eb4)	MH	Med. diff.
	Sustained.			

2000.	*Over the Steppe*			Schirmer
	Andante 4/4	(B2-F4)	MH	Med. diff.
	Sustained.			

2001. Koenemann, T.	*When the King Went Forth to War*			Marks+
(1873-1937) Russ.	Various tempo & meter	(A2-E4)	M-MH	Mod. diff.
	Vigorous and vocally demanding ballad.			

Mussorgsky, Modest
(1839-1881) Russ.

No bass should overlook the wonderful songs of Mussorgsky. Many of his songs in original keys are in ranges suitable for bass-baritone and many basses. His songs require interpretive and vocal maturity, but are approachable by intermediate level students. The songs listed below are in their original keys and constitute only a sampling of songs available in English translation. All of Mussorgsky's songs have been recorded by Boris Christoff (bass). (see also nos. 817-826.)

2002.	*After the Battle*			Schirmer
	Grave 4/4	(Bb2-Eb4)	M-MH	Med. diff.

Contained in "A Century of Russian Song" or "Masters of
Russian Song," vol. I; dramatic.

2003.   *A Vision*   Kalmus
                         Largo 4/4   (G2-Db4)   M-MH   Med. diff.
                         Contained in complete works; declamatory; subdued.

2004.   *Little Star*   Schirmer
                         Adagio 4/4   (Bb2-D4)   MH   Med. diff.
                         Not original key; a most beautiful, lyric melody; requires
                         command of soft dynamics.

2005.   *Silently Floated a Spirit*   Schirmer
                         Slowly 6/4, 9/4   (Db3-Eb4)   MH-H   Med. diff.
                         Contained in "A Century of Russian Song" or "Masters of
                         Russian Song"; flowing legato line; requires command of
                         soft dynamics.

2006.   *Song of the Flea* (Russ./Eng.)   Chester
                         Moderato giusto 4/4 (A#2-G4) M-H   Mod. diff.
                         Ballad from Goethe's "Faust"; vocally demanding with
                         shouted high G. (see Beethoven version, no. 57 or 174)

2007.   *Song of the Old Man*   Kalmus
                         Lento 4/4   (Eb3-Eb4)   MH   Med. diff.
                         Contained in complete works; somber; sustained.

2008.   *The Classic*   Kalmus
                         Andante 4/4   (B2-D4)   MH   Med. diff.
                         Contained in complete works; a satire.

2009.   *The Grave*   Kalmus
                         Adagio 3/4   (C3-C4)   M   Med. diff.
                         Contained in complete works; sustained; subdued.

2010.   *The Seminarian*   Schirmer
                         Allegro moderato 4/4 (B2-E4) M-H   Med, diff.
                         Contained in "A Century of Russian Song" or "Masters of
                         Russian Song"; humorous.

2011. Rachmaninoff, S.   *Come, Let Us Rest!*   B & H
      (1873-1943) Russ. Lento 4/4   (A2-D4)   M-MH   Mod. diff.
                         Contained in "S. Rachmaninoff Songs," vol. II; sustained;
                         original key.

2012.   *Love's Flame*   B & H
                         Lento 3/4   (A2-D4)   M-MH   Mod. diff.
                         Contained in (see previous listing, vol. I); sustained; original
                         key.

2013.	*Morning*			B & H
	Moderato 4/4	(A2-C#4)	M	Mod. diff.
	Contained in (see previous listing vol. I); flowing legato; original key.			

2014.	*O Thou Billowy Harvest-Field*			Schirmer
	Slow	(C#3-E4)	MH	Mod. diff.
	Sustained; dramatically intense.			

2015.	*The Soul's Concealment*			B & H
	Non Allegro 4/4	(C3-E4)	M-H	Mod. diff.
	Contained in "S. Rachmaninoff Songs," vol. II; passionate; original key; dedicated to Chaliapin.			

2016.	*When Yesterday We Met*			B & H
	Moderato 4/8	(D3-E4)	MH	Mod. diff.
	Contained in "S. Rachmaninoff Songs," vol. II; sensitive; declamatory.			

2017.	*With Holy Banner Firmly Held*			B & H
	Non Allegro 12/16	(C#3-E4)	M-H	Mod. diff.
	Contained in "S. Rachmaninoff Songs," vol. II; passionate; religious text; original key; dedicated to Chaliapin.			

2018. Tchaikovsky, P. I.	*A Ball Room Meeting* (Eng.)			Novello
(1840-1893) Russ.	Waltz tempo 3/4	(B2-E4)	M-H	Med. diff.
	Contained in "6 Russian Songs"; a very appealing love song.			

2019.	*Don Juan's Serenade* (Eng.)			Schirmer+
	Allegro 3/4	(A2-D4(E4))	MH	Mod. diff.
	Vigorous; vocally demanding; well-known.			

2020.	*None But the Lonely Heart* (Eng.)			Schirmer+
	Andante 4/4	(B2-D4)	MH	Med. diff.
	Somewhat sentimental; well-known.			

2021.	*Pilgrim's Song* (Eng.)			Schirmer+
	Andante 4/4	(A2-D4)	M-MH	Med. diff.
	Sustained; well-known; effective.			

SONGS IN SPANISH

2022. Obradors, F.	*La mi sola, Laureola* (Span.)			International
(1897-1945)	Various tempo & meter	(A2-D4)	MH	Med. diff.
	Contained in "Classical Spanish Songs," by Obradors; sustained; requires some flexibility. (see nos. 67, 68)			

APPENDIX A

SONGS WITH SPECIAL CHARACTERISTICS INDEX
(numbers refer to entries, not pages)

BALLADS
17, 24, 30, 40-4, 57, 87, 118, 168, 174, 199, 211-12, 221, 227, 229, 230-1, 233-5, 238, 473-4, 492, 494, 551-65, 614, 613, 726-9, 764-6, 817-20, 830-1, 888-91, 908, 1007, 1082, 1098, 1433, 1614, 1616, 1619, 1622, 1624, 1657, 1659, 1665, 1679, 1680, 1685, 1704, 1728, 1729, 1738, 1742, 1752, 1755, 1756, 1766, 1804, 1826, 1854, 1901, 1904, 1944, 1953, 1967, 1997, 2001, 2006, 2007, 2010, 2018

CHRISTMAS SONGS AND ARIAS
30, 108, 661-8, 1085, 1284-5, 1298-1300, 1349, 1358, 1361, 1379, 1396, 1400, 1406, 1408, 1412-14, 1416, 1422, 1436, 1438, 1557, 1570

EASY/MODERATELY EASY SONGS
1-9, 14-21, 23, 27-9, 31-9, 41-56, 60, 61, 65-6, 69, 72, 73, 81, 85, 89-91, 94-5, 98-100, 103-6, 108-111, 114-16, 118-22, 129, 140, 141, 145, 146, 150, 151, 154-6, 163-5, 169, 180-2, 187, 193, 208, 214, 223, 226-7, 307, 320, 348, 353, 356, 360, 364-5, 367-9, 385, 391, 394-5, 407-10, 414, 418-21, 429, 437, 439, 448-50, 454-9, 470, 481, 484, 496-7, 499-532, 561, 664, 667, 700-4, 706, 708, 710, 746-759, 827, 829, 834-5, 844, 848, 855, 857-9, 874-6, 972, 996-1000, 1002, 1028, 1260, 1385, 1386, 1387, 1389, 1390-9, 1402-5, 1407, 1412-17, 1422, 1424, 1427-8, 1430, 1434-6, 1495-1504, 1506, 1509-16, 1525, 1529-36, 1538-41, 1544-5, 1551, 1555-1561, 1564-1588, 1590-1, 1593-4, 1596-8, 1600-1, 1603, 1646, 1647-1710, 1713-14, 1717, 1720, 1727, 1734, 1739-43, 1750, 1767, 1773, 1778, 1784-5, 1791-3, 1798, 1802-3, 1806, 1814, 1819, 1826, 1834-5, 1839, 1847, 1849-52, 1967, 1982, 1984-85

HUMOROUS SONGS AND ARIAS
41-5, 57, 87-8, 118, 120, 154, 164, 173-4, 183, 186-7, 193, 565, 645-6, 685-8, 727, 768-770, 827-9, 843-8, 850-3, 855-6, 864, 873-7, 1079, 1127, 1133, 1135-7, 1139-41, 1143, 1154, 1161, 1165-8, 1180, 1182-4, 1212-17, 1238, 1240, 1247-8, 1250-1, 1253, 1258, 1265, 1270-1, 1531, 1542, 1649, 1679, 1680, 1688, 1704, 1719, 1722, 1736, 1748, 1751, 1757, 1769, 1771-2, 1791-2, 1794, 1796, 1801-4, 1815, 1825, 1843, 1847, 1850, 1854, 1899, 1977, 2010

SONGS EXHIBITING AGILITY
10, 19, 20, 26, 59, 74, 80, 87, 88, 92, 96, 123, 132, 135, 140, 142, 143, 147, 148, 149, 160, 170, 171, 178, 179, 183, 191, 211, 533-550, 566, 567, 568, 570, 571, 645, 646, 929, 930, 931, 1061, 1062, 1065, 1066, 1067, 1069, 1070, 1072, 1073, 1074, 1076, 1077, 1079, 1082, 1086-8, 1095, 1099, 1102, 1105, 1107, 1110, 1112, 1113, 1118, 1119, 1125, 1127, 1129, 1132, 1136, 1139, 1143, 1144, 1151, 1154-6, 1158, 1160, 1161, 1166, 1167, 1180, 1182, 1183, 1189, 1193, 1194, 1201, 1203, 1205, 1208, 1210, 1212, 1213, 1215, 1220, 1221, 1233, 1234, 1238, 1240, 1248, 1250-2, 1254, 1259, 1276-8, 1280-5, 1292-5, 1300-2, 1304, 1320, 1323-5, 1328-30, 1332, 1334-7, 1341-4, 1349, 1357-61, 1363, 1364, 1373, 1374, 1383, 1475, 1713, 1715, 1725, 1726, 1731, 1733, 1749, 1760, 1762-4, 1775, 1970, 1973, 1975, 1979, 2022

SONGS EXHIBITING LOW NOTES
Low note being F2 or E2: 88, 133, 142, 149, 156, 161, 181, 189, 191, 208, 212, 216, 217, 220, 254, 259, 261, 267-8, 271-2, 295, 303, 305, 307, 308, 330, 335, 338, 342, 346, 349, 350, 353, 354, 359, 369, 378, 379, 381, 385, 386, 395, 399, 411, 412, 432, 453, 469, 473, 474, 478, 490, 500, 507, 518, 520, 526, 527, 531, 543, 551, 558, 559, 562, 566-8, 580, 587, 613, 637, 689, 692, 704, 716, 719, 767, 785, 787, 788, 830, 833, 856, 875, 877, 917, 918, 920, 923, 926, 938, 967, 980, 981, 1012, 1013, 1031, 1032, 1041, 1066, 1069, 1071, 1072, 1076, 1077, 1081, 1095, 1096, 1103, 1104, 1110, 1118, 1122, 1132, 1134, 1138, 1141, 1150, 1159, 1160, 1165, 1179, 1181, 1183, 1202, 1203, 1206, 1214, 1216, 1220, 1227, 1237, 1246, 1249, 1251, 1275, 1277, 1286, 1302, 1309, 1350, 1385, 1725, 1730, 1762, 1865, 1903, 1904, 1908, 1909, 1910, 1913-15, 1925, 1927, 1930, 1931, 1942, 1946, 1961, 1965, 1966, 1981, 1997

Low note being Eb2: 86, 93, 200, 301, 331, 400, 524, 530, 681, 831, 1015, 1355, 1838

Low note being D2: 137, 157, 167, 310, 323, 351, 355, 362, 416, 430, 465, 487, 502, 556, 629, 673, 769, 1065, 1068, 1070, 1087, 1101, 1112, 1113, 1139, 1174, 1250, 1278, 1302, 1726, 1831, 1868, 1911, 1926, 1980

Low note being Db2: 876, 1353, 1950

Low note being C2: 138, 490, 629, 1094, 1802, 1803, 1976

Low note being B1: 799

Low note being Bb1: 134

SONGS EXHIBITING WIDE RANGE (two octaves or more)
86, 134, 136-8, 142, 157, 167, 189, 208, 212, 220, 254, 261, 323, 331, 338, 346, 351, 355, 359, 362, 381, 400, 416, 430, 465, 502, 556, 562, 629, 831, 853, 876, 877, 917, 1031, 1065, 1068, 1070, 1071, 1077, 1080, 1087, 1094, 1101, 1113, 1118, 1139, 1141, 1165, 1174, 1183, 1216, 1250, 1251, 1278, 1302, 1353, 1355, 1725, 1730, 1802, 1803, 1868, 1903, 1911, 1913, 1914, 1925, 1926, 1950, 1976, 1980

SONGS OF LIMITED UPPER RANGE (high note being C4 or below)
3-6, 13-15, 17-20, 22, 29, 30, 35, 36-39, 41, 44-46, 48, 54, 55, 59, 67, 72, 88-93, 95-100, 105, 113, 116, 121, 125, 129, 131-5, 140, 141, 146, 149, 151, 161, 195, 200, 204, 217, 219, 220, 227, 237, 268, 269, 272, 284, 342, 378, 382, 383, 385, 399, 432, 439, 448, 450, 454, 501, 507, 508, 515, 517, 525-527, 529-31, 561, 573, 576, 584, 588, 589, 596, 598, 614, 615, 625, 630, 664, 667, 669, 673, 675, 683, 706, 725, 732, 735, 746, 748, 755, 782-3, 785-8, 810, 812-14, 834, 843, 844, 846, 847, 848, 852, 855, 860, 871, 873-5, 883-5, 890, 900-2, 916, 918, 920, 923-6, 936, 938, 941, 956, 965, 1002, 1013, 1016, 1017, 1020, 1037, 1072, 1110, 1112, 1122, 1123, 1138, 1159, 1181, 1206, 1214, 1237, 1260, 1321, 1376, 1385, 1389, 1390, 1394, 1396, 1397, 1404, 1416, 1417, 1423, 1485, 1497, 1503, 1516, 1533, 1545, 1554, 1561, 1568, 1573, 1578, 1587, 1594, 1613, 1633, 1727, 1740, 1767, 1773, 1776, 1783, 1785, 1798, 1800, 1802, 1803, 1806-8, 1814, 1820, 1823, 1828, 1831, 1834, 1848, 1849, 1873, 1902, 1914, 1916, 1918, 1936, 1942, 1943, 1966, 1967, 1971, 1978, 1981, 1982, 1985, 1987, 2009

SONGS OF THE SEA
13, 54, 59-61, 70, 79, 85, 103, 112, 153, 160, 166, 191, 253, 254, 268, 270, 287, 292, 330, 353, 354, 356, 360, 466, 469, 505-7, 520-32, 563, 567, 605, 607, 700-704, 726-9, 730,

764-66, 785, 801, 1003-7, 1303, 1330, 1365, 1647-1710, 1711, 1733, 1735, 1740-42, 1747, 1751, 1753, 1765-6, 1768, 1770, 1779, 1789, 1793, 1795-6, 1800, 1804, 1818, 1826, 1835, 1840, 1852, 1859, 1865 1924, 1930, 1938, 1940

SPIRITUALS
32, 33, 75, 99, 1385, 1388-91, 1394, 1401, 1406, 1436, 1555-1602, 1727, 1739, 1785, 1806, 1819, 1820, 1823

APPENDIX B

COMPOSER INDEX

(numbers refer to entries, not pages)

186   Songs for Bass Voice

APPENDIX C

TITLE INDEX

In alphabetizing this index the initial article is disregarded in English and included in foreign languages. (numbers refer to entries, not pages)

APPENDIX D

PUBLISHERS

Alfred Publishing Co. Inc.
16380 Roscoe Bld., PO Box 10003
Van Nuys, CA 91410-0003
Ph. (818) 891-5999
Fax (818) 891-2182

Edwin **Ashdown** Ltd.
(see Brodt Music)

Ashley Dealers Inc.
133 Industrial Ave.
Hasbrouck Heights, NJ 07604
Ph (201) 288-8080
Fax (201) 288-0389

Associated Music Pub.
(see Hal Leonard)

Augener, London
(see ECS Publishing)

Bärenreiter
(see Foreign Music Distributors)

Belwin-Mills Publishing Corp.
(see CPP/Belwin)

Editions **Bessel**
78 Rue de Monceau
Paris, 8e, France

Edmund **Bieler** Musikverlag
Thürmchenswall 72
D-5000 Köln 1
Germany

Birch Tree Group, Ltd.
180 Alexander Street
Princeton, NJ 08540

C. C. **Birchard** & Company

(see Birch Tree Group, Ltd.)

Boelke-Bomart Music Publications
(see Jerona)

Boosey & Hawkes, Inc.
52 Cooper Square, 10th fl.
New York, NY 10003-7102
Ph. (212) 979-1090
Fax (212) 979-7056

Boston Music Company
172 Tremont St.
Boston, MA 02111
Ph. (617) 426-5100
Fax (617) 695-9142

Bote & Bock, Germany
(see Hal Leonard)

Breitkopf & Härtel
Postfach 1707
D-6200 Wiesbaden 1
Germany

Brodt Music Co.
PO Box 9345
Charlotte, NC 28299-9345
Ph. (704) 332-2177
Fax (800) 446-0812

Broude Inc.
141 White Oaks Rd.
Williamstown, MA 01267
Ph. (413) 458-8131
Fax (413) 458-8131

Wm. C. **Brown**
2460 Kerper Bld.
Dubuque, IA 52001

Chantry Music Press Inc.
PO Box 1101
Spring Field, OH 45501
Ph. (513) 325-9992

Chappell Music Co.
(see Warner/Chappell)

Chester Music Ltd.
(see Music Sales Corp.)

John Church Company
(see Theodore Presser Co.)

Classical Vocal Reprints
P.O. Box 20263
New York, NY 10023-1484

Concord Music Publishing Co.
(see Henri Elkan Music Pub.)

Concordia Publishing House
3358 S. Jefferson Ave.
St. Louis, MO 63118
Ph. (800) 325-3040
Fax (314) 268-1329

J. B. Cramer & Co. Ltd
(see CCP/Belwin)

J. Curwen & Sons
(see Hal Leonard)

Da Capo Press, Inc.
227 W. 17 St.
New York, NY 10011

Deutscher Verlag für Musik
Postschliessfach 147
Karlstrasse 10
DDR-7010 Leipzig
Germany

Oliver Ditson Company
(see Theodore Presser Co.)

Donamus Publishing House
(see Theodore Presser)

Dover Publications

31 E. Second St.
Mineola, NY 11501
Ph. (516) 294-7000
Fax (516) 742-5049

Durand Editions
(see Theodore Presser)

Eastlane Music
31 Bayberry Rd.
Trenton, NJ 08618

ECS Publishing
138 Ipswich St.
Boston, MA 02215-3534
Ph. (617) 236-1935
Fax (617) 236-0261

Henri Elkan Music Publisher
PO Box 7720
New York, NY 10150-1914
Ph. (212) 362-9357

Elkan-Vogel, Inc.
(see Theodore Presser)

EMI Music Publishing Ltd.
138-140 Charing Cross Rd.
London WC2H 0LD
England

Éditions Max Eschig
(see Theodore Presser)

European American Music Ditributors
Corp.
PO Box 850
Valley Forge, PA 19482
Ph. (215) 648-0506
Fax (215) 889-0242

Faber Music Inc., Boston
50 Cross St.
Winchester, MA 01890
Ph. (617) 756-0323
Fax (617) 729-2783

Carl F. Fischer, Inc.
62 Cooper Square
New York, NY 10003

Ph. (212) 777-0900
Fax (212) 477-4129

Foreign Music Distributors
13 Elkay Dr.
Chester, NY 10918
Ph. (914) 469-5790
Fax (914) 469-5817

Mark Foster Music Co.
PO Box 4012
Champaign, IL 61824-4012
Ph. (217) 398-2760
Fax (217) 398-2791

Galaxy Music Corp.
(see ECS Publishing)

General Music Publishing Corp.
145 Palisade
Dobbs Ferry, NY 10522

Musikverlag Hans Gerig
Drusugasse 7-11
5 Köln 1, Germany

H. W. Gray Co., Inc.
(see CCP/Belwin)

Gregg International Pub.
1 Westmead, Farnborough
Hants GU14 7RU
England

Hänssler-Verlag
(see Foster)

T. B. Harms
(see Warner)

Frederick Harris Music Co. Ltd.
PO Box 670
Oakville, Ontario, L6K 2G4
Canada

Heritage Music Press
(see Lorenz)

Heritage Music Publishing Co.
(see Ashley)

Heugel & Cie.
(see Theodore Presser)

International Music Co.
5 W 37th St.
New York, NY 10018
Ph. (212) 391-4200
Fax (212) 391-4306

Jerona Music Corp.
PO Box 5010
Hackensack, NJ 07606-4210
Ph. (201) 488-0550
Fax (201) 836-7927

Edwin F. Kalmus & Co.
6403 W. Rogers Circle
Boca Raton, FL 33487
Ph. (407) 241-6340
Fax (407) 241-6347

Robert King Music Co.
7 Canton St.
North Easton, MA 02356

Alfred A. Knopf
201 E. 50th St.
New York, NY 10022

Alphonse Leduc
(see Robert King)

Leeds Music Corp.
322 W. 48 St.
New York, NY 10019

Henry Lemoine et Cie.
(see Theodore Presser)

Alfred Lengnick & Co.
(see Theodore Presser)

Hal Leonard Publishing Corp.
P. O. Box 13819
7777 West Bluemound Road
Milwaukee, WI 53213
Ph. (414) 774-3630
Fax (414) 774-3259

Lorenz Corp.

PO Box 802
Dayton, OH 45401-0802
Ph. (513) 228-6118
Fax (513) 223-2042

MCA Music
(see Hal Leonard)

MMB Music Inc.
10370 Page Ind'l Bld.
St. Louis, MO 63132
Ph. (314) 427-5660
Fax (314) 426-3590

Magna Music
10370 Page Industrial Blvd.
St. Louis, Mo. 63132

Edw. B. Marks Music Corp.
(see Hal Leonard)

Masters Music Publications, Inc.
PO Box 4666
Miami Lakes, FL 33014-0666

McGinnis & Marks Music Pub.
236 W. 26 St. No. 11-S
New York, NY 10001-6736
Ph. (212) 675-1630
Fax (212) 675-1630

Mercury Music Corp.
(see Theodore Presser)

Merion Music Inc.
(see Theodore Presser)

Mobart Publications
(see Jerona)

Edition Modern
Musikverlag Hans Wewerka
Franz-Joseph-Strasse 2
8 Munich 13, Germany

Willy Müller Musikverlag
Marzgrasse 5
D-6900 Heidelberg
Germany

Music Press
(see Theodore Presser)

Music Sales Corp.
5 Bellvale Rd.
Chester, NY 10918
Ph. (914) 469-2271
Fax (914) 469-7544

W. W. Norton & Co., Inc.
500 5th Ave.
New York, NY 10003

Novello & Co. Ltd.
(see Theodore Presser)

Oxford University Press
200 Madison Ave.
New York, NY 10016
Ph. (212) 679-7300
Fax (212) 725-2972

Joseph Patelson Music House Ltd.
160 W. 56 St.
New York, NY 10019
Ph. (212) 757-5587 or 582-5840
Fax (212) 246-5633

Paterson Publications
(see Theodore Presser)

Peer International Corp.
(see Peermusic)

Peermusic
810 Seventh Ave.
New York, NY 10019
Ph. (212) 265-3910
Fax (212) 489-2465

C. F. Peters Corp.
373 Park Ave., South
New York, NY 10016
Ph. (212) 686-4147
Fax (212) 689-9412

Theodore Presser
Presser Place
Bryn Mawr, Pa. 19010
Ph. (215) 525-3636

Fax (215) 527-7841

Recital Publications
PO Box 1697
Huntsville, Tex. 77340

G. **Ricordi** & Co. Ltd.
(see Boosey & Hawkes and Hal Leonard)

Rouart-Lerolle & Cie
(see Hal Leonard)

R. D. **Row** Music Co.
(see Carl Fischer)

Editions **Salabert,** Inc.
(see Hal Leonard)

Edizioni de **Santis**
Via Cassia 13
00191 Rome, Italy

E. C. **Schirmer** Music Co.
(see ECS Publishing)

G. **Schirmer**, Inc.
(see Hal Leonard)

Schott & Co. Ltd.
(see European American Music)

B. **Schott's** Söhne
(see European American Music)

Seesaw Music Corp.
2067 Broadway
New York, NY 10023
Ph. (212) 874-1200

Shawnee Press Inc.
Waring Dr.
Deleware Water Gap, PA 18327
Ph. (717) 476-0550
Fax (717) 476-5247

Musikverlage Hans **Sikorski**
(see Hal Leonard)

N. **Simrock**
(see Hal Leonard)

Casa Musicale **Sonzogno**
(see Theodore Presser)

Southern Music Co.
PO Box 329
1100 Broadway
San Antonio, TX 78292
Ph. (800) 284-5443
Fax (210) 223-4537

Southern Peer Music Pub. Co.
(see Theodore Presser)

Stainer & **Bell** Ltd.
(see ECS Publishing)

Transatiantiques
(see Theodore Presser)

Transcontinental Music Publications
838 5th Ave.
New York, NY 10021
Ph. (212) 249-0100
Fax (212) 472-8280

Universal Editions
(see European American Music)

Viking Press, Inc.
625 Madison Ave.
New York, NY 10022

Warner Brothers Publications
265 Secaucus Road
Secaucus, NJ 07094

Warner/Chappell Music Inc.
10585 Santa Monica Bld.
Los Angeles, CA 90025-4850

Weaner-Levant
(see Theodore Presser)

Weintraub Music Inc.
(see Hal Leonard)

The **Well-Tempered** Press
(see Masters Music)

Wilhelmiana Musikverlag

(see MMB)

M. **Whitmark** & Sons
(see Warner Brothers Publications)

Suvini **Zerboni**
Galleria del Corso 4
Milano, Italy

ABOUT THE AUTHOR

ALAN ORD earned his B.A. in Voice from Brigham Young University, his M.S. in Voice from The Juilliard School, and his D.M.A. in Opera from the University of Southern California. He is an Associate Professor of Voice and Director of Opera at the University of Alberta, Edmonton, Alberta, Canada. In addition, Dr. Ord has taught at the University of Connecticut, the University of Utah, and Brigham Young University. He is an active member of The National Association of Teachers of Singing and currently serves as President of the Alberta North Chapter. As a performer, Dr. Ord has appeared as bass soloist in the United States and Canada in recital, concert, opera, on national radio and television, in plays, musicals, and is heard on several commercial opera recordings. He has performed as soloist in Carnegie Hall, Alice Tully Hall, and Avery Fisher Hall in New York City and appeared in American opera premieres of works by Darius Milhaud and Richard Rodney Bennett. He has performed under the baton of Leopold Stokowski, Jean Morel, John Nelson, and Anton Guardagno and has appeared in opera under the direction of John Houseman, George London, Christopher West, Titto Capobianco, and Lofti Mansouri. He has appeared with such organizations as The American Opera Center, The Metropolitan Opera Studio, and The American Opera Society. Dr. Ord studied voice with Alexander Kipnis and Giorgio Tozzi.